THE

MYSTICAL
CHORUS

Into this Dark beyond all light, we pray
   to come and,
      unseeing and unknowing,
  to see and
  to know
    Him that is
      beyond seeing and
      beyond knowing
  precisely by not seeing,
  by not knowing.
For that is truly to see and
        to know and
        to hymn transcendently
          Him that transcends all.
That is, negating, to do as sculptors do,
  drawing [from marble]
    the statue latent there,
  removing all that
      hinders or
      hides
    the pure spectacle of the hidden form and
  displaying, with this mere removal,
    the beauty hidden there.
One must, I think, hymn in
    negating and
    affirming
  for affirmations proceed
    from the topmost
    through the middlemost
    to the lowest.
  But here,
    from the lowest
    to the topmost,
  one denies them all, thus
    to lay bare the Unknowable who is
      by all known beings veiled,
    to see the transcendent Dark that is
      by the light of beings hid.

The Pseudo-Dionysius

THE
MYSTICAL
CHORUS

JUNG AND THE
RELIGIOUS DIMENSION

DONALD BROADRIBB

WITH CONTRIBUTIONS BY
MARILYN HOLLY & NORMA LYONS

MILLENNIUM
BOOKS

First published in 1995 by
Millennium Books
an imprint of E.J. Dwyer (Australia) Pty Ltd
Unit 13, Perry Park
33 Maddox Street
Alexandria NSW 2015
Australia
Phone: (02) 550-2355
Fax: (02) 519-3218

National Library of Australia
Cataloguing-in-Publication data

Broadribb, Donald, 1993– .
    The mystical chorus: Jung and the religious dimension.

    Bibliography.
    ISBN 1 86429 019 6.

    1. Jung, C.G. (Carl Gustav), 1875–1961. 2. Religions.
    3. Psychology, Religious. I. Holly, Marilyn. II. Lyons,
    Norma. III. Title.

200

Cover design by Megan Smith
Text design by Megan Smith
Typeset in Bembo 11/14 pt by DOCUPRO, Sydney
Printed in Australia by Griffin Paperbacks, Netley, S.A.

10 9 8 7 6 5 4 3 2 1

99 98 97 96 95

ACKNOWLEDGMENTS

The authors are grateful for permission to use material from the following:
Joseph Epes Brown (ed.), *The Sacred Pipe: Black Elk's Account of the Seven Rites of the Oglala Sioux*, University of Oklahoma Press, Norman, 1953.
The Spiritual Legacy of The American Indian, by Joseph Epes Brown. © 1982 by Joseph Epes Brown. Reprinted by permission of The Crossroad Publishing Company. The Crossroad Publishing Company, New York, 1982.
The paper by Chung-Yuan Chang "Tao and the Sympathy of All Things" is based on a lecture given at the Eranos Conference in Ascona in 1955 and was published in *Eranos 24–1955*, © Eranos Foundation, Ascona, Switzerland. The quotation from this paper that appears in the text is reprinted with kind permission of Eranos Foundation, Ascona, Switzerland.
Edward Conze (tr.), *Buddhist Scriptures*, Penguin Classics, Harmondsworth, 1959. © Edward Conze, 1959. Reproduced by permission of Penguin Books Ltd.
Dionysius the Areopagite, quoted by permission of The Shrine of Wisdom, Brook, Godalming, Surrey.
C.G. Jung Speaking, ed. William McQuire and R.F.C. Hull, Princeton University Press, Princeton, 1977.
The Collected Works of C.G. Jung, Routledge and Kegan Paul, London, 1959–1973.
Baba Kubi of Shiraz, "The Sufi Path of Love," tr. R.A. Nicholson, *Mysticism—A Study and an Anthology*, ed. F.C. Happold, Cambridge University Press, Cambridge.
John (Fire) Lame Deer and Richard Erdoes, *Lame Deer Seeker of Visions*, Washington Square Press, New York, 1972.
The paper by Paul Radin "The Religious Experiences of an American Indian" was published in *Eranos 18–1950*, © Eranos Foundation, Ascona, Switzerland. The quotations from this paper that appear in the text are reprinted with kind permission of Eranos Foundation, Ascona, Switzerland.
N.K. Sandars, *The Epic of Gilgamesh: An English Version*, Penguin Classics, revised edition, Harmondsworth, 1964. © N.K. Sandars, 1960, 1964. Reproduced by permission of Penguin Books Ltd.
Seven Arrows by Hyemeyohsts Storm. Copyright © 1972 by Hyemeyohsts Storm. Reprinted by permission of HarperCollins Publishers. HarperCollins Publishers Inc., New York, 1972.

Every effort has been made to trace and obtain permission from the copyright holders of material quoted in this book. In the event that any inadvertent omissions have been made, the authors apologize and would appreciate relevant information so that acknowledgments can be included in future editions.

CONTENTS

INTRODUCTION

Most readers of this book will have had some type of religious instruction. Whether as children we were taught at a church Sunday school or some other religious institution, or we absorbed simple social assumptions from the culture we live in, none of us grow up in a religious vacuum. Through most of history the majority of people appear to have been reasonably satisfied with the religious culture which went hand in hand with their social structure. It has been only in the past two or three centuries that religious questioning has occupied the minds and hearts of a large share of the population. Religious questioning is now a concern of the entire world, West and East alike. One sign of this is the extraordinary proliferation of new religious creeds and organizations. It sometimes feels as if there are as many religious creeds as there are adherents. It is true that the vast majority of Westerners continue to list themselves on the census forms as Christian or Jewish, but for many people these terms have come to lose nearly all meaning, except to identify them with a set of traditional festivals and a generalized "Yes," if asked, "Do you believe in God?"

I cannot claim to stand out from the majority of people in this. Like everyone else I have had my own personal experiences which have unquestionably colored my view. In order to help you understand my religious biases and to compensate for them in your own mind as you read this book, I wish to set before you a brief autobiographical religious profile, pointing out some of the possible preconceptions which may weave themselves into the fabric of the chapters to follow, even though in them I will try to be as objective as possible.

As a child I was reared in a fundamentalist Christian family which had little by way of formal affiliation with any particular church but which made a practice of going to *some* church each Sunday and of sending me to Sunday school. When I was about thirteen or fourteen I was baptized into a Baptist church—not, I must admit, out of religious conviction but because it was expected of me. With a small gnawing doubt which I did my best to push out of my mind, I looked forward to baptism by immersion as practiced in that church—desperately hoping that some sort of religious experience, or at least uplift, would come about, for the emptiness inside me was very great.

My disappointment after the baptism was equally great, though not totally unexpected. No tremendous experience took place. Following the baptism, when the minister asked me to tell the congregation how I had met Christ, I sat mute in my chair, for I had had no encounter. I nursed a small hope that first communion would bring about the longed for experience, but it passed without any feeling except one of disillusion.

For quite a few years I continued attending church each Sunday, still hoping to fill the hunger inside. Eventually I had tried every Christian church available. The conservative Protestant churches (such as Baptist or Salvation Army) left me feeling sad and lonely while everyone else in the congregation seemed to work up enormous enthusiasm. The liturgical churches—Lutheran, Catholic, Episcopalian (the name given to the Church of England in the United States) left me with a sense of coldness, making me feel a total outsider watching a stage play without a beginning, middle or end, in which I could only be part of the audience but never part of the cast. The liberal Protestant churches (e.g., Unitarian, Congregational and most community churches) I felt to be more social than religious gatherings. Whatever the church, I always left feeling empty and spiritually somehow cheated.

Once I was at university, philosophy seemed to me an obvious alternative to the churches. After all, theology had started as part of philosophy and the separation between the two of them is still not complete. I was already familiar with Plato. I could sense that he had come upon an insight which has its origins in something far deeper than mere intellectual reasoning. His mentor, Socrates, had known the *vox dei* (divine voice within) which gave him internal direction. But, as Plato reports Socrates as saying, he doubted whether anyone else could experience that same voice, and sadly I feared that he was right.[1]

Aristotle's writings made good sense, but I could never feel that his heart was in his subject as it was for Plato. Aristotle came across as regarding philosophy like an intellectual puzzle with which to play. For Plato it was a necessity of life.

For a long time I had felt that if I got to the roots of religious belief and practice I could find what I was missing in modern day religion. I enrolled in Union Theological Seminary in the city of New York for a post-graduate degree, hoping to fill the gap within me and then be able to convey spiritual assistance to others.

The historical and philosophical studies I undertook at Union Theological Seminary unexpectedly led me to search in a completely different direction than I had anticipated. The more I learned of the background of theological doctrines, the less relevant to life they seemed to be. I realized that to become a minister of religion would mean to live a lie, for I could not really believe in what I would be expected to preach.

The required courses in traditional theology brought home to me the problem of linking church doctrines with personal experience. I could learn the doctrines, but they did little to ease my feeling of inner emptiness.

I began to attend gatherings of the Riverside Meeting of the Religious Society of Friends, the Quakers. Riverside Meeting could not really be called a church. It had no membership. It had no budget. It had no teachings. It continued the traditional form of Quaker Meetings for Worship,[2] which consists of silent meditation that may continue for the full hour of the meeting. It was in the Riverside Meeting that my first experiences took place which I would now call "religious." What I experienced I later realized was typical in mystical religious movements, and Quakers are historically a part of the mainstream tradition of religious mysticism such as I will describe later in this book in Chapter 4 on Mysticism.

During the silence of a Quaker meeting a sense of harmony often comes to be felt. This sense of harmony is not only of person with person but equally with all that surrounds the person.

Looking back now from the perspective of having experienced the Quaker meetings, I think it might be wrong to say that these were my first religious experiences. As a child, as I lay beside a river looking up into the clouds and merging into the world around me, I had rather similar experiences. And many, many years later, on one occasion a dream left me with a lasting afterglow of the same feeling of Oneness. (I have printed this dream on pages 108–9.)

The Master of Divinity degree from Union Theological Seminary (UTS) left me confused. I had failed to find anything similar to what others called God and had lost all faith in organized religion, though I stayed with the Quakers for about eighteen years. Eventually I found myself teaching at the University of Melbourne in Australia and moving gradually from teaching biblical studies and languages (which I had studied at UTS) to teaching the history of pre-Christian civilizations and religions. It was not long before I discovered Carl Jung's book *Symbols of Transformation*.

Although at UTS a friend had introduced me to Jung's short book *Modern Man in Search of a Soul* which became a very close friend of my own soul, I only now began to follow up on Jung's ideas. *Symbols of Transformation* is devoted to a discussion of the meaning and feeling-value of symbols in personal life, as well as in culture generally. Jung was, with

Sigmund Freud, a cofounder of psychoanalysis. I had since childhood been acquainted with Freud's *The Interpretation of Dreams*. From Freud I now learned why it is that old beliefs persist in the face of scientific refutation. But Freud seemed to have no insight into how religious experiences affect those who have had them. As the son of a Swiss Protestant minister, Jung was particularly interested in this aspect. From Jung I began to understand something of what I had experienced.

It is almost a cliché to say that to understand a person's writings you must know the person who wrote them. It took very little time for me to realize that neither Freud's nor Jung's works can be understood outside the context of their personal lives and experiences. I devoured everything available from and about both men, a process I continued for decades, until I felt that I knew them both intimately, and respected them both equally for what they felt and knew. I even polished my German, a language I particularly disliked when I studied it in university, to be able to get back to their own distinctive styles and feeling-worlds by reading their own words as they wrote them.

There is a major step to be taken after working through Jung's *Symbols of Transformation*. This can be a sideways step to the right into his other studies of religiously related subjects, his various volumes on the symbolism used in alchemy, his many studies of the underpinnings of Christian doctrine, and his excursions into the conceptual worlds of oriental religions, particularly Buddhism. These I found very helpful in understanding what symbols relate to. But I quickly discovered that to understand their effect you must take a step to the left into his studies of psychiatry, abnormal psychology, and the structure of the personality. This particular step is not popular among the public, for it requires not only taking a very close look at others but particularly at yourself.

This was really no problem for me. What is the value of studying symbolism if it is only to lead to replacing a set of religious symbols with an equivalent set of psychological symbols? This is, in effect, what Freud had done. Superego had replaced Father God, castration complex replaced the threat of hellfire because of your sins. The feeling was the same and it did not seem to me to make much difference which world of symbols you preferred. When I was a teacher I came across a young woman who cried amidst much suffering: "Oh that Oedipus Complex! It's torturing me. I can't get away from it, it pursues me wherever I go!" She was in the care of a Freudian psychoanalyst, but it could as easily have been a New Guinea shaman telling her about the malevolent spirit of her dead grandfather. Or a Christian priest warning her about the Almighty Creator who wants vengeance and can never be fully appeased. How she was feeling seemed to me to be the same, regardless of the cultural indoctrination. As far as I could see the content hardly seemed to matter. Three thought systems, with three different sets of symbols, but for all that, with little difference in their effect.

As I made my way through the psychiatric volumes and experimental researches in Jung's *Collected Works* I found in them the sound of authenticity for which I had been waiting. For example:

> However abstract this may sound, practical experience shows
> that many neuroses are caused primarily by the fact that people
> blind themselves to their own religious promptings because of a
> childish passion for rational enlightenment. It is high time the
> psychologist of today recognized that we are no longer dealing
> with dogmas and creeds but with the religious attitude per se.
> *(Jung, C.W., vol. 16, paragraph 99)*

It is because of statements such as this that Jung has frequently been called "mystical" in a pejorative way, because in modern Western scientific civilization there is no room for subjective experience or for the importance of attitudes.

Jung validated what I had felt. Freud had authoritatively pronounced that the religious experience does not exist,[3] which seemed to me to reflect a rather closed mind. From Jung's autobiography, as from Plato's writings, I got the feeling that he did know of the religious experience, though perhaps in a different way.

But religious experiences were for me very elusive, in fact serving to highlight the feeling of inner emptiness in that spot where others seemed to place religion. Plato was still whispering in my ear: "If we imagine we can discover Truth in this our life on earth, then we are the most deluded of all creatures. But unless we search we will not even know that much." The Buddha had said the same a century or so earlier, but knowing no Sanskrit and thus unable to hear his voice as it leapt from the page, I could feel him as only a rather distant cousin, compassionate but elusive; unlike Plato who had become my close friend through my studies of Greek.

Might Jung, with his statements about the hopelessness of ever achieving individuation, but the necessity of searching for it nonetheless, have been expressing this same insight in his own fashion? Jung, like the Buddha and

Plato before him, had expressed the problematic character of the desire for a leader.[4] The quest for Reality could be undertaken only through life's everyday experiences, it could not be found in teachings or in books, all three men had come to realize that. Plato had found it through the death of his father while he was a small child and Socrates had stepped in more as a substitute father to love him than as a teacher to inculcate truths.[5] Even so, it took Plato most of his lifetime to understand the meaning of the motto Socrates had adopted from the Oracle at Delphi, "Know yourself." Jung joined in with the same motto. The Buddha might well have used this motto also, had he added "as long as you remember that there is no you," but to explain that will require a chapter on its own.

My own efforts to know myself had led me to realize that this could not be achieved without help. Despair had swept over me, making life intolerable. The meaninglessness of my personal life and my career led me to analysis as a way of coming to cope with myself. I began to see life in a new way, and eventually this led me to enrol in the analytical institute which Jung had established in Zürich for the multi-year training leading to a diploma in psychoanalysis.

About this time I severed my connection with the Quakers. I was discovering that the attainment of "oneness," which is what the word "individuation" means, is a life-long process that has its own timetable and cannot be fitted even into a system of meditation. Perhaps I should explain that for Jung "individuation" meant attaining a state of unity not only within yourself but with the whole of the cosmos, including people as much as things. This is more or less what Martin Buber, a modern Jewish writer, meant when he spoke of changing one's perception of the world, including all of humanity into a "Thou" instead of an "It." This is a major theme which we will meet time and time again in this book, particularly in the chapters on American Indian and Australian Aboriginal beliefs.

Analysis "in Jung's manner" is not, as popular fantasy has it, grandiose philosophy, esoteric teaching, or great illuminations, but very prosaic dissection of everyday events and how you react to them. Plus, equally important, why you react to them the way you do.

Here was no philosophy and no creed. The religious attitude Jung spoke of is one of looking at life as if it was made for you, as indeed it is as far your own experiences go. Dreams may be the starting point for discussion, but they are not the "voice of God." They are an attempt within you to re-establish emotional equilibrium.

The requirement of study and experience in psychiatry is given equal footing with undergoing analysis, a reminder that Jung was first and foremost a psychiatrist. Who are you to say how a schizophrenic feels? Stop talking at the person and start to listen. How does it feel to weep nonstop for months at a time? If you haven't discovered that in your own sufferings, in or out of analysis, then meet it head on in someone else, listen to it day by day, month by month. If you do not have the patience for that, then try a different trade, this one is not for you. One suffering person will teach you more than a million books. If you are that suffering person, so much the better. But you need to learn what other sufferers experience also.

During the years in which I have accompanied many suffering people as they try to find their way back to peace—or, for many of them, to find inner peace for the first time—I have found that the lack of some kind of "religious attitude" has a great deal to do with their suffering, and the finding of some form of "religious attitude" has much to do with their discovery of some kind of release from their suffering. By this term "religious attitude" I do not mean the religions and philosophies of the past or present, or any kind of religion or philosophy at all. I mean the ways in which individual persons come to discover their own niche in their ongoing participation in the more than five billion years of the evolution of life on this planet—a solution to the sense of alienation that seems to be the price we pay for the legacy of a human world split apart and a physical world which we are slowly bringing to destruction. And also the faint possibility that we have means to repair the damage that we have done.

The one feature which I have found in all the religious systems I have studied is the theme of being at one with the reality in which we live, no matter what fantasies or beliefs we have about the nature of that reality. To me this is the goal of religion as much as it is of psychology. We have all been burdened with the task of making whole the world which is under severe stresses that could lead to its ruin. Whatever fantasy or belief about how we came to have this burden, it rests upon our shoulders and the real question is not "why" but "how" to manage this burden.

THE CONNECTION BETWEEN PSYCHOLOGY AND RELIGION

What then is the connection between psychology and religion if the purpose of our study is not to substitute psychological jargon for theological jargon as so many people assume? For me the "oneness" which we sometimes experience has been the goal of the religious quest from time immemorial. This is also a major goal of psychoanalytic therapy. Again I stress that "oneness" is not restricted to within ourselves but applies to our relation with the whole of what is, both "internal" and "external." In this book I want to show you some of the variety of ways this quest has been undertaken, and to relate religious beliefs and actions to the ways in which we experience them. How we experience and interact with the events of life is the realm of psychology, and religion is a central part of the experience of life.

It has only been a century since the idea took hold that it might be possible to study the religions of the world in a systematic and, hopefully, unbiased manner. One of the hopes, which still inspire many investigators today, was that through such study it would be possible to grasp the nature of religion as a human experience, so that, divested of its elaborations, the skeleton common to all the world's religions could be discovered. Obviously it would be impossible to have a truly unbiased view. By virtue of having grown up in some culture every student inevitably has bias and preconceptions. Nevertheless if due allowance is made for this, it might be possible to discover some features of religion that have general validity.

The establishment of a Department of Comparative Religion at the University of Chicago in 1892 might be said to have inaugurated the study of Comparative Religion as an academic discipline in its own right. This happens to have been the same time that the first major steps were being taken towards establishing psychology as a study in its own right, especially the various forms of Depth Psychology. Pierre Janet and Sigmund Freud were already publishing or preparing their major works and it was but a few years before William James and Carl Jung came on the scene.

Probably the first major study of the interrelationship of Depth Psychology and religion, with a view to understanding the human side of the experience, was William James' *The Varieties of Religious Experience* published in 1902. It was the same year in which Carl Jung's doctoral thesis *On the Psychology and Pathology of So-called Occult Phenomena* was published. James attempted to cover the field of religious experience in general and to establish the guidelines for the new study of the application of psychology to such experience. Jung provided a detailed description and analysis of the seances of a young medium, examining the structure of her experiences and their probable background.

The study of religion and religious experience was, of course, not something newly invented for the twentieth century. People in the West and East had always known that religious systems other than their own existed. Westerners were well acquainted with the existence of Judaism, though very few Christians had much conception of why and how Judaism continued to exist two thousand years after the time when, according to Christian teaching, it had been superseded by Christianity. Many of the basic religious concepts of India had been popularized in the West, with Buddhist and Hindu doctrines being widely known—even though for the most part poorly understood and often greatly distorted. The existence of Islam was also well-known, principally because of the Crusades and other wars past and present. Just what Islam taught and practiced was, however, little known in the West. By and large the tendency among Western religious writers was to divide the world's religions into two camps: Christians and Jews on the one hand, and "pagans" or "heathens" on the other. On the relatively few occasions that studies of another religious culture such as Islam were made, it was largely for the purpose of finding out only enough about it to use in attempts to make converts, usually to some form of Christianity. Even now books concerned with Comparative Religion or the History of Religions tend to devote the giant's share of their content to the development of Jewish and Christian thought, which is then used in turn as a basic outlook from which to view and compare other religious thought.

The study of religions covers many topics. The philosophical assumptions underlying religious and theological systems have been the interest of most of the major Western philosophers throughout history going as far back as Plato twenty-four hundred years ago, and is still continuing. Even to attempt to outline the course of such philosophical studies systematically would be an enormous task. In growing numbers, particularly in the last two centuries, the rise of science has brought conflicts between "scientific truth" and "religious truth," almost always with the conclusion that you must opt for one or the other, but not both. In retrospect, it seems that it was almost inevitable that with the rise of Depth Psychology and psychological examination of religious experiences it would be claimed that religious experience can be "reduced to" psychological processes going on within the person. Unfortunately, this view was also espoused by Sigmund Freud, the best known of the Depth Psychologists, with the result that for many decades religious bodies and individuals have treated Depth Psychology with deep suspicion.

Earlier in this Introduction I quoted from Carl Jung a passage to the effect that the time of "rational enlightenment" has long since passed and it is no longer on dogmas and creeds that we should focus our attention, but on the religious attitude *per se*. By this he meant that the religious attitude is concerned not with specific doctrines but with the way in which we approach life, within or outside of a particular religion's framework. This book is an attempt to explore this domain.

Chapter 1 is concerned with the basic problem of the differing meanings that people give to the word "religion," along with examples to illustrate each of these concepts. There is an attempt in this chapter to lay the groundwork for the discussions of religion that will be followed through in the remainder of the book.

Chapters 2 and 3 deal with two specific religious systems, Buddhism and Christianity. Chapter 4 deals with Mysticism, in which many of the main themes already discussed are put in the context of other world religions. Furthermore, as a transcultural phenomenon, mysticism is closely examined with some suggestions of the psychology underlying it. This chapter on Mysticism has in many respects been the most difficult portion of the book to prepare. Because it cuts across all religious cultures, and views of its nature vary radically, it bears the stamp of my own particular personality perhaps more than any other chapter.

The study of Mysticism is followed by examination of two indigenous populations: Chapter 5 discusses American Indian, and Chapter 6 Australian Aboriginal religious cultures. These specific religious cultures were selected with a special purpose in mind: to present completely separate, yet remarkably similar, millennia-old religious cultures, each of which is very rich in its all-encompassing attitude towards the meaning and purpose of life.

I am responsible for the content of the introductory chapters, the chapters on Buddhism, Christianity, Mysticism, and the Conclusion. My sister, Dr Marilyn Holly of the Philosophy Department of the University of Florida, a specialist in the philosophical bases of American Indian thought, has kindly contributed Chapter 4, "A Chorus of Powers: American Indian Belief." Chapter 5, "The Sacred Land: Australian Aboriginal Religion," has been contributed by Norma Lyons, who discusses the highly sophisticated culture of the Aboriginal peoples for whom the continent of Australia is not merely their home, but a part of themselves. Norma's interest in her subject arose from her study of Australian history out of a concern for past and present mistreatments of Aborigines through ignorance of their values. I must, however, bear the brunt of criticism of the editing of these two chapters. Both Dr Holly and Ms Lyons have read, criticized, and contributed to the remainder of the book as well, throughout all its stages of preparation.

The Conclusion is in many ways a summary of what has been observed in the earlier chapters but presented from a very different standpoint. In this chapter my intent is to present a psychologist's view of what is taking place in these religions, and indeed in religion generally, attempting to draw together the strains of experience and thought that have gripped humankind for so many centuries and to help integrate them into our overall, even though still quite scanty, understanding of the nature of human life.

One technical comment: endnotes have been limited to points directly relevant to the subject under discussion. Reference sources have been grouped together at the end of each chapter. Translations from the Greek are my own, except in a few instances specifically noted in the references.

I wish to thank Dr Gertrude Spencer, who read through the book in manuscript and gave me much good advice in clarifying and expressing otherwise obscure points. And finally, I wish to express special thanks to Peter Broadribb for his editing of the manuscript.

REFERENCES

Carl Jung, *On the Psychology and Pathology of So-called Occult Phenomena*, in *The Collected Works of C.G. Jung*, vol. 1, Routledge and Kegan Paul, London, 1957.
William James, *The Varieties of Religious Experience*, Harvard University Press, Cambridge, Mass, 1905.

NOTES

1. Socrates is reported by Plato as claiming that at times he sensed a supernatural voice within himself forbidding him to undertake some action, though it never attempted to persuade him to undertake an action. His comment that he supposed it unique to himself is in *The Republic* section 496c.
2. The term "Quaker Meeting" refers both to an organization of Quakers and to a specific gathering of Quakers for some purpose, such as worship (silent meditation).
3. In *Civilisation and Its Discontents*, (original 1930), the first two pages, in reference to a suggestion by Romain Rolland. In vol. 21 of the *Standard Edition of the Complete Psychological Works of Sigmund Freud*, Hogarth Press and the Institute of Psycho-Analysis, London, 1953 onwards.

4. See the long discussion in Jung, *C.W.* vol. 17, paragraphs 300–311.

5. This despite the fact that Plato almost never describes Socrates in any other role than as a teacher. Plato rarely reports himself as present at any of the dialogue gatherings which he describes, even though he and Socrates had been in a de facto son and father relationship for many, many years. He seems to have wanted to keep his personal relationship with Socrates a completely private matter.

THE COLLECTED WORKS OF CARL JUNG

All references in the body of this book to the works of Carl Jung refer to the following volume numbers of *The Collected Works of Carl Jung*, ed. Sir Herbert Read, Michael Fordham, Gerhard Adler and William McGuire, published by Routledge and Kegan Paul, London. Works are referred to in the text as Jung, *C.W.* and are followed by the relevant volume and paragraph number.

Volume	Date of publication	Title
1.	1957	*Psychiatric Studies*
2.	1973	*Experimental Researches*
3.	1960	*The Psychogenesis of Mental Disease*
4.	1961	*Freud and Psychoanalysis*
5.	1956	*Symbols of Transformation*
6.	1971	*Psychological Types*
7.	1953 (2nd ed. 1966 used)	*Two Essays on Analytical Psychology*
8.	1960	*The Structure and Dynamics of the Psyche*
9.	Published in two separately bound and paginated parts:	
	PART 1 1959	*The Archetypes and the Collective Unconscious*
	PART 2 1959	*Aion*
10.	1964	*Civilization in Transition*
11.	1958	*Psychology and Religion: West and East*
12.	1953	*Psychology and Alchemy*
13.	1968	*Alchemical Studies*
14.	1963	*Mysterium Coniunctionis*
15.	1966	*The Spirit in Man, Art, and Literature*
16.	1954	*The Practice of Psychotherapy*
17.	1954	*The Development of Personality*
18.	1976	*The Symbolic Life*
19.	1979	*General Bibliography of C.G. Jung's Writings*
20.	1979	*General Index to the Collected Works*

CHAPTER ONE

WHAT IS RELIGION?

... there came to me, I cannot tell whence, a most powerful
sweetness that had never come to me afore. It was not religious,
like the goodness of a text heard at a preaching. It was beyond
that. It was as if some creature made all of light had come on
a sudden from a great way off, and nestled in my bosom. On
all things there came a fair, lovely look, as if a different air
stood over them. It is a look that seems ready to come
sometimes on those gleamy mornings after rain, when they say,
"So fair the day, the cuckoo is going to heaven."

Only this was not of the day, but of summat beyond it. I
cared not to ask what it was. For when the nut-hatch comes
into her own tree, she dunna ask who planted it, nor what
name it bears to men. For the tree is all to the nut-hatch, and
this was all to me.
[From Mary Webb, Precious Bane, (1924), Virago Press
Ltd, London, 1978, pp. 58–59.]

From the earliest times, religion has been a feature of human activity, yet we
have detailed knowledge of only recent manifestations of religious thought.
The principal reason for this is that writing—and thus writing down of religious thought—is, at most, only five thousand years old. This is a very short
time in view of the fact that archaeologists have unearthed the remains of
complex civilizations from up to ten thousand years ago. Remains of religious
paintings and icons—both painted and sculptured—have been found, in what
appear to be religious chapels, even in very early village buildings. However,
their specific significance and the religious thought systems which they represented are largely a matter for guesswork. The same must be said of the interpretation of most of the cave paintings found scattered throughout the world.
That many of these cave drawings had to do with religion seems very likely.

Unfortunately the earliest of them appear to date back only some twenty to forty thousand years, a brief period if we consider the two million years of existence of human beings. Although it is plausible to speculate that religion has existed in one form or another for at least as long as human beings have had the capacity to think, for most of that period no religious traces are known to have survived. The importance of this fact is that where known religious icons and (in more recent times) writings do survive, it is likely that there is up to two million years of history behind them, a history of which we know literally nothing.

DEFINITIONS OF RELIGION

We use the word religion for a number of related but distinct concepts. It takes but little reading in the literature to discover, for example, discussions debating whether indigenous groups such as the traditional clans of Aborigines in Australia have a religion, or religions, at all, since for the most part there is no concept among them of God or gods. Similar questions have also been raised in regard to whether Buddhism and Confucianism are entitled to be called religions, for they involve no belief in God, even though they may tolerate coexistence with religious systems that are God-based. Freud held that Marxism should be considered a religion,[1] though this idea has not been generally accepted. Freud came to this conclusion through considering the role that Marxism plays in the minds of committed Marxists.

From some points of view, Freud's own development of psychoanalysis has characteristics of a religion, and the same has often been said of the form of psychoanalysis developed by Jung. In these two instances, as with Freud's evaluation of Marxism, the definition of *religion* is stretched to include the intensity of devotion of its adepts as a primary characteristic of religion, together with a certain unwillingness on the part of the founders to acknowledge the possibility that many of their claims are theories rather than established facts. I would like to invite you to accompany me in considering what the word religion implies to us who live in the tail end of the twentieth century in a time when so many questions—ranging from the question of the meaning of life to the very practical question of exactly when life begins and ends—create an enormous muddle of confusion.

Religion may be variously defined as a way of life, a type of belief, or a particular orientation of your innermost being. In a legal sense, it can refer to an incorporated body recognized by the state, sometimes on the basis of what appears to be a mere technicality. For example, Dianetics (Scientology) became incorporated as a church in California after it ran into legal difficulties because it was presenting itself as a form of psychology. As the "Church of Scientology" it has presented a legal conundrum. Similarly, in the Australian state of Victoria, a psychologists' registration act was enacted specifically to outlaw Scientology; but the constitutionally guaranteed freedom of religion made the state powerless when Scientologists shortly returned as the Church of Scientology.

The State government of Western Australia decided that it would determine whether an organization should be granted legal status as a religious group on the basis of whether it taught the worship of God. This was an ill-informed decision, which has proved impossible to implement, because by that standard neither Buddhism nor indigenous Aboriginal tradition would qualify. Aboriginal tradition has presented a particularly difficult, ongoing legal problem, because in Aboriginal culture many geographical areas are considered sacred sites and therefore off-limits to industrial or housing development. The difficulty of finding an overall definition of "sacred" has meant that legal authorities have regularly been forced to consult professional anthropologists to decide the status of particular areas. In Australia, rather frequently, anthropologists consulted by the Federal government give a much wider meaning to the word "sacred" than those consulted by the State governments. Similar problems arise with American Indian tribes.

To a large extent such problems arise because, for the majority of Westerners, religion is taken as a specific area of life, separate from everyday secular living. This is particularly evident in countries in which there is a strict separation between Church and State. We do not have to look far, however, to discover that this is not the case all over the world. In modern Israel several groups reject such separation of religious and secular life, and also wield considerable political clout. At the time of writing these words, military conflicts based on religious differences plague Lebanon and former Yugoslavia. When this chapter was first formulated, nine years of war had just ended between Iraq and Iran which, among other causes, found a basis in conflicting views on how the regulations of Islam should be implemented in daily social and political life. These religious conflicts have fairly firm foundations. For example, currently—as in the past—Judaism and Islam prescribe quite closely how life is to be lived, not only on what might be called a spiritual level, but also in terms of everyday activities such as what is to be eaten, how it is to be cooked, what clothes are to be worn, how judicial systems are to be organized, and much else. Small groups such as the Old Order Amish, in the eastern United States, are striking examples of Christian traditions which define the details of daily life. On a larger scale, many readers will remember that within the general Christian tradition the Roman Catholic Church, until very recently, retained some vestiges of food and clothing regulations, if only in the form of eating fish on Fridays and the use of head coverings in church.

When it comes to indigenous populations, it becomes virtually or totally impossible to distinguish between daily life and religion. This is a point discussed in considerable detail in Chapter 5 on American Indian beliefs and in Chapter 6 on Australian Aboriginal culture, both of which not only continue in full strength on their respective continents, but are steadily gaining in importance as minority groups challenge central governments on fundamental issues.

Generally, in cultures where daily life and religion are indistinguishable from each other, daily activities are governed not only by rituals, but particularly by a special type of relationship with other people and with the physical world as a whole. For such groups there is no distinction possible between the religious and the secular, because the whole of life is, so to speak, religion. Theology and beliefs in general play little role in this aspect of religion. The question of God arises within some groups (e.g., Jews, Muslims, Hindus, various African tribes, some varieties of American Indian culture), while other groups conceive of reality as a continuum incorporating both earthly and spiritual aspects, and have no need to postulate a separate supernatural realm.

A different point of view from that outlined above is found among religious traditions which make a sharp distinction between the visible world and an ultimate reality which transcends the universe. This group of traditions distinguishes between the material universe and a second, spiritual, realm outside space and time. Religious systems such as mainstream Christianity have tended to emphasize the distinction between the secular and the sacred to a point where the material world frequently becomes devalued in favor of the spiritual. Because the material world is not considered to be sacred, there is very little restraint on its exploitation, which even verges on the total destruction of parts of nature. By and large, conservation, which is central to the life patterns of American Indians and Australian Aborigines, is not considered a religious issue among the major God-focused traditions.

THE SPIRITUAL AND MATERIAL WORLDS

As we will have frequent occasion to see during our survey of individual religious traditions, the words *God* and *spirit* mean many things to many people. For the moment I will merely make the observation that two major concepts of God have played a prominent role in the history of religions:

1. Many participants of religious traditions hold that there is an impalpable and invisible power or energy which penetrates the whole of the universe and gives it cohesion, meaning, and purpose. For those who hold such a belief, God is—to a very important extent—a fact of the material world as well as possibly of a spirit world. The power may be personalized in order to make it easier to relate to.

2. For the many people who make an absolute distinction between the material and the spirit realms, religion is a particular type of relationship with God, or, in more general terms, with spirit beings held to be different in nature from anything found in the material universe to which we are accustomed. This viewpoint holds that there is a realm which transcends the material universe which, however, is also the essential foundation of the material universe. Generally, it is postulated that while God and other spirit beings have some activity in the material world, there exists an unconnected spirit world in which the spirit beings exist apart from humanity and matter.

The distinction between the two ways of viewing reality is easily seen if we consider the Australian Aboriginal traditional view that the material world was not only created by special Beings in The Dreaming[2] but also embodies those Beings in material forms such as rocks, hills, and most other natural objects, as well as in individual people, plants and wildlife, and also as the Rainbow Serpent which lives in many bodies of water such as sacred springs and streams. This is in direct contrast with the popular religious view that the material world, as well as human beings, are the creation of a spirit or spirit beings but separate and distinct from them.

In Western thought there are, of course, also varieties of belief which deny a reality beyond the natural world because they do not acknowledge that matter and spirit are different things. These views, which include Marxism and most branches of Western science, have generally not been considered part of the religious scene. But some religious groups also do not assume a difference between matter and spirits, including Westernized forms of Zen, and the relatively modern Church of Christ, Scientist (the Christian Science Church).

RELIGIOUS BELIEF SYSTEMS *VERSUS* AN EMOTIONAL RESPONSE TO GOD

Unlike indigenous religious cultures, most modern religious systems place great stress on the acceptance of beliefs. For many people, religion is synonymous with a particular set of beliefs. Beliefs may be intellectual statements, but just as often they are statements which try to convey an experience and only become philosophically formulated when they are taken over by those who have inherited the beliefs without a prior experience of what they refer to. As examples I would point to the Buddhist teachings of nirvana and karma, and the Christian doctrines of the Trinity and of predestination, discussed in Chapters 2 and 3 on Buddhism and Christianity respectively.

The distinction between belief as an attempt to express a personal feeling-experience and as an attempt to make an intellectual statement might best be illustrated by a specific example. The statement "God is Love" may hold quite different meanings for persons who use the phrase. The two principal meanings may be expressed as:

1. "God" is a word used to indicate that the only important principle of religious life is love;
2. God is the supreme example of how the act of loving is made manifest.

At first glance the two statements appear virtually identical. But when we examine how they are used, we find that quite different meanings may be intended.

Those who assume the first meaning (that "God" refers to the emotion of love) often find it pointless to delve into theological discussion. Because love is a natural emotion, they understand the essence of religion to be a particular emotional framework. No particular intellectual or philosophical statements need be attached. Martin Buber's seminal book *I and Thou*[3] has become a classic expression of this approach. Kindred feelings are found among the Quakers in the West and in Zen in the East. All three regard discussion of the "supernatural" (however it may be defined) with great distrust because they regard it as detracting from, or even replacing, the crucial essence of religion. Their principal concern is that religion should not be a venture into anything other than a direct personal experience. It is interesting that this concern is shared by many who otherwise find themselves at the opposite pole to Buber, Quakers, and Zen, namely, those who voice the "Evangelical Christian" emphasis. That emphasis is on direct personal experience as a vital requirement without which no religious involvement is possible. The mystics also generally expound this view, a point we will examine in considerable detail in Chapter 4 on Mysticism. All of these groups also share the view that a specific type of experience is intended, even though they may differ as to the details of the experience.

The second meaning of "God is Love" (that God is the supreme example of how the act of loving is made manifest) does not understand "God is Love" to be a kind of definition, but rather a description which characterizes, but does not limit, God. In this meaning, "God is Love" is considered to be part of a large system of descriptions of God, which include doctrines about God's activities and our corresponding human responsibility. There is a creed which is accompanied by a set of intellectual teachings about God. Virtually from their beginning, mainstream Judaism and Christianity placed almost exclusive emphasis on this second meaning of "God is love," as did Islam when it came into being in the seventh century AD. The mainstreams of these three religions continue today to stress that intellectual definitions and beliefs are of immense importance.

There are, of course, religious systems which do not find a need to include a concept of God. For simplicity's sake I am using the term "God" to include also a group of "gods," i.e. so-called polytheism as well as monotheism. Religions without a God-focus often emphasize specific items of belief and faith to which intellectual as well as emotional assent must be given. Mainstream Mahayana Buddhism is a prime example.

Other systems place more or less equal emphasis on personal experience, including that which takes place during rituals, and a belief system which may be explicit or simply taken for granted. Prime examples of these are the traditional American Indian and Australian Aboriginal traditions.

We must also keep in mind that many people deny that they hold religious *beliefs* because they are fully convinced that they are involved with self-evident truths. In view of this, we might better define belief as "presumed truths of which the person is aware and totally convinced."

RELIGION AS AN ORGANIZED SYSTEM

Usually there is a more or less formal organization of people holding to kindred beliefs or claimed knowledge about nonmaterial reality. This organization may be a whole social system or culture, or an ill-defined grouping of people to whom it is convenient to give a common name such as "Jewish" or "Shinto." What is more usually intended is very well-defined, organized groups which distinguish between members and nonmembers, have definite regulations, codes of conduct, practices of worship, and usually legal status.

Religions as organized systems with some sort of formal central coordinating bodies are by no means a recent invention, although the proliferation of such organizations within a single, social system is somewhat modern (with notable exceptions as in India). The history of most of the "major" or "minor" religions of the world, present and past, indicates a high level of organization tracing back a very long way.

The development of religious systems

The various aspects of religion so far discussed in this chapter (religion as a way of life, attitudes towards and relation with the world, a relationship with God, systems of belief and formal organizations) are, of course, in practice not as clearly delineated as they have been described here. Individual groups, and particularly individual adherents of a religious system, commonly construct for themselves a system combining several of these aspects of religion.

Throughout history there has been a tendency for new religions to grow out of older ones sometimes replacing, but more usually competing with, the religion(s) from which they originated. Religions as organized systems never exist in isolation. They are heavily influenced, or even formed, by the social system in which they operate. In addition, the interaction of social systems with each other, as well as the crossing of boundaries between religious systems, produces profound changes which often eventually lead to distinct and often opposing systems. As an example, let us look at Figure 1 which is a highly simplified sketch of a "family tree" of one interrelated group of religious systems, each of which was or became highly organized and often a corporate body.

Figure 1 shows how the interaction of organized religious systems in contact with each other comes to produce as their offspring other well organized religious systems which eventually come to be seen as independent identities. The diagram has been simplified in that many branches have had to be omitted for the sake of legibility and comprehension, and only one of the many possible religious family trees, most of them interrelated as well, is portrayed.

Egyptian + Palestinian + Arab + Mesopotamian Cultures

Hebrew

Hebrew + Zoroastrian + Greek + Gnostic

Judaism   Christian

Christian + Arab

Christianity

Islam

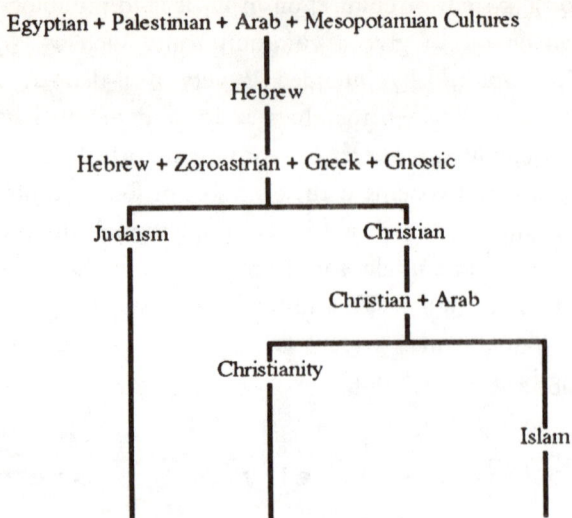

Figure 1: An example of interrelated religious systems

To explain the family tree in Figure 1, some basic historical information is required. On the first level we find Egyptian religion of approximately 1400 BC which became codified and highly organized under King Akhenaton.[4] It was later blended with religious elements from ancient Palestine of about the same era, as well as with organized Arab religious movements, and with a very old, long-standing Mesopotamian religious culture, to form the Hebrew religion. In describing these religions as "organized," various degrees and types of organization are implied. King Akhenaton's religious reformation in Egypt appears to have been tightly organized and unified throughout Egypt by a highly centralized government and civil service. The Palestinian religious movements were also organized, but on a less intensive scale. They appear to have been primarily organized on a city to city, or town to town, basis with local shrines, temples, and priesthoods which held much in common but were relatively independent of each other. Much the same is true of the Arab culture of the period. Mesopotamian religion was, like the Egyptian, organized on a higher state level, though apparently not as closely knit as in Egypt.[5]

From this blend of religious cultures developed the early Hebrew religious culture. In its initial stages Hebrew religious culture was organized along clan and village/city lines. It became progressively more unified and centralized until it was formed into a unified system with its own distinct bureaucracy under King David and his successors in the general period 800–700 BC. Hebrew religious culture did not exist in isolation, but our chart does not allow room to show the numerous influences which gave it its distinctive character, in particular the continuing and at times very pervasive influence of Mesopotamian culture.

During the period 800–500 BC, a creedal statement of vast proportions emerged and was eventually codified in writing, something which had also been done, to a much lesser degree, in King Akhenaton's system in Egypt. The Hebrew and Egyptian examples are at present the first known written linkage of creedal statements with formal, legally sanctioned and regulated religious organization.[6]

In the general period 500–200 BC three major new influences impinged upon the Hebrew system in Palestine and elsewhere in the Babylonian, Egyptian, and later Persian, and eventually Macedonian empires. The first influence was a religious system which traces itself back to the work of an individual, Zarathustra, about 600 BC, often known by the Greek spelling of his name as Zoroaster. Zoroaster's religious system swept to legal status and ultimately governmental promulgation as the official religious system of Persia and then of the Persian empire.[7] This system today is continued by a very small group principally located in Bombay and known as the Parsees, and is the only one of the group of religious cultural traditions on level three of our diagram to survive to the modern day. Zoroastrianism was highly creedal, that is, it postulated doctrines proclaimed to have originated by revelation from God. This was not the first time that this had happened. Tradition ascribes a similar role to Moses[8] in the foundation of Hebrew religious culture, and some religious historians feel that the limited historical material resulting from the Egypt of King Akhenaton's day implies a similar claim to divine revelation by King Akhenaton. Through the influence of Zoroastrianism and through the second major influence—the writings and schools of classical Greece—came a new, carefully defined system of Hebraism which can lay claim to being the direct progenitor of modern day Judaism.

The third major influence at this time was the Gnostic schools, which were a very loose grouping of philosophical and in some cases organized religious systems incorporating many influences from Indian Buddhism, Persian Zoroastrianism, and Graeco-Roman philosophy. They gained prominence during the first centuries AD and continued in some instances to survive for many centuries as organized systems and as philosophical concepts which exerted not only great influence on the development of classical Judaism, Christianity and Islam, but have continued into modern times where they have been incorporated into a number of new religious movements such as the Rosicrucians, Christian Science, and the Gnostic Church, especially during the nineteenth and twentieth centuries.[9]

An intermixture of the same religious, cultural and organizational movements from which modern Judaism developed, also gave birth, almost simultaneously, to another independent religious movement—Christianity. As in the development of Zoroastrianism and the Hebrew religion, known historical individuals had a major hand in shaping the emergence and development of Christianity.[10]

Within a very few centuries, eastern Christianity—in both an ideological, and to some degree organizational, sense—was mixed with Arab traditions, and promulgated primarily by Muhammad, c. AD 600, who claimed divine inspiration as had the founders of the earlier religions. From this beginning, the system known as Islam quickly emerged as an intricately organized ideological movement, which, within a very short time became a major world religion. This, in its turn, spawned a variety of independent movements. Some of these, such as Baha'i, continue to the present day along with their parent Islam which continues to be a driving force in modern world secular and religious culture.

From this discussion of the "family tree" of one interrelated group of religious systems, each of which was or became highly organized and often a corporate body, we can understand how often relatively amorphous religious traditions may become more or less formal organizations of people committed to specific beliefs or knowledge about nonmaterial reality.

The interrelationship of organized religion and social organization has barely been touched in this discussion, despite being a field of extreme importance, a field about which a massive amount of literature already exists. Suffice it to say that no religious tradition originates or flourishes in a social vacuum. The degree to which social and political involvement determines its shape and development should not be underestimated.

What does become clear is that "religion" means different things to different people, and confusion can easily arise when religion is discussed. For some people "religion" means a basic attitude towards life, an attitude which can be expressed in many types of social systems and which defies any attempt at intellectual definition. Zen and Quakers typify this meaning. For others, "religion" means first and foremost a specific group which holds certain customs and specific beliefs in common. Jews, Christians, Muslims, Parsees, and perhaps the bulk of Buddhists align themselves with this viewpoint. Yet others feel religion to be a type of experience which in its essence is separate from attitudes and groups alike, whether cultural or ethnic. The mystics, by and large, epitomize this emphasis. And for others, a history of continuous, relatively isolated culture with all of its characterizations constitutes "religion." Into this category American Indians and Australian Aborigines and most other indigenous groups are fitted by sociologists and many historians of religion.

In the chapters which follow, we will see the interweaving of the many concepts of religion and, it is hoped, come to a broad view which will encompass all the varieties of religious thought and experience that are such a striking feature of human beings.

NOTES

1. Sigmund Freud, *New Introductory Lectures in Psychoanalysis* (1933) lecture 35 in *Standard Edition of the Complete Psychological Works of Sigmund Freud*, vol. 22, Pelican Books edition, Penguin Books, Harmondsworth, 1973.
2. For Australian Aborigines The Dreaming is the joining of time and space. Totemic Beings gave the landscape the form it has, and became transformed into the specific features of the landscape, while also continuously becoming the various animal and vegetation species, and animating individual human beings, so that (according to our concept of time) past, present, and future are combined in The Dreaming.
3. Martin Buber, *I and Thou*, T & T Clark, Edinburgh, 1959.
4. Details in Cyril Aldred, *Akhenaten*, Thames and Hudson, London, 1968; Henri Frankfort, *Ancient Egyptian Religion*, Harper Torchbooks, New York, 1948; A.H. Gardiner, *Egypt of the Pharaohs*, Oxford University Press, Oxford, 1961.
5. Details in Henri Frankfort, *Kingship and the Gods*, Book II, University of Chicago Press, Chicago, 1948.
6. For the overall development of ancient Hebrew religion see Helmer Ringgren, *Israelite Religion*, Fortress Press, Philadelphia, 1966. German original, 1963.
7. For a detailed discussion of Zoroastrian origins, concepts and history see R.C. Zaehner, *The Dawn and Twilight of Zoroastrianism*, Weidenfeld & Nicholson, London, 1961.
8. As described in such literature as the Bible, in the book of Exodus.

9. See particularly Hans Jonas, *The Gnostic Religion*, Epilogue to the second revised edition. Beacon Press, Boston, 1962.

10. See Evaldo Pauli, *Mil Jaroj de Kristana Filozofio* (especially chapters 1 and 2), Eldonejo Simpozio, Florianópolis (Brazil), 1985.

CHAPTER TWO

BUDDHISM

The basis of religious criticism is: man makes religion.
Religion does not make man. And indeed religion is the
self-consciousness and self-regard of man who has either not
yet found or has already lost himself ... The struggle against
religion is therefore indirectly the struggle against the world
whose spiritual aroma is religion.

Religious suffering is the expression of real suffering and
at the same time the protest against real suffering. Religion is
the sigh of the oppressed creature, the heart of a heartless
world, as it is the spirit of spiritless conditions. It is the opium
of the people.

Karl Marx[1]

Buddhism can be traced back to Gautama Siddhartha (c. 620–540 BC) who is titled The Buddha (Sanskrit for "The Awakened").[2] Most historians place Gautama in the sixth century BC in India. There are no written teachings from the hand of Gautama or his immediate followers. Their teachings were preserved by word of mouth and many came to be written down a few centuries after Gautama's lifetime. The various biographies of Gautama also date from long after his death, so that it is difficult to know how much of them are reliable. However they share enough facts in common for it to be reasonably probable that Gautama's father was a prominent and reasonably wealthy aristocrat in a small state in India. Gautama's mother is said to have died shortly after his birth leaving him to be reared by his sister. He eventually married and had at least one son. Tradition also holds that he left his wife and son—and perhaps other children—while in his early thirties, to go on a quest for Truth.[3]

Just what the religious situation was in India at that time in history, is very difficult to determine. As a rule, religious historians assume that early forms of the same Hindu teachings as are found in the sacred writings the *Vedas* and the *Upanishads* were already standard belief in India, and that Gautama's teachings can best be seen as a protest against these early Hindu traditions. It is therefore desirable that we first look briefly at these Hindu beliefs.

HINDU BELIEFS

Hinduism is a God-centered religion, in which communion with God is all-important. According to Hindu tradition, God (titled Brahman) exists outside, and independently, of the universe, while at the same time being the origin and support of all existence, both natural and supernatural. The various aspects of God have various names. God is understood as being at the heart of every person and in that aspect is termed the Self (in Sanskrit, *Atman*), which is a pure manifestation of Ultimate Truth beyond all description. Every living being has the quality and potential to come into communion with the Atman through meditation. The often quoted phrase "You are That," which comes after a discussion of the attributes of God, emphasizes the Divine Center in every being. Many Westerners are under the impression that Hindus worship a multitude of gods, but properly speaking Hinduism is not polytheistic. The Supreme Godhead (Brahman) is but one Being who may be glimpsed through many forms. Vishnu (in many branches of Hinduism) or Shiva (in other branches) has traditionally been the name used for the form which the Brahman takes within the created world. All other "gods" are names used to personify the activities of this Supreme Godhead.

Hindu theology and tradition have been elaborated in countless writings by Indian religious philosophers over the centuries. For the purpose of examining the background of the basic teachings of Buddhism, three Hindu concepts are most important:

1. The universe is eternal. It undergoes an endless series of cycles of birth, progress, decay and annihilation, a series of cycles which has neither beginning nor end.
2. There is a never-ending cycle of reincarnation of all living beings. The personality of every individual being is born in a body, lives, dies, and is reborn in yet another body throughout all eternity. Because it is the same personality which is reborn, the individual's personal nature during a previous lifetime, and the effects of that person's actions, remain when

the person is reborn. This is the doctrine of *karma* which played one of the central roles in the origins of Buddhist teaching.

3.   There are detailed teachings about the aspects of God, Brahman, Atman, and a spiritual world which may intervene in human or other worldly affairs. How we are to relate to them, as well as the conduct of prayers, rituals and festivals, form the center of religious faith.

THE ESTABLISHMENT OF BUDDHISM

Gautama initiated a religious revolution against the very premises of Hinduism, and established the world's first known atheist religion. In this he was prompted by the impression made upon him by the living conditions of the times. Buddhist tradition is unanimous in portraying his lifelong concern with the poverty, disease, and death he saw all about him, and with the inequity that some few elite classes should live in luxury while the vast majority lived, starved, and died in a virtual state of endless slavery to the wealthy. Buddhism has always held close to its heart the demand that its true practitioners take care to keep to the "middle way," that is, to live a life that is neither luxurious nor a burden on society, but one in which compassion for one's fellow beings replaces the desire for wealth and influence.

Gautama began his search for Truth and the way of right living in the traditional Hindu fashion. He became an extreme ascetic, a hermit, and devoted himself to meditation, trances, and fasting. Through meditation he succeeded in bringing on visions which terrified him. Despite the terror they brought him, he continued to induce visionary experiences which came to take the form familiar to mystics the world over, although colored by Hindu teaching—visions of the cosmos, the sense of being immortal and memories of having been reborn on this Earth countless times, visions of the gods, and experience of powers of extra-sensory perception and of magic feats. Following upon these visions there came, as if in complete refutation of the visions, an experience so powerful that it overturned his whole conception of life. As he sat beneath a tree in meditation there dawned upon him the realization that everything he had believed and all his religious experiences were an illusion and that what he had been attempting to achieve, in effect, perpetuated the very situation from which he wanted to escape—the pain, the misery, and the ignorance that inevitably afflict all those who live in this world.

Gautama's reaction to this realization was to discard, as much as he found possible, all the religious teachings and practices of his day and to start afresh, because he came to realize that it was the religious beliefs and the social system that supported them that were the root of the misery and suffering.

The nature of the break from Hinduism

From the distance of time, we can see that Gautama did not succeed in freeing himself from traditional beliefs as much as he thought he did. The three central points of Hindu faith were modified rather than fully abandoned in his teaching. Nevertheless, the effect of the modifications was to make his teaching radically incompatible with the Hindu belief of his times.

The eternal universe

Though Gautama accepted the common belief that the world is eternal and undergoes an endless cycle of beginning, progress, decay, and annihilation repeated ad infinitum, he became aware that our main problem is that we are trapped in this cycle. Rather than attempt to manipulate the world—as the Western cultures came to do—he turned his attention to finding an escape from our entrapment. This was not to be an escape to some purported spirit world, but an escape from existence itself into total extinction (i.e., "nirvana," a concept that we will be examining at length later in this chapter).

We who live in the modern West sometimes find it difficult to understand just what Gautama's goal was, because we are not used to the premise—accepted unquestioningly by the culture in which Gautama lived—that we, as individuals, live and die only to be born, live, and die again endlessly. In that culture, the prospect of death as final escape from existence did not seem plausible.

Gautama could not fully free himself from belief in the Hindu teaching that after death we are reborn into a life commensurate with our character in the life just finished. Hindu teaching did, however, hold open the possibility that we might be reborn on a higher level than the world we knew, that is, in a spirit world in which we could conceivably even attain to the rank of gods. Existence, as understood by Gautama, included not merely the individual lives we lead now, or in the past or future, but also the entire system of spirit, God, heavens, hells, and death itself. His was an all-out assault on what religious ideology assumed as common sense—the desirability and ultimate reality of life and death. It was an assault on the very concept of existence.

Why was it that the idea of death did not bring the sense of finality which seems so obvious to many of us in the West now? In some cultures it was assumed that life continues, after death, in another world, often a spirit world. But careful thought put forward a different and excellent reason; namely, that experience showed that everything which dies returns again to life. How else are we to explain why it is that a child may have the same talents, features, or temperament as someone who died perhaps years before it was born? Only two and a half thousand years later did a scientist in the West propose a different explanation—the theory of genetics. (Even so, many intelligent thinkers in the East believe that genetics only answers some questions. Eastern traditions generally maintain that no single view of reality can be the only true one. Thus, it is easy for many in the East to view genetics as a complement to reincarnation, rather than as a substitute for it.)

Reincarnation

The premise, accepted by East and West alike, that we are individuals with an inner soul was firmly rejected by Gautama. Nevertheless, Gautama could find no way out of acknowledging that there is a modified type of reincarnation that takes place. Just as we in modern times find ourselves faced with what to us seems the indisputable fact of heredity, so Gautama could not avoid the fact that, within the framework of the material world, reactions to past events brought about by now dead persons do indeed take place and reappear generation after generation. For this phenomenon, the traditional Hindu term "karma" was used. Gautama proposed a paradoxical compromise between reincarnation of a soul and pure materialism. He proposed that karma, which ultimately determines the nature of personality and therefore of life, has its antecedents in the character of some person now dead, but that there is no soul or spirit or personality which is reincarnated. What was done in the past irrevocably changes the future, every action calls forth a pattern of reaction, no matter how long delayed. It is the *pattern of cause and effect* holding sway, and it is this pattern that is called karma. A person is "reincarnated" in the limited sense that the after-effects of that person's life influence the nature of some other person's life in a later time. This is the meaning of the teaching of karma which appears to have been one of the basic elements in original Buddhist thought. It has posed many difficulties for later Buddhist thinkers. If there is no physical or "spiritual" connection between the person who acted in the past and the person whose life is affected now, how is it possible that the effect is only on an individual rather than on society as a whole? There must be some kind of personal quality to karma which has an existence separate from the human beings who bring it into being. Indeed, many Buddhist writings do come perilously close to connecting karma with some sort of personal soul. However, in classical Buddhist thought karma is a nonpersonal element, like a gene, although, unlike a gene, it is nonmaterial. The closest a Westerner can get to the basic Buddhist message may be to understand it as saying that the effect of how a person lives, although non-material in itself, becomes a reality and is absorbed by the personality of someone born in a later age. Some forms of modern materialism come close to Gautama's insight, except for the materialists' assumption that long-term improvement of the quality of life is possible, a view which Gautama rejected as pure illusion.

The move from viewing karma as the result of reincarnation to being the after-effects of people's actions, did not really answer the observation that it *appears* as if fundamental personality characteristics keep reappearing gener-ation after generation, which is the keystone of belief in reincarnation. To say that karma is reincarnated says very little. What is it that carries this karma? Gautama's experience led him to insist that this question is unanswerable. Nevertheless the problem of "what is it that is reincarnated, if there is no soul or personality?" has continued to plague Buddhist thinkers up to the present day. Later I will discuss some attempts to solve this conundrum.

The spiritual dimension

According to tradition, Gautama himself taught pure atheism; that is, that nothing divine exists. How far-reaching this conviction really was is imposs-ible to tell. We do know that frequently Buddhism in later centuries, and in other cultures, did come to accept the existence of gods and spiritual planes. The emphasis remained, however, on the original insight that since the ulti-mate goal is escape from existence, this includes escape from any god or spirit world, for they too are entrapped in the experience of existence.

Modern psychology has had the misfortune to have evolved exclusively in the West, taking into itself many Western presuppositions which owe their origin to the work of Western religious philosophers. The effect of this is that we have virtually no formulated concepts which will help us to understand how radically new the conception of the world brought about by Gautama was. It may be for similar reasons that modern psychology, particularly psychoanalysis, and depth psychology in general, have found virtually no acceptance among peoples which have a long-standing Buddhist tradition. There is considerable risk in examining the psychology of Buddhist beliefs, because we have no way of assimilating them to our own conventional beliefs without trying to force them into an alien mould. This may require revising some of our psychological conceptions currently assumed to be axiomatic.

GAUTAMA'S SYSTEM IN PRACTICE

Although Gautama held that suffering is inevitable, he did not intend this to be taken as excusing us from alleviating, to the best of our abilities, the sufferings of others. Gautama is frequently described as The Compassionate Buddha. He instituted a system of social reform which, if tradition is to be believed, was manifested in an organization of his followers. Compassionate regard for the welfare of all living beings was the duty of all those who would follow the Buddha. Their credo was: Our work and our efforts will no longer be directed towards "self-realization" or towards accumulation of possessions and wealth, but towards sharing what we have with others. Our thought will no longer be centered on our will, or anyone else's will, but on finding the path to end suffering. Our religion will no longer be founded on the myth of God and the fulfilment of God's imagined will. True insight knows that there is no God to appeal to, and the path leading to the end of suffering is one we must reach by ourselves. Of this Gautama was convinced.

Tradition holds that Gautama organized a large body of followers over whom he firmly kept control. These followers were meant to set into motion a society based on the renunciation of wealth and self-aggrandizement, on the principle of communal living and sharing, and on abolition of all forms of priesthood and the Hindu caste system, as well as ending all the traditional religious rituals and teachings.

It seems clear, however, that though Gautama may have wished to abolish the systems of worship, priesthood, and theological doctrines common in his time, the illumination which he had experienced was not readily available to all who yearned for it. We must remember that his own illumination required a long and arduous quest. This inevitably led to a division between those who could devote themselves entirely to the quest of illumination through meditation and those who could only do so vicariously; that is, by helping to support the new system of meditating monks. The principles of chastity and segregation of monks, and of maintaining a standard of living similar to that of the people they serve, have remained constant to the present day. Those who cannot dedicate their lives to meditation must be content to carry out the social values enjoined by the Buddha; that is, avoidance of any kind of violence including violence towards animals (an avoidance that necessarily requires the adoption of vegetarianism), the offering of compassionate relief, as far as possible, to those who suffer more than you, and the hope for illumination.

To what extent Gautama had in fact set up an organized movement which included a system of monasteries and systematic meditation before his death is unknown. It is clear, however, that Gautama had not made any provision for a successor to guide the movement, so that upon his death factions appeared among his followers and Buddhism has been divided ever since.

THE DEVELOPMENT OF BUDDHISM SINCE GAUTAMA

Within the next two or three centuries the Buddhist movement achieved astounding success in India. Westwards, Buddhism had to confront the new and well organized God-focused system of Zoroastrianism which had quickly gained the official support of the Persian empire. For reasons not quite clear, this prevented the establishment of Buddhist influence as a major religion in the West, although its basic concepts gradually became well known, particularly during the time of the Macedonian and Roman empires. By about 300 BC Buddhism had become a major social and religious force in India. King Asoka (c. 270–220 BC), ruler of a portion of India, made Buddhism a state religion. In India, Buddhism continued for several centuries as a major religion, but eventually came to be replaced by a resurgence of Hinduism and the rapid spread of Islam from the seventh century AD onwards. Today Buddhism is a minority religion in India, although north and eastwards throughout all of Asia it has become the dominant religion. Westwards of India, Christianity and Islam, strongly opposed to Buddhist teachings, eventually came to replace Zoroastrianism as state religions.

As stated before, the origins and early spread of Buddhism are best understood as a reaction to, and negation of, early Hindu preoccupation with the spirit world. Popular religion in India was in the process of introducing a seemingly endless number of gods. Indian gods generally portray natural realities such as fire, sun, death, aggression, thunder, power, and all the rest of the universe and its contents. One of the major psychological functions of religion is to link us with the world and to give us our orientation, the sphere normally occupied by instincts in the animal world, and in the human world in so far as we have kept some natural life in our artificially contrived civilization. The many, almost countless number of Hindu gods and the rituals associated with them played this role in Hindu life. They were not carefully separated from each other, but tended to blend in with one another and, as already pointed out, should be understood as the Supreme Reality viewed from its many angles. (Conze, *Thought*, part 1)

Though theological philosophers in India came to understand the gods to be the many various ways in which the Supreme Godhead is manifest in forms to which human beings can relate, it is unclear to what extent popular piety understood the subtleties involved. In the eyes of traditionalist Hindus, Buddhism offered a very different, much simpler form of religion. The Buddha's teachings proposed no God or gods, no spirit or spirits, no "other world," no soul, and nothing beyond what we can see and touch in the course of everyday life. Nor did it require or depend upon the performance of rituals or (except in the original organizational stages controlled by Gautama) obedience to the commands of a leader or master. Liberation is to be in a state of nirvana which is totally beyond all human conceptual abilities, the state into which The Buddha, Gautama Siddhartha, entered at the end of his life on earth. The same potentiality is within the grasp of all people even though, in the world as we know it, it is difficult to believe that such an attainment is possible.

WOMEN IN BUDDHISM

There was and is, however, a serious social hurdle which, because of its general familiarity both in the past and in the present tends to escape due attention. The introduction of monasteries for men was fairly easy, but the finding of a role for women proved difficult. Buddhism was a child of its times, when male domination was even more prevalent and taken for granted than now. Very little allowance was made for women and, according to tradition, Gautama had grave doubts as to the desirability of allowing women to play a prominent part in his movement. A traditional account of the conflict which arose when it was suggested that women be admitted to the monastic order reads:

*When the Buddha was visiting his native town his aunt and
foster mother, Mahaprajapati, thrice begged him to grant this
privilege to women but was thrice refused and went away in
tears. Then she followed him to Vesali and stood in the
entrance of the Kutagara Hall "with swollen feet and covered
with dust, and sorrowful." Ananda, who had a tender heart,
interviewed her and, going in to the Buddha, submitted her
request but received a triple refusal. But he was not to be
denied and urged that the Buddha admitted women to be
capable of attaining saintship and that it was unjust to refuse
the blessings of religion to one who had suckled him. At last
Gotama yielded—perhaps the only instance in which he is
represented as convinced by argument—but he added "If,
Ananda, women had not received permission to enter the
Order, the pure religion would have stood fast a thousand
years. But since they had received that permission, it will now
stand fast for only five hundred years."*
(Eliot, vol. 1, pp. 156–60)

The order of nuns soon died out, however, and it was possible for tradition to record a dialog claimed to have taken place while Gautama was on
his deathbed:

*"How, Lord, are we to conduct ourselves with regard
to women?"*
"Don't see them, Ananda."
"But if we see them, what are we to do?"
"Abstain from speech."
"But if they should speak to us what are we to do?"
"Keep wide awake." (Eliot, vol. 1, p. 159)

Consequently, from the beginning to the present, contact of monks
with women has been frowned upon. A popular anecdote illustrates the attitude that monks are supposed to have:

*Tanzan and Eido were once traveling together down a muddy
road. A heavy rain was still falling.*

Coming around a bend, they met a lovely girl in a silk kimono and sash, unable to cross the intersection.

"Come on, girl," said Tanzan at once. Lifting her in his arms, he carried her over the mud.

Eido did not speak again until that night when they reached a lodging temple. Then he could no longer restrain himself. "We monks don't go near females," he told Tanzan, "especially not young and lovely ones. It is dangerous. Why did you do that?"

"I left the girl there," said Tanzan. "Are you still carrying her?" (Reps, p. 28)

Is it the social role of women that determines their place in religious systems, or does their place in the religious system determine their social status? The origins of male dominance are lost in the mists of time, proposed explanations are mere conjecture. Frequently it is women who provide the greatest ritual involvement in religious practice, but it is men who determine the nature of the beliefs and rituals and direct their practice. Just as in Christian tradition God is "He" and Christ a man, so in Buddhist tradition the Buddha is—with one important exception—male. The exception is Kwan-yin, a name which originated in India as the name of a male Bodhisattva but which gradually came to be used for a female Bodhisattva as Buddhism spread.[4]

We may wonder why Buddhism, as adopted by modern Westerners, retains the original concept that a Buddha must necessarily be a man, in contrast to the Oriental feeling that a Buddha might equally well be a woman. The explanation may be simply that Buddhist converts in the West come from a Jewish or Christian background in which the masculinity of God has until recently been virtually unquestioned. That the Buddha is merely another name for the concept of Christ, and thus of God, is a prevalent Western misconception.

Although an apparent holdover from Hindu beliefs, it generally remains unquestioned in Buddhism that reincarnation in the form of a male is a state superior to reincarnation in the form of a female. In Buddhism this is something of a paradox, since reincarnation is held not to be of physical anatomy.

THE ROLE OF PARADOX

Many of the basic Buddhist teachings seem paradoxical. Paradoxes are by no means special to Buddhism, but have a major role in all the world's religions.

Buddhism, however, more than most tends to emphasize them, largely in an attempt to dethrone rationalism in that part of human life which it holds should be devoted to feeling-experiences that transcend all human reason. Because, to a large extent, Buddhism was a reaction to what Gautama considered to be an overly rational philosophical speculation rife in Hinduism, the dethroning of rationalism in Buddhism is stronger than in most religious traditions. In his remarkable application of Jung's theory of psychological types to the classification of religions, Toynbee saw Buddhism as being of the introverted intuitional type;[5] that is, introverted in that it looks to no outside savior figure and does not require rigid adherence to a set of teachings imposed by a hierarchy outside the individual, intuitional, also, in that its anti-rational and personally acquired insight is considered to be the highest goal.

There is a paradoxical quality in all of the basic Buddhist statements, best illustrated by an anecdote from the most paradox-loving of all Buddhist traditions—Zen. Zen demands that we accept statements which give the impression that they should be meaningful, while any attempt to understand them in logical terms is fruitless:

> When Banzan was walking through a market he overheard a
> conversation between a butcher and his customer.
> "Give me the best piece of meat you have," said the customer.
> "Everything in my shop is the best," replied the butcher. "You
> cannot find here any piece of meat that is not the best."
> At these words Banzan became enlightened. (Reps, p. 41)

This is a fairly typical Zen paradoxical anecdote, which defies rational interpretation but conveys a particular feeling which is at the heart of Buddhist teaching. One of the most important points to learn in working with Zen paradoxes is to puzzle over them as much as you possibly can until you reach the point of absolute despair of ever understanding it, for only then will you be open to the uninterpreted feeling experience which it is intended to evoke.

All of classical Buddhism is founded on a logical paradox: the teaching that there is no soul, no self, no independent personality, alongside the teaching of reincarnation. Gautama and, generally speaking, his followers made no attempt to explain. Gautama's teaching was based on his experience during his enlightenment which transcended all rationality. A classical illustration put in pure terms of feeling also comes from the Zen tradition:

> *The mind functions through the sense-organs, and thereby an*
> *objective world is comprehended—*
> *This dualism marks darkly on the mirror;*
> *When the dirt is wiped off, the light shines out;*
> *So when both the mind and the objective world are forgotten, the*
> *Essence asserts its truth. (Suzuki,* Manual, *p. 99)*

As a philosophical statement the poem above could give rise to much discussion, but philosophical discussion is precisely what Zen does not want. It is the grasping of the feeling of the experience that leads to understanding, not the other way around. As I will point out in the next chapter, this was also the original premise in primitive Christianity, though the Christian emphasis on feeling soon turned into an emphasis on intellectual belief.

THE WHEEL OF REBIRTH

As already mentioned, Gautama became a buddha at the moment when he experienced consciously that he had lived countless times before; nevertheless as a person he was a simple, physical living being, rather than a soul encased in a body. As in the poem quoted above, it is vital for us to begin with realization of the nature of ourselves as living beings that are mentally conditioned to create for ourselves the objective world. The objective world is not "really Real." Nor are we concerned with anything that is potentially beyond the objective world. There is no Mind which belongs to an ultramundane Reality. Mind and body are inseparable. We hurt or feel pleasure, we perceive, we have emotions. We are body-mind units. How could there be anything more? Yet Buddhist writers often speak of our "buddha nature." There is something about us that is neither divine (as in the Hindu teaching of the Atman) nor a soul (as in Christian belief), or even a distinct self (as in materialist "common-sense"). There is nothing we can point to that is able to escape bondage to the universe of time and space. There is no "I" or "We" which experiences the annihilation that is the closest approximation to a description of nirvana which human language can express. Nevertheless, there is something inexpressible about us. The problem is that we are slaves to the conviction that all experience can be portrayed in words, thoughts, and concepts. How very, very wrong we are.

In an inexpressible fashion, the Buddhist tradition holds, we are eternal. After we die we eventually enter new bodies and the endless cyclic sequence of birth, life, and death continues on through all eternity. The wheel of rebirth is a much favored image of Buddhists. Many Buddhists claim that it is possible to remember previous lives, although there is no value in doing so. Buddhism teaches that many extraordinary feats can be performed; yet if they become our goal, we are sunk in the bitter abyss of total delusion.

The Western religions think in terms of body and mind. Some of them, like Judaism, Christianity, and Islam, expect a resurrection (a bodily survival after physical death) either immediately (perhaps in heaven) or at the end of the world. Others hold that a life-principle which they call "soul" survives, either as an independent entity, or perhaps merged into a general life-force. These religions are all trapped in the myth that Supreme Reality can somehow be described, or at the very least pointed to. They leave no room for experience of the inexpressible—but it is the inexpressible which is reincarnated and longs for release from anything we can conceive of as existence.

Eastern Buddhists have their own illustrative anecdotes to convey the feeling of finding release from the wheel of reincarnation. One ancient writer in the West has attempted to lead us to grasp what this means, but even he is seldom understood, because, as with Buddhist writers, what he wanted to say is beyond expression. That writer is Plato who held, like the Buddhists, that we are trapped in this world for all eternity, of our own free will, until and unless we come to the dawning of realization of true Reality. Let us look at what he has to say. It comes in the form of a parable which Plato portrays as being told to his brother Glaukon by his own close friend and teacher, Socrates.

[We are in the other world. The dead are all gathered together in an assembly where they have been told they must now choose the lives they wish to lead when they return to earth. They are cautioned to be very careful in their choice, because once they have chosen they will have to live out that life whether or not they like it. They draw lots to determine the order in which they will choose. Socrates comments on this:]

"There, my friend Glaukon, appears to be the greatest danger
for a person. That is why each of us must strive to the utmost,
even at the expense of other learning, to learn this—to spend

our lives as disciples of a person, if only we can find such a
person, who can make it possible for us to understand and
distinguish between a life which is good and one which is bad,
so that we can always choose the best that is possible ... "

Socrates then describes a scene in which:

... the person who drew the first lot immediately chose to be
an absolute dictator. Because of his recklessness and greed he
took it without examining it carefully enough and did not
notice that it involved the fate of eating his children, and other
terrible things. When he examined it at his leisure, he beat
himself to despair over his choice ... Because he refused to
blame himself for the horrors, he blamed his luck and the
divine powers and everything except himself ...
(The Republic 619b–d, author's translation)

The parable goes on to add that before being reborn into the life which has been chosen, the dead must drink from the "water of forgetting" so that in the new life there will be no memories of the past, nor a realization that this type of life was intentionally chosen.

Socrates' point is that the character which we strive to develop in this life determines how we will spend our next life—the basic nature of karma. In his parable he assumes a great degree of voluntary choice, something also stressed in classical Buddhism, in contrast to the traditional Western concept of fate which became embedded in the Christian doctrine of predestination (discussed at length in the next chapter).

The biggest difference between the parable as relayed by Plato and the traditional Buddhist teaching of karma is that, in the parable, the dead have the opportunity to choose carefully what their fate will be, while in most Buddhist traditions that choice comes only during life on earth. However, the gap is narrowed when we realize that according to Socrates/Plato it is the degree to which we devote ourselves to discovering true Reality that determines our character and thus the kind of choice of lifestyles we would make.

THE ESSENCE OF BUDDHISM

Exactly what is it that the Buddha Gautama would have us strive for? It is to give up our craving for life, to experience that release from suffering which is nirvana (Sanskrit for extinction, like extinguishing the flame of a candle). Nirvana is a state—not exactly a state of being, for it is quite beyond and apart from existence in any way we could conceive of. The effect of attaining nirvana is to attain complete release from life and death, from the cycle of rebirth, and from karma. Nirvana is not equivalent to death, it is escape from life, death, suffering, space, and time. It is total liberation from existence on Earth and whatever other worlds, physical or spiritual, there might be. And, yes, liberation from all the gods and spirits there might be, from God itself if there is such a thing. It is the discovery and entry into True Reality which is like nothing the mind can conceive of, it can only be experienced.

Is there anything within our own experience that can help us to identify what the Buddha is pointing towards with these teachings? We are so used to considering the material world as all-important—and those among us who adhere to one of the Western religions usually add a spiritual world as a goal for which we are to strive, or at least experience. The one point Western religions have in common is the claim to certainty about the existence and nature of the world, no matter whether they have in mind our present material world, a spirit world, or both. The Buddha stands out in refusing to discuss the nature of nirvana. There is therefore no point in talking about it. All that is possible for us is to experience a conviction that an indescribable state is possible. How then can we come to experience this conviction? We cannot. It must come to us. This quality of nirvana comes close to Rudolf Otto's idea of "The Wholly Other"—that for which there is nothing known to us which can help us comprehend it—except that Otto had in mind God as postulated in Christianity, while the Buddha has in mind our own becoming "the Wholly Other"; that is, to enter buddhahood.

This conclusion is not as foreign to us in the West as we might suppose at first. In the Western religions, salvation from evil is a gift from God, something that cannot be striven for, an act of grace (that is, a free and unearned gift from God). To put it simply, salvation in Western religious terms, and liberation in Buddhist terms cannot be acquired by trying.

The Concept of Buddha

There is also a similarity between the Christian concept of Christ and the concept of the Buddha, though not as usually supposed. Christ is unique, according to Christian teaching. The Buddha is unique, according to

Buddhist teaching, only in so far as we are talking about Gautama Siddhartha, who once lived on Earth. Both Christ and Buddha are totally outside of the space-time continuum. In purely human terms the closest we can come to this is to say that both are prior, as well as subsequent, to the earthly lives of Jesus and Gautama.

Christian teaching makes no allowance for more than one Christ. Buddhist teaching makes room for an infinite number of Buddhas; nevertheless, there is no known Buddha who has lived on this earth except for Gautama. As Christians look forward to the return of Christ, so traditionally Buddhists look forward to the coming of another Buddha, popularly named Maitreya. However, Christianity is God-centered, and Christ is one of the "persons" of God, while Buddhism knows that, whether Buddha or Bodhisattva, such a being is demeaned if called God. Such beings are beyond God.

There is, however, a parallel between Buddhism and Christianity which must not be overlooked. It is to be found in the negative theology of the mystics. One such writing has become a classic; it comes from the hand of a Christian writing under the pseudonym of Dionysius the Areopagite, about 500 AD in, presumably, Syria. His topic is the nature of God:

> *Again, ascending yet higher, we maintain that He is neither*
> *soul nor intellect; nor has He imagination, opinion, reason or*
> *understanding; nor can He be expressed or conceived, since He*
> *is neither number, nor order; nor greatness, nor smallness; nor*
> *equality, nor inequality; nor similarity, nor dissimilarity;*
> *neither is He standing, nor moving, nor at rest; neither has He*
> *power, nor is power, nor is light; neither does He live, nor is*
> *He life; neither is He essence, nor eternity, nor time; nor is*
> *He subject to intelligible contact; nor is He science, nor truth,*
> *nor kingship, nor wisdom; neither one nor oneness; nor*
> *godhead, nor goodness; nor is He spirit according to our*
> *understanding, nor filiation [being the child of someone], nor*
> *paternity; nor anything else known to us or to any other*
> *beings, of the things that are or of the things that are not;*
> *neither does anything that is, know Him as He is; nor does*
> *He know existing things according to existing knowledge;*
> *neither can the reason attain to Him, nor name Him, nor*
> *know Him; neither is He darkness nor light, nor the false nor*

the true; nor can any affirmation or negation be applied to
Him, for although we may affirm or deny the things below
Him, we can neither affirm nor deny Him, inasmuch as the
all-perfect and unique Cause of all things transcends all
affirmation, and the simple pre-eminence of His absolute nature
is outside of every negation—free from every limitation and
beyond them all.[6]

With writings like this in mind, the suggestion has been made that perhaps we have been asking the wrong question. Our question should not be whether the Buddha and the Christ are two versions of the same concept and experience, but whether nirvana and God correspond to one another.[7]

Nirvana

Let us examine a description of nirvana from a major Buddhist document, *The Questions of King Milinda*.

According to Buddhist tradition, King Milinda (c. 155 BC) was a local ruler of a province in India that had been part of the conquests of Alexander the Great (d. 323 BC). Archaeological evidence indicates that Buddhism had reached some degree of official status under King Milinda.[8] Popular Buddhist legend recounts that in his constant search for new truths, King Milinda asked a number of fundamental questions about the basic teachings of the Buddha, and the answers to these questions provide us with a relatively early picture of Buddhist thought. The text is preserved as a dialog between King Milinda and Nagasena, a representative of Buddhism. The dialog, which is divided into individual topics, preserves for us a fairly succinct and carefully worded set of "definitions," more exactly, descriptions, which we may use for our understanding of the idea of nirvana:

> *King Milinda said: "I will grant you, Nagasena, that Nirvana*
> *is absolute Ease, and that nevertheless one cannot point to its*
> *form or shape, its duration or size, either by simile or*
> *explanation, by reason or by argument. But is there perhaps*
> *some quality of Nirvana which it shares with other things, and*
> *which lends itself to a metaphorical explanation?"*
>
> *"Its form, O king, cannot be elucidated by similes, but its*
> *qualities can."*

"How good to hear that, Nagasena! Speak then, quickly, so that I may have an explanation of even one of the aspects of Nirvana! Appease the fever of my heart! Allay it with the cool sweet breezes of your words!"

"Nirvana shares one quality with the lotus, two with water, three with medicine, ten with space, three with the wishing jewel, and five with a mountain peak. As the lotus is unstained by water, so is Nirvana unstained by all the defilements.—As cool water allays feverish heat, so also Nirvana is cool and allays the fever of all the passions. Moreover, as water removes the thirst of men and beasts who are exhausted, parched, thirsty, and overpowered by heat, so also Nirvana removes the craving for sensuous enjoyments, the craving for further becoming [the craving for reincarnation], the craving for the cessation of becoming [the craving for the end of reincarnation].—As medicine protects from the torments of poison, so Nirvana from the torments of the poisonous passions. Moreover, as medicine puts an end to sickness, so Nirvana to all sufferings. Finally, Nirvana and medicine both give security.—And these are the ten qualities which Nirvana shares with space. Neither is born, grows old, dies, passes away, or is reborn; both are unconquerable, cannot be stolen, are unsupported, are roads respectively for birds and Arhats [Someone who is or is becoming a Buddha (Conze, Thought, pp. 166–9)] to journey on, are unobstructed and infinite.— Like the wishing jewel, Nirvana grants all one can desire, brings joy, and sheds light.—As a mountain peak is lofty and exalted, so is Nirvana. As a mountain peak is unshakeable, so is Nirvana. As a mountain peak is inaccessible, so is Nirvana inaccessible to all the passions. As no seeds can grow on a mountain peak, so the seeds of all the passions cannot grow in Nirvana. And finally, as a mountain peak is free from all desire to please or displease, so is Nirvana."

"Well said, Nagasena! So it is, and as such I accept it."

(Conze, Scriptures, pp. 156–7)

It is clear that nirvana is a condition, not a thing; it is the condition reached on attaining buddhahood.

If we set aside for a moment the Western notion that God is a sort of person, even if only metaphorical, the Christian and the Buddhist descriptions show a great similarity. Both are saying that Ultimate Reality is totally beyond all human comprehension. The Christian writer tends to turn to philosophical terms in an effort to define Ultimate Reality. In this, Christianity shares with Hinduism a passion for definition and logical precision—even its innermost paradoxes are carefully worded and made into creeds. In Toynbee's application of Jung's theory of psychological types, Christianity is defined as an extroverted, thinking religion. It treats its principles as objects, rather than experiences, and prefers definitions to subjective accounts of how experiences feel. However, as we will see in Chapter 4 on mysticism, Christian mystics are far less prone to do this than the theologians, as illustrated by Dionysius' essay in which his purpose is to deny the validity of any attempt to give a definition based on a description of God. All traditional, positive statements are renounced along with their opposites, emphasizing that the human mind is incapable of making any statement that is true of God. This is in line with the Buddhist writer, who will only describe Buddhist principles in terms of the subjective effect they have on the person experiencing them, while refusing any statements that give a palpable meaning to nirvana.

As stated at the beginning of the previous paragraph, the comparison between Christian and Buddhist notions of ultimate Reality was made with the proviso that we set aside the questionable assumption that God is some sort of person. At first glance, Dionysius appears to be obviously talking of Ultimate Reality in terms of a person, for God is "He" throughout the discussion. We cannot, however, be sure how much of that impression is due to the translator, and whether it is the translator's presuppositions that make the English text read "He" rather than "it." In the same way, it is unclear how much of the "it" in the translation of King Milinda's questions is due to the translator's assumptions. While reading the descriptions we get a gnawing feeling that if asked, Dionysius would not mind including in his text "neither is He a person, nor is He not a person, nor has He human qualities, nor non-human qualities ... " And Nagasena would likely not be unhappy with some such statement as "Nirvana shares with a river the quality that it is in constant flux, and with a rock that it is motionless and never changing. As a King is the bulwark for his people, so is Nirvana the protection against all craving."

Although neither of these additions was made, they would not be totally foreign to the ways of thinking of Dionysius and of Nagasena. It is very unlikely that Dionysius would conceive of God as a condition, yet it is clear that for Dionysius God is unconditioned. Nor would Nagasena be likely to confuse nirvana with a person or any kind of object, yet it is clear that in order to communicate his experience he was forced to resort to concrete analogies.

For the God-centered religions, in their traditional forms, Ultimate Reality is usually spoken of in personal terms, while for the atheistic Buddhism, Ultimate Reality is spoken of as a state, a condition that is achieved by opening oneself to it. We cannot say that Buddhism had no opportunity to define Ultimate Reality as a person. The temptation was, in fact, very great and some Buddhist scriptures come perilously close to speaking of the Buddha as the Ultimate.[9] At the same time, some Western theologians come more than perilously close to speaking of God as a process.[10] Is not the similarity of God and nirvana that they are two ways of speaking about a Reality which cannot find any satisfactory counterpart in human thought or imagination? Perhaps both might be understood as an attempt to express the intuitive feeling that, as human beings are only one part of reality, so human reason is also but one part of reality and cannot encompass the whole. Put into the conceptual framework of current Western Depth Psychology, it would be the acknowledgment that the entire capacity for human thought has evolved in unison with the environment which is the world, making it impossible to express any other type of human experience apart from using weak analogies taken from life.

But what are we to make of the claim that through one procedure or another, Ultimate Truth has become known to someone, generally the founder of the religious system? The God-centered religions usually speak of this as "revelation," other types of religious systems may speak of "enlightenment" or the acquisition of supernatural "knowledge." It is difficult to deal with such claims in abstraction, somewhat easier in specific terms.

For much of Buddhism, as for much of Hinduism, there is a series of procedures collectively known as yoga and claimed to make it possible for a practitioner to reach, if not full enlightenment, then at least considerable progress along the path to enlightenment.

BUDDHIST YOGA

Yoga is a type of meditation. The point of departure for Buddhist yoga is concentration on a single object. This may be a specific object or thought, it may be a religious image. The immediate result of such intense concentration is withdrawal from distractions and a loss of interest in what is happening around you. Reaching such a depth of concentration is difficult, particularly if you are not used to it. It is made easier by rituals which guide you. Rituals of purification of both body and mind are important. Along with these go a careful observance of basic morality including: no killing—either of people or of animals—truthfulness, honesty, generosity, an ascetic way of life and—in most yogas—avoidance of sexual activity.

The most common techniques require the posture of sitting in the lotus position. Great stress is placed on breathing control. The ultimate ideal would be not to need to breathe at all, but the practical goal is to slow down the rate of respiration.

Motionless, breathing rhythmically, eyes and attention fixed on a single point, you begin to turn inwards into yourself with the goal of no longer having conscious thought. Attaining this state may take a very long time for the novice.

So far what has been described is generally valid for most meditation procedures, Buddhist and non-Buddhist. The particular posture demanded by yoga is especially helpful in shutting out external distractions. The efforts made, with a little practice, succeed in turning off directed thinking, and at the same time sensory input is minimized. If at this point in reading this book you stop and attempt the procedure (though leaving out the lotus position), turning your concentration towards looking as closely as you can at the tip of your nose while ensuring that your eyes remain fully open, you will discover the onset of a special mental state. To some people this comes easily, to others it requires a considerable amount of practice. The danger of falling asleep in the process must be avoided or the meditation will fail.

The reason for leaving out the lotus position is that for Westerners unaccustomed to the position, the initial pain the lotus position causes can quickly override falling into meditation. Properly speaking, anything could serve as a point of departure. The value of staring at the tip of your nose is that it requires immense concentration, so strong that conscious thinking is virtually forced to stop if you are to keep staring without interruption.

Most meditation systems use some variation of this procedure. The point of concentration can be a mantra (a special selected syllable, word or name), a picture or small statue, or simply staring off into space and concentrating on listening to every sound with no attempt to consciously identify what sound it is.

In the yogas the next stages are fairly standardized, but they receive their specific form from the type of yoga being undertaken. It is easier to describe the experience of doing a yoga than explain it. I will take as an example one of the more interesting yogas, the Yoga of Psychic Heat.[11]

Alexandra David-Neel, a French Buddhist, describes the practice of this yoga as she found it while investigating psychic phenomena in Tibet. In greatly abridged form her description is as follows:

> The novice must begin his training each day before dawn and finish the special exercise relating to tumo [empowerment] before sunrise, because as a rule he has to perform one or another meditation at that time. The practice must be done in the open, and one must be either naked or clothed in a single cotton garment.
>
> Beginners may sit on a straw mat ... More advanced disciples sit on the bare ground, and at a still higher degree of proficiency, on the snow or the ice of a frozen pond or stream. They must not breakfast or even drink anything, especially any hot drink, before practicing ...
>
> Various breathing drills are first performed which aim at clearing the passage of air in the nostrils.
>
> Then pride, anger, hatred, covetousness, sloth, stupidity are mentally rejected with the rhythmic breathing out ...
>
> ... Having become perfectly calm, one imagines that a golden lotus exists in one's body, on a level with the navel. In this lotus, shining like the sun, stands the syllable ram. Above ram is the syllable ma. From ma, Dorjee Naljorma (a feminine deity) issues.
>
> These mystic syllables, which are called "seed," must not be regarded as mere written characters, or symbolic representations of things, but as living beings standing erect and endowed with motive power. For instance, ram is not the mystic name of the fire, it is the seed of fire ... Tibetans identifying ram with the fire, think that he who knows how to make mental use of the subjective image of that word, can set anything ablaze or even produce flames without apparent fuel ...

*Slow, deep inspirations act as bellows and wake up a
smouldering fire, the size and shape of a minute ball ...
Then each deep inspiration is followed by a retention of the
breath. Gradually the time spent holding in the breath is
increased more and more ...*

*The exercise goes on, through ten stages, but one must
understand that there exists no pause between them. The
different subjective visions, as well as the sensations which
accompany them, succeed each other in a series of gradual
modifications. Inhalations, retentions of the breath and
expirations continue rhythmically, and a mystic formula is
continually repeated. The mind must remain perfectly
concentrated and "one pointed" on the vision of the fire and
the sensation of warmth which ensues.*

Summarized, the stages of the exercise are as follows: a central nerve which
distributes psychic energy is visualized, first as thin as thread, then increasingly
thicker until it fills the whole body and the body becomes "a kind of tube
filled with blazing fire and air." The nerve is then "enlarged beyond all measure" and "engulfs the whole world" while the meditator "feels himself to be
a stormbeaten flame among the glowing waves of an ocean of fire."

*Beginners whose mind has not yet acquired the habit of very
protracted meditation go more quickly through the five stages
than more advanced disciples, who progress slowly from one to
another, sunk in deep contemplation. Yet even the quickest
ones take about an hour to reach the fifth stage.*

*Now the subjective visions repeat themselves in reverse
order. [At the final stage] the fire ceases utterly to be perceived,
as well as all forms, all representations whatsoever. All ideas of
any kind of objects vanish likewise. The mind sinks into the
great "Emptiness" where the duality of the knower and the
object perceived does not exist any longer.*

*It is a trance which, according to the spiritual and psychic
development of the [magician], is more or less deep and more
or less prolonged.*

*The exercise, either with or without the five last stages,
may be repeated during the day or whenever one is suffering*

*from cold. But the training, properly speaking, is done during
the early practice before dawn.*

...

*Inhalations, retentions and expirations of the breath are
accomplished mechanically, in the prescribed order, by those
who are already well trained in the* tumo *practice. They do
not break the concentration of the mind on the mirage of the
fire, nor the repetition of the mystic formula which must
accompany the contemplation. These advanced students do not
need to make any effort of imagination to see the growing
intensity of the fire. In their case, the process goes on by itself
as a result of habit which they have acquired, and a pleasant
feeling of warmth spreads gradually all over the body, which is
the aim of the practice.*

*Sometimes a kind of examination concludes the training of
the* tumo *students.*

*Upon a frosty winter night, those who think themselves
capable of victoriously enduring the test are led to the shore of
a river or a lake. If all the streams are frozen in the region, a
hole is made in the ice ... [s]heets are dipped in the icy water,
each man wraps himself in one of them and must dry it on his
body. As soon as the sheet has become dry, it is again dipped
in the water and placed on the novice's body to be dried as
before. The operation goes on in that way until daybreak
... It is said that some dry as many as forty sheets in one night.
One should perhaps make large allowances for exaggeration, or
perhaps for the size of the sheets which in some cases may have
become so small as to be almost symbolical. Yet I have seen some
respas dry a number of pieces of cloth the size of a large shawl.*

(David-Neel, pp. 207–8)

Just what is, in fact, happening in this yoga? Alexandra David-Neel con-
templates the question:

*It is not impossible that here, as in many other cases, certain
elements of the training have been borrowed from the
autochthonous Bonpos occultists [a pre-Buddhist tradition in
Tibet]. One of the latter once told me that it is the*

visualization, rather than the motion of the breath, which produces warmth during the trance. As I did not agree, he added: "A man may be killed by suggestion, he may kill himself by autosuggestion. (I need not to say that the terms suggestion and autosuggestion are mine. The Tibetan used the words 'killed by the power of mind'; kill himself 'by his own imagination.') If death can be produced in that way, so much more easily may heat be generated."

She herself was eager to participate in this meditation:

I do not know whether, when yielding to my pressing requests and shortening my time of probation, the venerable lama who "empowered" me only wanted to get rid of me or not. He simply told me to go to a lonely spot to bathe there in an icy mountain stream, and then, without drying my body or putting on my clothes, to spend the night motionless in meditation. Winter had not yet begun, but the level of the place, about 10,000 feet high, made the night rather chilly, and I felt very proud of not catching cold.

Later on I took another bath of the same kind, this time involuntarily, when I lost footing as I was fording the Mekong River, near Rakshi in Northern Tibet. When I reached the shore, in a few minutes my clothes froze on me … I had no spare ones. (David-Neel, p. 200)

REINCARNATION

There has been an enormous amount of interest in the West in the practice of yoga. Generally the purpose has been to obtain "magical" powers, or simply to obtain more complete control over the body, rather than as a preparation for religious enlightenment. In a Buddhist religious context the value of such practices is highly questionable. Generally the view held by Buddhists who value yoga as a religious practice, is that since true enlightenment is impossible for us in this world, we may make ourselves more prepared for life in a "higher" world in our next reincarnation by mastering "psychic" powers.

Such a belief reflects the amalgamation of original Buddhist tradition with popular acknowledgment that the actual experience of enlightenment seems to be an impossibility in this world in which we live. If only one person in known history has succeeded in attaining nirvana, then what realistic hope is there for us? There has been a decided popular tendency to reintroduce the concept of a soul. Particularly in the Mahayana[12] areas, the feeling that there is a personal self, contingent as it may be on the physical universe, has tended to dominate, so that hope may be held out that your own particular soul may in a future incarnation have a better prospect of encountering nirvana. This is the premise which pervades *The Sutra of the Lotus Flower of the Wonderful Law*, particularly popular in Japan. Nevertheless belief in permanent, ultimate individuality such as is assumed in Western religions is regarded with suspicion, and serves primarily as an analogy to aid in understanding the doctrine of karma.

The belief in personal reincarnation makes certain changes in the conception of the world necessary. If a person has bad karma from a previous lifetime but seizes the opportunity of a new life to learn from past errors, then that person's karma will improve and in a subsequent reincarnation a higher level of character and life will be achieved. But if the choice is to continue with impure living, there will continue to be degeneration in this and later lifetimes. However, there are practical limits to what can be attained on this our planet.

In religions which do not teach some form of reincarnation, there is typically a teaching of a three-tiered universe consisting of earth in this lifetime, a spiritual heaven or paradise for existence after death (alternatively, a purified and regenerated earth at the end of time) and hell, a state of unmitigated misery. This three-level doctrine is not limited to the major religions of Zoroastrianism, Judaism, Christianity and Islam, but traces back far into antiquity among the Egyptians and Mesopotamians, and is also basic in many lesser-known cultures.

Popular Buddhism has frequently made its own use of the theme of the three-tiered universe, accommodating it to belief in reincarnation. The presumption is that there exist many worlds in the universe. If a person reaches the limits of good or evil character that are possible on this earth, the next reincarnation will be on a world where further development may be made in either direction. According to those branches of Buddhism which stress the concept of bodhisattvas, ultimately the universe will be emptied as all beings fulfil their buddha nature. There is an interesting parallel here, which we will examine in more detail in the next chapter, with an early Christian controversy over the question of whether ultimately all human souls will be saved by Christ. The background of this controversy is found in the summary of Christian doctrine known as the Apostles' Creed, which includes the statement that Christ "descended into hell" between his execution and return to life. Many early Christian theologians held that this means he preached to, and converted, all who were in hell.[13] The Christian doctrine of Christ's mission to save all souls is a parallel to the Buddhist doctrine of bodhisattvas, which in turn is a logical outcome of the claim that the Buddha is all-compassionate, so that anyone who reaches the state of possible buddhahood is filled with compassion for all of humanity. In Christianity, the argument focused on the unlimited love which is held to be characteristic of God, of which Christ is a manifestation.

ZEN

In this chapter it has been possible to discuss only the most basic aspects of Buddhism, and little attempt has been made to consider the many divergent schools of thought within Buddhism. However, I do not wish to finish this discussion without some reference to Zen, not only because it is the best known form of Buddhism in the West, but also because it epitomizes the fundamentals which distinguish Buddhism from all other religions.[14]

Zen has its home in Japan, although originally it came from India via China. Among the streams of Buddhism, Zen is perhaps the most radical, for in principle it does away with the distinction between monks and laity. For Zen, a monastery is not conventionally a place for life-long meditation, but more a training school from which it is expected that the individual will eventually return to the ordinary pursuits of life in traditional society, albeit with a difference in attitude. Ideally, Zen is a discipline which requires the full-time dedication of its participants in a very rigid system of work and meditation over a period of ten to twenty years or more. Zen makes no promise of bringing you to nirvana, but it holds out the hope of *satori*; that is, enlightenment which transforms everyday life. In practice, Zen monasteries may be frequented for a shorter period of time, to get the taste of the process of Zen meditation if not all its fruits.

I have already pointed out, in speaking of yoga, that Buddhist meditation is a form of organized mysticism, with what to the outsider appears to be the attempt to clear the mind of all conscious thought. In Zen, an elaborate system of *koans*, a special type of questions on which to meditate, is set out for progressive contemplation. The novice is given a koan and told to appear before the Zen master at regular intervals to report progress on explaining the koan. The koans are designed to appear to have a possible meaning if enough thought and consideration is given to them. Traditionally, one of the first koans given is:

> When your mind is not dwelling on the dualism of good and
> evil, what is your original face before you were born? (Suzuki,
> Introduction, p. 104)

This appears to require very profound philosophical—in the next chapter I will say even theological—thought, though the task of giving a simple, clear answer seems quite daunting. The question must be taken very seriously, and a very serious attempt be made to answer it. Another "beginner's koan" runs:

> When Joshu was asked about the significance of Bodhidarma's
> coming East (which, proverbially, is the same as asking about
> the fundamental principle of Buddhism) he replied, "The
> cypress-tree is in the courtyard."
>   "You are talking," said the monk, "of an objective
> symbol."
>   "No, I am not talking of an objective symbol."
>   "Then," asked the monk again, "what is the ultimate
> principle of Buddhism?"
>   "The cypress-tree is in the courtyard," again replied
> Joshu. (Suzuki, Introduction, p. 106)

This koan seems a bit more amenable to explanation than the one about your original face. It looks like it may contain a very profound meaning. Many modern Westerners understand oriental religious philosophy, including Zen, as having the goal of being at one with the universe in which we live, of reaching supreme tranquillity, of being a part of nature, tranquil and unselfconscious as a cypress tree. Frequently they turn to Zen because of its strong stress on the Buddhist teaching that there is no God, no supernatural something which must be obeyed, and that contains no commands claimed to be given voice by some sacrosanct book or person. To these people there is appeal in Zen's teaching that there is no need for convoluted philosophical arguments and seemingly incomprehensible doctrines. Zen offers an escape from what they feel to be worn out Western creeds and rituals. They understand it as reaching within yourself, finding your own depths and, some add, perhaps even becoming part of a universal Soul that fills the universe. Zen is frequently felt as offering a place for this yearning for mysticism which is denied Westerners by virtually all the traditionally recognized religious movements of the West.

In the koan, Joshu rejects a suggestion that actually seems quite reasonable, that the cypress tree in the courtyard is an objective symbol of the inner depths of Buddhist experience. An "objective symbol" would be something concrete, palpable, representing in physical form the inner meaning of true Reality. In this case it would mean that all reality, including human beings, are one, and a natural part of a natural world. Objective symbols as such are an important part of many religions. For example, in Christian tradition there is such an objective symbol, namely the Host which represents the physical presence of Christ in a Catholic church. (The Host is a consecrated bread wafer which according to Catholic Christian theology becomes, when properly consecrated by a priest, the physical body of Christ. It is a symbol in the sense that it indicates a reality which cannot be adequately conveyed by any framework of thought; it is objective in that it truly is that which it represents, and is not merely a reminder, such as an icon would be. This is in contrast to a crucifix for a Christian, for example, or for a Buddhist, a statue of the Buddha or one of the Bodhisattvas. A crucifix or statue can be understood as a symbol, but it is not called "objective" in the special sense because it is merely a pictorial image and not the reality itself.) To say that the cypress tree is an objective symbol would mean that pure nature, meaningful in itself without philosophical reflection, delivers to you the key to discovering your own innermost buddha nature. But Joshu rejects this interpretation, and the koan then leaves us to ponder over his unchanged statement, that the ultimate principle of Buddhism is the cypress tree in the courtyard. We are, so to speak, defied to find in what way the cypress tree is the embodiment of the basic principle of Buddhism.

D.T. Suzuki, the most renowned and respected representative of Zen to the West, attempts to explain the point of this koan as seen with Zen eyes:

> Joshu ... was not a philosopher even in its broadest and most popular sense; he was a Zen master through and through, and all that comes forth from his lips is an utterance directly

ensuing from his spiritual experience ... If it is an intellectual
or conceptual statement, we may endeavor to understand its
meaning through the ratiocinative [logical] chain of ideas as
contained in it, and we may come to imagine that we have
finally solved the difficulty; but Zen masters will assure you
that even then Zen is yet three thousand miles away from you,
and the spirit of Joshu will be heard laughing at you from
behind the screen, which after all you have failed to remove.
The koan is intended to be nourished in those recesses of the
mind where no logical analysis can ever reach. When the mind
matures so that it becomes attuned to a similar frame to that of
Joshu, the meaning of the "cypress-tree" will reveal itself, and
without further questioning you will be convinced that you now
know it all. (Suzuki, Introduction, *p. 107)*

Zen is not something that can be learned. The purpose of the koans is, in part, to force this realization upon you. They are designed to force the mind into accepting that there is simply no answer which any amount of reason can attain. The purpose is to break the stranglehold of reason on the mind. In this koan, the reaction of the master, Joshu, is confined to the mere statement that the monk has failed to understand. What would a "correct" answer be?

All that really can be said is that there is no "correct" answer, by which I mean no answer which can be worked out and will be valid for everyone. In the Zen anecdotes, the reaction of the master upon hearing an answer is a spontaneous reaction in keeping with the nature of both the answer and the attitude of the student. The "correct" answer is, paradoxically, the spontaneous expression of the student's realization that there is no correct answer, because the question (koan) is intended to be, in its very heart, logically meaningless. If some logic can be teased from it, that logic is irrelevant. There is no way to circumvent the problem by trying to discover what the master wants to hear and give that answer. Being yourself can not be faked. Premeditated spontaneity is a contradiction in terms. As long as it is believed that it is possible to please the master the procedure is bound to fail; for, in simple terms, an attempt to please the master is to miss the point of the exercise. You must in full honesty consider in detail in your mind all the possible meanings the koan might have, even though your every attempt may be rejected. Only when your mind has genuinely reached the breaking point and moved beyond, can the most appropriate answer—appropriate for you—be given. Obviously what might be the most appropriate answer for you might be completely inappropriate for someone else. It is, if you like, a catch 22 situation; that is, no answer you can give will be right, but you must give the right answer. The solution to this situation is itself paradoxical: only through years of attempting to find a solution to the meaning and purpose of life can you truly experience the fact that no solution exists. And only when you truly experience the fact that no solution exists can you find the solution. This is a description of the point of Zen. But you will go wrong if you suppose the description I have given to be the reality. Another famous statement points up the difficulty: all teaching, all explanation, all help is merely a finger pointing to the moon; but as for seeing the moon, only you can do that for yourself. Sometimes it all seems very simple:

> *A monk asked the master: "It is some time since I came to*
> *you to be instructed in the holy path of the Buddha, but you*
> *have never given me even an inkling of it. I pray you to be*
> *more sympathetic." To this the following answer was given:*
> *"What do you mean, my son? Every morning you salute me,*
> *and do I not return it? When you bring me a cup of tea, do I*
> *not accept it and enjoy drinking it? Besides this, what more*
> *instructions do you desire from me?"*
>
> (Suzuki, Introduction, p. 83)

The obvious point being made is that Zen is not a series of teachings to be learned, it is an attempt to destroy the self-observing, self-critical, self-conscious way of living and to become what you really are, something nobody can teach you. Thus the motives which cause Westerners to turn to Zen are quite right—even though the initial understanding of what is needed to achieve their goal may be very far from the truth.

Zen is by no means merely a passive system of meditation. In the West, Herrigel has brought out vividly the application of Zen to archery,[15] and it has often been pointed out that Zen has been used in times past as a part of the training of warriors. These applications are not Zen itself, but a method of approximating to what Zen is all about. Some people achieve more by doing than by contemplating, although the end result may be the same.

To the Western observer, it appears that the goal is to remove the distinction between conscious planning and the native unconscious responses and patterns of "mental" activity inside us. Probably the closest we can come to it in Western developmental psychology is the concept of individuation as proposed by Jung. Individuation is the goal—albeit a theoretical goal which can never in reality be reached—of integrating *all* aspects of the body-psyche unit which we call a human being. This is neither a totally introverted approach (self-examination by, for example, studying your dreams in order to discover how your emotional system is functioning) nor is it a totally extroverted approach (examining the relationships between you and the world—material and human—around you), but is a breaking down of the barriers which have been erected within and around us that make us feel like isolated minds encased in a prison, a prison which is at the same time our bodies and the world around us. This goal is theoretical, because, like nirvana, there is no hope of truly reaching it in this our life on earth. Yet it gives us something to live for, and it is something that on very rare occasions we can momentarily glimpse. In this respect it may be likened to satori, the Zen experience of "enlightenment" which is not absorption into contemplation but a shift in our entire psychological makeup and approach to all aspects of living. I think there is no better way to describe it than with a poem from a thirteenth century Zen master, Dai-o Kokushi:

> There is a reality even prior to heaven and earth;
> Indeed, it has no form, much less a name;
> Eyes fail to see it;
> It has no voice for ears to detect;
> To call it Mind or Buddha violates its nature,
> For it then becomes like a visionary flower in the air;
> It is not mind, nor Buddha;
> Absolutely quiet, and yet illuminating in a mysterious way,
> It allows itself to be perceived only by the clear-eyed. It is
> Dharma [ultimate reality] truly beyond form and sound;
> It is Tao [the Path] having nothing to do with words.
>
> Wishing to entice the blind,
> The Buddha has playfully let words escape his golden mouth;
> Heaven and earth are ever since filled with entangling briars.
>
> O my good worthy friends gathered here,
> If you desire to listen to the thunderous voice of the Dharma
> [ultimate reality],

Exhaust your words, empty your thoughts,
For then you may come to recognize this One Essence.
Says Hui the Brother, "The Buddha's Dharma
Is not to be given up to mere human sentiments."
                                    (Suzuki, Manual, pp. 145–6)

Zen is not typical Buddhism, but it enshrines some of the innermost experiences which Buddhism attempts to express. Yet we need to place it in its proper perspective, as a part of the much wider religion which we call Buddhist.

BUDDHISM AND JUNG

If the whole essence of Buddhism were to be summarized in words, it would probably be something like this: the conviction that suffering is an inevitable aspect of life, the fruitlessness of attempting to gain an intellectual understanding of what lies beyond the bounds of the intellect, the stress on karma, and the hope of nirvana.

In the West, until quite recently, all of these basic points had fallen into oblivion, although they were familiar in the early centuries AD. Recently, we have finally begun to rediscover the need to question our axiomatic belief that we are on a one-way road of continual progress, at least in the material sphere.

Buddhism was not, however, based solely on material distress. It was also based on the realization that inner distress and misery are the inevitable concomitants of living, such that no amount of positive thinking or faith in a merciful God can alleviate. Those who deal with inner human misery are well aware that it is as plentiful now as always. Yet when Sigmund Freud introduced the concept of the death instinct into psychology in the early 1900's, it was received with a general skepticism which has continued unabated. Yet Freud's concept of the death instinct was based simply on the experience that all tendencies towards the continuation and preservation of life are counterbalanced by tendencies towards the annihilation of life, and these two tendencies are built into the very structure of the universe, with nonexistence the inevitable outcome. In one way Freud was merely outlining the psychological bases for the necessary feeling of hopelessness that must come before there can be change. His denial of ultimate, permanent solutions to human misery, while in no way taken from Buddhism, reflect much the same emotional situation.

Joy must always succumb to sorrow. Like Gautama's insights, Freud's experience of the death instinct was not the result of scientific study, but of personal experience. It was directly following the death of one of his daughters that he first published his reflections on the inevitability of death and its miseries.[16] His second, more lengthy discussion of the death instinct directly followed the death of his much loved grandson, and also the first of numerous operations for cancer of the palate.[17] There is nothing like personal experience of death to bring home the reality of annihilation and, like Gautama, Freud could find no comfort in the traditional teaching that the dead are not really dead but simply with God. For Gautama, as for Freud, suffering and death are ultimate facts unmitigated by any hope. When we strip away the cultural trappings, is there any emotional difference between the perpetual cycle of birth, suffering and death as envisaged by Gautama and Freud's conception? In one respect, however, Gautama knew better than Freud. Freud hoped, and may have actually believed, that human reason could bring us to our senses. Gautama realized that belief in reason, like belief in religion, is purely an illusion.

The inability of the human intellect to understand the depths of Reality has not yet been accepted by the larger share of the "developed" world. The discovery of unconscious mental processes near the end of the nineteenth century brought into question the view, which had until then reigned supreme in the West, that human intellect is the psychological faculty which is, at least potentially, in ultimate control of life. Belief in the inevitable triumph of the human intellect is still in its agonizing death throes.

By 1921 Jung had become known for his suggestion of the four aspects of ego functioning: thinking, feeling, sensation, and intuition. For the first time in modern psychology, reason was placed alongside other mental functions as equal but not dominant.

Like Freud, Jung seems to have been largely unfamiliar with Buddhist concepts in 1921, though he was familiar with Schopenhauer's writings which had introduced to the West some of the basic concepts from India. By placing feeling—by which Jung meant emotional value—alongside reason, as its equal, Jung dethroned the intellect as supreme arbiter of reality. Ultimate truths cannot be known solely by intellect. Though arrived at by a different route, Jung's suggestion came very close to Gautama's postulate, a fact which was eventually brought to Jung's attention and which he later discussed at length.[18]

To be fully convincing, an experience must appeal to the feeling, and the intellect follows rather than precedes the feeling. This is very likely the reason for the observation that mystics from all traditions report quite similar experiences, yet when describing them phrase their descriptions in terms familiar from the intellectual teachings of their cultural or religious tradition. This is a point to which we will return in considerable detail in Chapter 4, on mysticism. As Dai-o Kokushi said in the poem with which I ended the discussion of Zen, the feeling of something ineffable and supremely real is a genuine feeling and, as among most mystics everywhere, the attempt to put a name and definition to it is bound to be fruitless if the feeling of the supremely real is not to be denatured.

REFERENCES

Edward Conze (tr.) *Buddhist Scriptures*, Penguin Classics, 1959. (Referred to in the text as "Conze, *Scriptures*.")

Edward Conze, *Buddhist Thought in India*, George Allen & Unwin Ltd, London, 1962. (Referred to in the text as "Conze, *Thought*.")

Edward Conze, I.B. Horner, David Snellgrove, Arthur Waley (eds) *Buddhist Texts Through the Ages*, Oxford, 1954. (Harper Torchbook reprint, 1964, used. Referred to in the text as "Conze, *Texts*.")

Alexandra David-Neel, *With Mystics and Magicians in Tibet* (1931). (Penguin reprint of 1936 used.)

Charles Eliot, *Buddhism and Hinduism*, three volumes, Routledge & Kegan Paul Ltd, London, 1921.

W.Y. Evans-Wentz (ed.) *Tibetan Yoga and Secret Doctrines*, second edn. (1935). (Oxford University Press Paperback of 1967 used.)

Paul Reps (ed.) *Zen Flesh, Zen Bones* (1957). (Penguin Books reprint of 1971 used.)

Daisetz Teitaro Suzuki, *Introduction to Zen Buddhism* and *Manual of Zen Buddhism*, combined into a single volume in the Causeway Books edition, New York, 1974. (These two originally separate publications retain their separate page numbering in this edition and are referred to in the notes as "Suzuki, *Introduction*" and "Suzuki, *Manual*.")

NOTES

1. Karl Marx, *Writings of the Young Man on Philosophy and Society*, ed. and tr. by Loyd D. Easton and Kurt H. Guddat. (German original, 1843), Doubleday & Company Inc., Anchor Books edition, Garden City, N.Y., 1967, p.250.

2. Properly speaking Buddha is a title, not a name. It can be applied to any person who has reached the stage of full enlightenment. According to Buddhist tradition a large number of persons, apart from Gautama (often spelled Gotama), have also attained the status of Buddhahood. However, within known historical times only Gautama has reached this state, and is therefore popularly called *The* Buddha.

3. This section is primarily a summary from Eliot, vol.1. book III, chapter VIII. For a popular Buddhist legendary account of the Buddha's life see Conze, *Scriptures*, pp.34–66.

4. A Bodhisattva is a person who has reached the state necessary to enter into nirvana, but who has postponed the final step of entering into nirvana in order to first aid the rest of humanity. Although technically only a person who has entered into nirvana is entitled to the title of Buddha, in practice Bodhisattvas are felt to be a sort of "living Buddhas" and they are often called "Buddhas" in popular speech.

5. Arnold Toynbee, *A Study of History*, vol.7, Oxford University Press, London, 1957.

6. Quoted from F.C. Happold, *Mysticism*, Harmondsworth, Penguin Books, 1964 edn., p. 196.

7. Detailed discussion in Wilfred Cantwell Smith, *Religious Atheism? Early Buddhist and Recent American*, Australian Society of Comparative Religion, Melbourne (Australia), 1966, an offprint from *Milla wa-Milla* 6/1966, Melbourne.

8. For a traditional Buddhist legend about King Milinda, see Conze, *Scriptures*, pp.146–7.

9. See Myoho-Renge-Kyo, *The Sutra of the Lotus Flower of the Wonderful Law*, Tokyo, Rissho Kosei-Kai, 1970, pp. 307–8.

10. For example, Paul Tillich, *Systematic Theology*, 3 vols.

11. The technical details of this yoga are presented in detail in Evans-Wentz, pp.155–209.

12. Buddhism has traditionally been separated into two widely popularized forms, the Mahayana and the Hinayana (also called Theravada), one of which tends to dominate in any given Buddhist country. Loosely speaking, the

Mahayana tends to stress the possibility of immediate enlightenment more than does the Hinayana, and to place more emphasis on the concept of multiple Buddhas or near-Buddhas in giving aid to the individual human person.

13. A summary of the debate is to be found in Martin Werner, *The Formation of Christian Dogma*, Adam & Charles Black, London, 1953. See especially pp.100ff.

14. The following description of Zen is primarily based on Suzuki, *Introduction* and *Manual*.

15. Eugene Herrigel, *Zen in the Art of Archery*, Routledge & Kegan Paul, London, 1953.

16. Sigmund Freud, *Beyond the Pleasure Principle* (German original 1920: "Jenseits des Lustprincips" in vol. 13 of Sigmund Freud, *Gesammelte Werke*, S. Fischer Verlag, Frankfurt am Main, 18 vols.

17. Sigmund Freud, *The Ego and the Id* (German original 1923: "Das Ich und Das Es") in vol. 13.

18. There are no references to Buddhism in any of Jung's published writings before 1921. For his eventual discussions of Buddhist topics see Jung, *Collected Works*, vol. 11.

CHAPTER THREE

CHRISTIANITY

*I cannot conceive of a creator who could condemn
forever to an infinity of grief a finite creature who
is the work of his hand.*

Morris West[1]

ORIGINS

Christianity had its origins in Palestine and the areas immediately north. In the first century AD this area was one of the outposts of the Roman Empire. Because this was the site of major trade routes with Africa and Asia, Roman garrisons were stationed throughout the area, and though the details of conduct of day to day life were left to local governments appointed by Rome, matters of overall policy, trade, and major political decisions were administered by the Roman occupying forces. Generally speaking, local religious customs were tolerated, often encouraged, except when they infringed on what were regarded by the Romans as political issues or social activity which might threaten the stability of the Empire or its grip on the territories.

Judaism was the major religious and social influence in first century Palestine, and Christians at the time regarded the sacred scriptures of Judaism as their own. The Christian sacred scriptures, which now constitute the New Testament in the Bible, were not compiled into a single book for several centuries after the foundation of Christianity. The Bible is divided into two sections, the Old Testament which deals with Jewish history and beliefs up until the period of the Roman occupation, and the New Testament which consists of writings selected from texts composed by Christians during the first two centuries AD.

Details of the founding years of Christianity are few. For virtually all of its first century we are limited to writings written in Greek and preserved in the New Testament. Somewhat more is known from the second century, and from the third century to the present historical documentation is abundant.

Unlike the situation in Buddhism, the first accounts of the founder of Christian teaching, Jesus, were written only a few decades after his death. They are, however, of limited value with respect to information about contemporary historical events, since their content is largely concerned with the teachings of Jesus during his last one to three years of life, and very rarely mention datable events or persons.

During the first century AD, Judaism in Palestine consisted of a number of competing sects. The two main religious movements in Palestinian Judaism were the Sadducee and Pharisee groups. While both groups based themselves solidly on religious tradition handed down over the centuries, the Sadducee form of Judaism focused on the Temple in Jerusalem, with its accompanying system of animal sacrifice and priesthood. The Pharisees had little to do with the Temple and the priesthood; their leaders, called rabbis, led worship in small local buildings (synagogues) involving neither sacrifices nor priests. The records portray Jesus as participating both in Temple worship and in synagogues. When Christianity moved into countries far from Palestine, the traditional Jewish form of worship in the Temple was impractical. Christians for a time continued to worship in the synagogues, but as the number of Christians who had no Jewish background grew, separate Christian churches became the norm. Nevertheless, the pattern of worship in the new Christian churches was modeled on that of the synagogues and the similarity continues to the present day.

Strange as it may seem, there are no known references to Jesus or his teachings in any documents dating from the first century apart from the writings in the New Testament. Archaeological finds for this initial period of Christianity are also completely lacking. For this reason, a great deal of information about Jesus comes from later centuries, and from a historical point of view is necessarily speculative.

According to the traditions written in the New Testament, at some time about the year 30 AD, a Jewish religious teacher named Jesus began itinerant preaching and teaching throughout Palestine. As he moved from spot to spot he gradually collected a following, part of which came to constitute a close inner circle around him. These persons, including twelve men—who came to be called the "apostles"—and also a number of women, eventually became the nucleus of an organized movement. Large numbers of the public became associated with the movement. However it appears that during Jesus' lifetime no formal organization was set up.

The traditions go on to relate that Jesus' teachings involved a degree of social reform, and questioned many of the Jewish teachings of the time. He is said to have claimed as his authority, not the traditional sacred writings but inspiration direct from God. He is also said to have frequently used as a title for himself the phrase "The Son of Man," which had been used in a number of Jewish writings as a title for a prophet who would come to restore political sovereignty to Palestinian Jews and, ultimately, bring in the Kingdom of God on earth. However, a more popular title for the expected prophet was "Messiah," a term used in the Aramaic language, which translated as "Christ" in Greek. In most of the New Testament writings, and for Christians generally, "Messiah" and "Christ" came to be used exclusively to refer to Jesus, its origin as a title was quickly forgotten, and "Jesus," "Jesus Christ," and "Christ" came to be felt as interchangeable proper names.

Of considerable importance in the narratives is a series of miracles performed by Jesus. These consisted, for the most part—but not exclusively—of healing sick persons by word or by touch, and on a few occasions of restoring a dead person to life.

Eventually the Jewish establishment came to feel severely threatened by the new movement, which was seen as undermining their authority, although the Christian writings claim that Jesus was careful not to disobey or teach disobedience to any of the Jewish religious and social traditions. After a few years Jesus was formally charged with sedition and handed over to the Roman authorities. Following a summary hearing he was found guilty and executed.

The accounts continue with a vital sequel. They state that when friends and associates of Jesus visited his tomb some two to three days after the execution, they found the tomb open and empty and were informed that Jesus had returned to life. Various episodes are then related in which Jesus was seen alive by these friends and others. To what extent the return to life was understood as being in a material body is unclear. Although most of the episodes claim or imply a material return, a few do not. From the writings of the Apostle Paul in the New Testament it is clear that there were conflicting views on this point.

There has been much debate over the centuries, and continuing on into the present day, about the historical truth of the accounts of the life of Jesus. Although historians state that there is in fact no proof, Christian believers are adamant that the life of Jesus as told in the Bible is a true record. Even so, it is worth noting that many Christian theologians are not greatly concerned whether the accounts are true or not. They point out that the Apostle Paul's writings in the New Testament make no reference to events in the life of Jesus. Presumably this is because Paul had experienced the presence of Christ in his spiritual life, and it is clear that it was spiritual experience that was foremost in his mind and emotions.

Whether historically true or legendary, are events claimed to have taken place two thousand years ago actually vital for the religious experience of people who live now? Christians usually find it hard to see how there can be an experience of Christ if there was no (Jesus) Christ. But let us pause for a moment. We have religious experiences, but people around the world give very different "historical" statements to account for their experiences. Is it possible to divorce a present-day experience from the historical explanation given to account for it? I think the answer must be yes.

There is a vivid example of religious experience which remains valid, even though the history which appeared to give it validity is no longer considered to be true, in the case of Saint Christopher. Saint Christopher was supposed to have lived in the third century AD and for over sixteen centuries he has been venerated and prayed to by countless Christians. In some respects he has been the most popular of the saints, particularly for traveling Christians, because of the story that he had once carried Christ, then a child, across a river. (The name "Christopher" is Greek for Christ-carrier.) Saint Christopher became the patron saint of travel, and Saint Christopher medals are often prominent in Christians' cars. Nevertheless, in the late twentieth century, after carefully considering the documentation and traditions, the Roman Catholic Church theological authorities came to the conclusion that the story of Saint Christopher is merely a popular legend, and that no such saint ever existed.

Now, the decision that Saint Christopher never existed is interesting in its own way, but what of the numerous accounts, both past and present, by Christians of having received help from him? It seems a bit too much to ask that we conclude that they have all fabricated their experiences, or experienced delusions, or merely interpreted natural events as the saint's intervention in their lives. But what is it that they experienced if it was not help from a historical person named Christopher?

Some sort of intervention into their consciously lived lives had taken place, but the interpretation of how and where this intervention originated must be changed. A Christian theologian might say that because these people prayed to and invoked Saint Christopher in good faith, God intervened in their lives to fill the role that the fictitious Saint Christopher was believed to fulfil. A psychologist might say that given the fairly certain existence of ESP (extrasensory perception), the kind of help supposed to have been given by Saint Christopher might be due to ESP potential within the believer. For example, a person who, through some obstacle, failed to board an airplane which subsequently crashed, might think that Saint Christopher had saved her/him, when actually what had happened was unconscious precognition of the catastrophe about to happen to the airplane. That psychologist might point to experimental evidence that ESP is more likely to occur when there is very firm belief. Another psychologist might point to the fact that safe travel is to a large extent determined by the conduct of the traveler. Although this normally has relevance more to automobile travel than air travel, a good case could be made for combining the two psychological suggestions: a person who had, through an unexpected obstacle, failed to make it to an airplane which subsequently crashed may have had an unconscious ESP premonition of the crash-to-be and unconsciously arranged to encounter that obstacle. No doubt other suggestions could also be made. The point is that the Christian's faith in Saint Christopher was effective, despite the fact, paradoxically, that there had never been a real Saint Christopher.

Could then Christianity itself also prove effective even if it were discovered that no Jesus ever existed? Although I do not wish to follow up on the point quite yet, some major Christian theologians have held that no historical truth in the story of Jesus is really necessary, because what Christians experience is the Christ who is eternal and does not depend on events in history in order to be experienced. This viewpoint goes so much against the grain of traditional Christian thinking that it will be necessary to examine fairly closely Christian beliefs and experiences before this suggestion can be properly evaluated. I will set it aside for the moment, in order to return to it later in this chapter. For the present we will continue with our examination of Christian tradition.

Whatever the original facts, our thumb-nail sketch of the traditional beliefs about Jesus has special importance for understanding the development of Christian thought. Like Gautama, Jesus is said to have given numerous social and ethical teachings. But unlike Buddhism, Christianity is a God-focused religion, and the teachings are held to be, therefore, God-given and obedience to them is considered vital. In Buddhism independent ways of viewing the basic teachings often sprang from the previous religious views held in the countries to which Buddhism spread, and the precise nature of these views is held to be of little or no importance. In Christianity the extraordinary proliferation of separate Churches is based on differing claims of what precisely the basic beliefs are and how they are to be expressed. Consequently, although by and large there is no feeling of a duty among Buddhists to convert other Buddhists to their particular interpretation of the beliefs, much of the energy of Christian groups is spent in attempting to persuade other Christian groups to adopt their particular form of worship or interpretations of the beliefs.

BASIC BELIEFS

The basic claim the earliest Christians made was of having witnessed divine intervention through God's restoration of Jesus to life. For many years, to be a Christian meant simply to claim that Jesus had been shown to be the Christ. In contrast to Buddhism, in which Gautama was considered to be but one example of a Buddha, Christian belief adopted from established Jewish belief that there could be only one Christ and after him there would never be another. Jesus had been returned to life and—it was said—rose into heaven in his body. The belief was that Jesus' life on earth was a preliminary to a full-scale return by Jesus as the Christ, God's officially ordained representative, to bring about the end of the world, the purification of society, punishment of evil-doers, restoration to life which would be eternal of all worthy believers who had died as well as those still alive, and an endless reign of God on earth.

The Pharisee Jews, in particular, believed that after death God punishes all evil-doers by consigning them to the eternal flames of hell. Jesus is also reputed to have taught this. In Pharisee belief, only the strictest observance of God's laws, as found in what we now call the Old Testament, could make it possible for a person to avoid such condemnation to hell.

The newly evolved Christian teaching claimed that such punishment by God is averted, not by observance of religious laws but through what has come in English to be called the "atonement" by Christ. The word "atonement" in English was made from the words *at-onement*. The idea is that of being-at-one with Christ. Jesus was sinless, this was taken as axiomatic. Generally speaking the moral rules as taught by Judaism were taken for granted as necessary for an acceptable life, but the Jewish rituals and prayers were not. The Jewish system of morality along with belief and faith in Jesus Christ's execution and resurrection were, in the early years of Christianity, the only requirements for salvation; that is, salvation from eternal punishment by God.

From perusal of the writings in the New Testament, and comments made by Christian writers after New Testament times, it would appear that the earliest Christians simply accepted the traditional Jewish ideas of God as self-evident. For some time in the early years, Roman Empire officials considered Christians to be merely another Jewish group. It was only when Greeks and Romans who had no background in the Jewish religion began to predominate in the Christian Church that the Jewish ideas no longer seemed so self-evident, or, for that matter, even known to all Christians.

By the year AD 70, the Empire had decided to clamp down on the Jewish community in Palestine, which had been in a state of insurrection against Roman rule for some years. Gradually the Roman authorities came to outlaw, or at least force underground, the public practice of Judaism. Christians, who by and large had no complaint with the government of the Empire as such—and who for the most part lived in Rome, Greece, and Turkey—sought to distance themselves from the public perception of them as a Jewish sect. As a consequence, Christians with no Jewish religious heritage gradually became the theological leaders in Christianity, and the teachings of Greek and Roman philosophers came to predominate in an uneasy blend with traditional Jewish presuppositions. Of all the philosophical heritage of Greece and Rome it was Plato's teachings, as taught and expanded by the Academy which he had founded, that dominated.

Christian belief as we know it today traces back directly to a series of official Councils of Christian leaders and thinkers, the first of which was convened in the year 325 in the city of Nicaea, in what is now Turkey, at the behest of Emperor Constantine. Christian belief, and organized Christian groups, had been steadily gaining strength over the intervening years. The establishment of a uniform, official religion of the Roman Empire had long been a goal of the emperors. Emperor Constantine had cast his lot in with the Christian movement as the most prevalent religious movement of his time and the most likely to succeed. He promoted the Christian religion to be the official state religion of the Empire, thus making available to it financial and legal privileges it had never enjoyed before. In addition, he bequeathed to posterity a uniform, philosophically worded set of religious doctrines, largely hammered out as a compromise between competing views held by diverse Christian groups and writers throughout the Empire.

Christian belief before the Nicaean Council

From the point of view of the development of Christian belief and practice, the most important of the doctrines hammered out at the Council concerned what precisely was the relation between Jesus, Christ, and God. With no clear-cut discussion of these terms in the biblical writings, a variety of contradictory viewpoints had sprung up during the first two centuries of the Christian Church. The principal viewpoints were:

1. Jesus was a divinely inspired prophet. That miracle working was a major element in the accounts of Jesus along with his teachings posed no problem. Miracle working by the prophets is recorded in the Jewish sacred writings, and teaching was their main purpose. It is worth noting that the belief in Jesus as a major prophet in the same line as the other biblical prophets, was the belief later stated in the Koran, the sacred scripture of Islam pronounced by Muhammad about three centuries after the Nicaean Council. For Islam, the teachings and work of Jesus were divinely inspired. Not so the theological doctrines promulgated after his death.

2. Jesus was more than an ordinary mortal man. By divine design, although he began as a normal human being living a normal human life, he acquired a supernatural quality which became manifest in his offering of divine guidance and the possibility of salvation from sin and its punishment by death. The usual claim was that Jesus acquired this supernatural status at the time of his baptism. (This view was eventually elaborated, as discussed in point 4 below, to claim that not merely supernatural status but divinity itself was bestowed on him.) Such a suggestion was far more credible at that time than it would be now. Greek religious tradition, taken over and expanded by the Romans, was familiar with "heroes"—human persons who through their nature and actions acquired a type of divine status and as such continue on in the heavens with the gods. This suggestion, like the first one, preserved the basic Jewish emphasis that there is only one God, with one single form.

3. Jesus was God, who had for a brief period descended to earth, taken the form of a human being and eventually returned to heaven. Both Greek and Roman popular religious traditions were familiar with the teaching that God—specifically Zeus for the Greeks, and Jove for the Romans—from time to time comes to earth and takes on the guise of a normal

person. This viewpoint was also highly appealing, for it preserved intact the Jewish stress that only one God exists, a view that most non-Jewish philosophers and intellectuals had already come to accept, yet at the same time it allowed for God to have taken an active part, in human form, in human history. The greatest difficulty with this otherwise appealing view was that it was extremely difficult to square with what is said of Jesus in the New Testament, for example that Jesus is frequently recorded as speaking of, and even to, God as a separate being.

4.   Jesus was a man who became divine by the intervention of God's spirit.[2] In the New Testament writings Jesus frequently refers to God as "Father," and in many texts the specific phrase "son of God" is applied to Jesus. In a Semitic language, such as Hebrew or Aramaic, such a phrase would usually be taken to mean "a divine person," and not necessarily a god—a view only marginally different from that of seeing Jesus as a "hero" in the Greek religious meaning of the term. But in Greek culture, familiar with the concept of a hierarchy of divine beings descended from an original father-god, the phrase "son of God" tended to be taken literally. Despite apparently widespread popularity, this view could not be accepted by main-stream Christian theology without modification, primarily because it runs counter to explicit statements by some New Testament writers. In particular it contradicts the first part of the "Gospel According to Saint John" (the fourth of the "biographies" of Jesus in the New Testament) and statements by Paul the Apostle, whose writings in the New Testament served as the basis for much official Christian theology. Nevertheless among some early Christians it was held that Jesus was a man who became divine by the intervention of God's spirit which entered him at the time of his baptism and later entered his followers after he had ascended into heaven following his return to life, and thereafter this Spirit came to all believers at the time of their baptism.

However, as much or all of the New Testament was originally written in Greek, to a reader schooled in Greek or Roman culture, the New Testament references would inevitably lead to the conclusion that there are three distinct beings: the Father (God), God's son (Jesus), and God's spirit. In the early centuries Christians made many attempts to get out of this seemingly inescapable trap of ending up with three Gods. The simplest and, for a time, possibly the most popular solution was that these are three forms of one God. This would not be particularly different from the Hindu concept of one

Supreme Reality (Brahman) understood as manifested in a variety of ways in the world we know. But, while this is a possible, perhaps even inviting interpretation of many New Testament texts, it runs counter to the overriding conviction that Jesus Christ was the whole of God, not merely one aspect.

The Nicaean Council Compromise

The conclusion reached at the Council of Nicaea in 325, and passed on to all of subsequent Christianity, was a compromise which turned away from the philosophical traditions—which called for a water-tight logical argument—to an analogy. Although this analogy may be difficult, even impossible, to argue in philosophical terms, it is relatively easy to grasp if it is taken as a statement of experience rather than of logic.

The analogy came, unexpectedly, from Greek drama which had had to face a very similar dilemma. A drama usually included a number of roles or characters to be played on stage, yet tradition demanded that the actual number of actors be strictly limited to two, or at most three. How is it possible for there to be, let us say, nine characters in a drama while using only three actors? The obvious solution was to double up on roles, so that one actor might take on three roles. It would even be possible for one actor to play two or three roles simultaneously on stage by using a simple device which would also make it possible for the audience to know which role a particular actor was playing at a particular moment. The solution was to use masks. The actor would hold the mask of the character he was playing before his face (only men were allowed to act on stage). He could easily speak to another character, which he also played, either by speaking to it as if off stage, or by changing masks. The Latin word for mask was "persona," from which our English word "person" derives.

Let us imagine that, by analogy, the roles played by God can be compared with those played by an actor in a play. The single actor (God) takes on three different roles, which are seen by the audience as the Father, as that Father's son, Jesus Christ (a human yet eternal manifestation of God) and as the Spirit of God. If this were to be portrayed on stage by a single actor, the audience would be accustomed to accept the viewpoint that, for the purpose of the drama, the one actor is in fact three persons. God is three "persons" in the drama of the universe, but only one actor, unchanging. As one person on stage may speak to another person on stage, both played by the same actor, so too can God in his three persons communicate with himself. We must suspend logic for the purpose of viewing the staging of a Greek-style divine play. We must, for the sake of the play, believe in the independent reality of the three characters, while for the sake of our own sanity we must also know in our minds that there is really only one actor.

This was an analogy ordinary people of the Greek and Roman worlds could easily understand. While philosophers might and did argue endlessly about how to present the concept in appropriate logical categories, it was simplicity itself to experience the reality: God, the Father; Jesus, the eternal Christ; and God's Holy Spirit—these are all the divine One, which we encounter on the divine stage in the role of three distinct and simultaneous persons. Thus the tri-unity, or Trinity, doctrine of God became the official Christian teaching. For seventeen centuries Christian philosophers have argued how to express, explain and justify a doctrine that eventually came to be called a "divine mystery" beyond human understanding, a "mystery" which originally was no mystery at all but simply made use of an easily understood analogy to satisfy the need to be able to present a standard account of early Christian experience.

I have, without explicitly saying so, shifted from the early view that the resurrection of Jesus and eventually of all true believers was the only necessary belief in order for a person to be called a Christian, to the development of a doctrine about the nature of God which came to replace the resurrection in importance. Such a shift in Christian thinking was probably inevitable in view of the fact that the resurrection of Jesus receded more and more into the past and no sign of the world's coming to an end was in sight. While still required to believe in the resurrection—both of Jesus and eventually of all believers—Christians were now judged primarily on their willingness to accept the doctrine of the Trinity, the three-fold nature of God. This did not happen overnight. Actually, the Council in the year 325 was more concerned to spell out official doctrine about the nature of Jesus Christ than to worry about the third role of God, the Holy Spirit. It was left to later councils to place God's Holy Spirit on a par with God the Father and God the Son.

A psychological examination of the Trinity

While it is not difficult to see how the doctrines arose, it is difficult to present them in an understandable way in the modern era. We are, after all, not accustomed to the dramatic practices of the early centuries, and with the changing meanings of the word "person" the doctrine of the Trinity leaves us confused. Consequently Depth Psychologists have attempted to examine and explain what the experiences were that brought about the doctrine of the Trinity. We can come up with some intriguing suggestions, at any event, even though not outright conclusions. The primary question is: what, from the realm of psychological observations, corresponds to the *experiences* that were behind the theological doctrine of the Trinity? I am assuming that the Trinity doctrine was not an arbitrary invention out of thin air by fevered overworked bishop-theologian-philosophers, but in reality became important because it actually did reflect real, frequently felt, experiences at that time in history and place in the development of Western religious culture.

It has occasionally been pointed out that Sigmund Freud's formulation of his psychological theories, in particular his "trinity" of ego/superego/id might be brought onto the scene in explanation of the Christian theological Trinity. This is not fanciful. Freud himself in his book *Moses and Monotheism* (1939)[3] attempted to examine the background and development of Jewish and Christian beliefs, including the Christian theological presentation of Jesus. Jung also tried his hand at a psychological interpretation of the Trinity doctrine, in a lecture and article: "A psychological approach to the dogma of the Trinity" (1941/1948).[4] Jung's "psychological trinity" of Consciousness, the Personal Unconscious, and the Collective Unconscious, has also, in turn, been brought into service as a clarification of the theological doctrine.

Without attempting to review or summarize the above mentioned writings of either psychologist, I would point out that it has frequently been said that "man has made God in his own image," and to a certain extent there may be some truth in saying that conventional ideas of God are, metaphorically, a projection onto a heavenly screen of an image which reflects human makeup. For example, the superego—which essentially is each person's internalization of society's *do*s and *don't*s—does fit reasonably well with the picture of God presented in the Old Testament, if we allow for a bit of artistic license. It is certainly not out of the question that Yahweh (the Old Testament Hebrew name of God) and God the Father in the New Testament and Christian doctrine really are faltering attempts to express the partly unconscious experience of the superego in each of us, commanding what we should and should not do or think. Could this hold also for the ego as God the Son? Freud's exposition of the development of the Jesus legend in *Moses and Monotheism*, is far more intricate than I could relay here. But we might just notice that the expression "Son of Man," already mentioned as a title frequently used by Jesus to refer to himself in the Bible, more idiomatically means "human being." For twenty centuries now Jesus has been held up as a model human being, the ideal of what a person should be like. While this is taking matters a bit further than Freud did, it is an intriguing suggestion.

If we were to follow this analogy through, it would leave the id as the origin of the concept of the Holy Spirit. Freud understood the id as consisting of instincts of a definite antisocial and immoral nature, which is hardly applicable to the Christian experience of the Holy Spirit. The problem might be met by reinterpreting the id in terms of Jung's "two million year old person" within us; that is, a personification of our instinctual development which aligns the natural human character with the natural environment, both human and nonhuman. "Inspiration from the Holy Spirit" would then be the feeling of instinctual "knowledge" of how to deal with a situation. This would be, in effect, to replace Freud's concept of the id with Jung's understanding of the collective unconscious. The feeling of influence by the Holy Spirit has many similarities with the feeling of influence by the collective unconscious, our natural instinctual heritage in other words. Both concern the totality of life—the physical world, the social world, and the inner world. Religious believers would add "the spiritual world."

Might the Holy Spirit, as described in trinitarian religious beliefs, be connected with the feeling that each of us has of always having existed, while paradoxically knowing that we came into existence at a certain time and place? We may feel we have a predetermined psychological pattern and fate for which we are not individually responsible—the Buddhist concept of karma, and the Christian belief in predestination.

Death and resurrection

In the present day there has been great difficulty, among would-be religous believers, in accepting both the doctrine of Jesus' resurrection and the doctrine of the Trinity, and this has led to the formation of a number of Christian Churches which deny, or at least ignore, these two doctrines. The teaching of the eventual resurrection of all true believers has also posed a problem in the light of current scientific knowledge. Alongside the doctrine of resurrection, the concept of an immortal soul was introduced fairly early on in the two thousand years Christianity has been developing, and has subsequently, to a greater or lesser extent, been introduced into Church theologies. Many Christians find it easy to combine biological science with a nonbiological essence which they can call soul, which permits their acceptance of a religious Christian viewpoint.

In the Bible itself the question of life after death is addressed at length only in the New Testament, but there is some latent uncertainty about its nature. This appears to be due to the assumption by most of the New Testament writers that the "Second Coming" of the Christ (Jesus' life being the first coming) would take place during their lifetime, so that the problem of just what happens when you die was irrelevant in view of their belief that they would not, in fact, die. The belief in the eventual resurrection of all Christians, or the alternative view that everyone has an immortal soul which returns to the hands of God upon death, gradually became necessary as the early generations of Christians died despite their original belief. By and large, belief in an immortal soul was the viewpoint which came to predominate.

Freud pointed out that the id, which is that hereditarily determined aspect of the mind which is unconscious, does not appear to include any concept of that person's own death.[5] The fear of your own death is a function of conscious mental activity and, he suggests, very closely linked with anxiety, presumably due to having experienced the death of others. But unconsciously we all assume that we ourselves will not die. Jung made the same point, commenting in a TV interview:

Well, you see, I have treated many old people, and it's quite interesting to watch what the unconscious is doing with the fact that it is apparently threatened with a complete end. It disregards it ... Of course, it's quite obvious that we're all going to die, and this is the sad finale of everything; but nevertheless, there is something in us that doesn't believe it, apparently.[6]

This may help to explain why it was that Christians of the earliest period were able to believe that their own deaths would not take place, even though others had died. Avoiding death is a major emphasis in most religious belief-systems, and plays a central role in some of the offbeat yet highly successful modern Christian Churches—from Father Divine's extraordinarily successful movement in New York City, to Christian Science which is a world-wide movement. Our funeral ceremonies also paradoxically deny the reality of death.

It is interesting to speculate as to why there is apparently no unconscious belief in one's own death in that stratum of mental activity which is transmitted by heredity. The simplest explanation may be correct: that the beginning form of all life is a single cell—both historically and in the case of each individual being. Since the original cell does not die but simply divides into two, and since—as is obvious—there is no reproduction of organisms after they die, there would be nothing to enable a genetic inheritance of an inbuilt, unconscious expectation of death. Freud's introduction of a "death instinct" into psychological theory stands in curious opposition to his simultaneous statements that the id, the instinctual aspect of the mind, has no concept of death, and to my knowledge he never attempted to reconcile this apparent self-contradiction.

Research in the area of ESP has brought out new possibilities that are still to be fully explored. In 1958 Jung addressed the question of whether ESP and the concept of life after death might be related:

> ... the question of immortality is so urgent, of such immediacy, that one ought ... to give some kind of answer ... we have irrefutable evidence that at least parts of our psyche are not subject to the laws of space and time, otherwise perceptions outside space and time would be altogether impossible—yet they exist, they happen ... I have been able to verify this from countless experiences, not to mention Rhine's experiments ... quite apart from the numerous instances of prediction, nonspatial perception and the like.
>
> This offers the clearest and most incontrovertible proof that our conceptions of space and time ... are incomplete. To get a complete picture of the world we would have to add another dimension, or we could never explain the totality of the phenomena in a unified way ... We must reckon with the fact that this empirical world is in a sense appearance, that is to say it is related to another order of things below or behind it, where "here" and "there" do not exist; where there is no extension in space, which means that space doesn't exist [and] that time doesn't exist.
>
> We are not in a position to prove that anything of us is necessarily preserved for eternity. But we can assume with great probability that something of our psyche goes on existing ...

In other words, it goes on existing relatively outside space and time, which would by no means be a proof of immortality, but rather of an existence for an indefinite time after or before death.[7]

Another obvious comment is that perhaps religions are right, and there is no total death of the individual—a point we must be prepared to entertain, no matter what our personal religious beliefs or nonbeliefs might be.

The personal soul which is the life force that animates the body was also the topic of the teachings of many of the Mystery Religions (religious movements which taught supposedly secret doctrines and truths to their initiates) which were immensely popular throughout the Roman Empire in the period of the growth of Christianity. These Mystery Religions taught, as a rule, that through participation in their rituals immortality in a spiritual form could be guaranteed. In a Christian form, those who held to this teaching went one step further by saying that if found to be worthy, the soul would continue to live eternally alongside God; while if judged unworthy, the soul would be sent to hell, a place of punishment which might be temporary or permanent.

The details of the teaching of an immortal soul originated in Zoroastrianism and became popularized all through the Roman Empire in the centuries immediately before Christianity. This belief in an eternal soul could also be blended with belief in resurrection. It could be held that the eternal soul lived in the spirit world in the interim between death, and the resurrection which would occur at the end of the world. Alternatively, it could be held that the eternal soul is given a "spiritual body" whereby it lives in bodily form in the spirit world. The judgment by God as to a soul's worthiness might take place immediately after death, or might be postponed until the end of the world. Christian theology has never arrived at a doctrine which has found general acceptance throughout the Christian community as a whole.

Despite a lack of consensus concerning details of the nature of life after death, Christian theologians and churches are for the most part consistent in holding that belief in survival after death is an integral part of being a Christian. We saw that in Buddhism as a whole nirvana is held to have been experienced by Gautama, and is the raison d'être for Buddhist faith today. The large majority of Buddhists believe that the buddhas and boddhisatvas are guiding them to eventual attainment of nirvana. Similarly, in Christianity the continued life of Christ after his death and the attainment of eternal life by believers, through the act of Christ, is both the central teaching and the central belief.

THE CENTRALITY OF BELIEFS

Why are beliefs so important in Christianity? Most Westerners take for granted that a religious system is something to be believed in. While we could describe any religious system in such a way that it resembles a series of propositions about the nature of reality, this is not the normal practice in most religious systems. Of the major religious systems, and most ethnic religions, only two, Christianity and Islam, place primary emphasis on belief. As we saw in examining Buddhism, overall beliefs are few and far between, and traditional Buddhism is quite unconcerned whether doctrines or historical claims are believed. Since the absolute Ultimate Reality is by definition unknowable in any intellectual sense, specific beliefs are held in Buddhism to be of secondary interest.

Perhaps not so surprizingly, the development of an emphasis on belief in Christianity is due to its amalgamation of Jewish traditional teachings with insights from Greek and Roman writers. This becomes clear when we compare the history of Christianity with that of Buddhism. Buddhism began with the declaration that liberation from suffering is possible, but, if tradition is to be believed, no system of beliefs accompanied this declaration. To be sure, the earliest converts to the Buddha's teachings were, presumably, Hindus who already had a surfeit of philosophical doctrines about the supernatural. It could be said that the Buddha was liberating the people from doctrines as much as from suffering—because continued existence in the world, which is the direct cause of suffering, depends on being attached to beliefs and craving for life at all costs. The Buddha was substituting direct experience for doctrines and belief. To a certain extent it is likely that the very first Christians, those of the first generation, had a similar approach. Very few of the teachings attributed to Jesus in the New Testament have to do with doctrines. Most of his teachings are in the moral sphere and directed towards the social obligations which spring from love of fellow human beings—very little different, in fact, if at all, from Gautama's moral teachings. Also, in whatever way we wish to explain the origins of the accounts of the resurrection of Jesus, those who experienced the events felt liberation to be within their grasp. Judaism held strongly to the teaching that death occurs as punishment from God. Christians argued that the escape of one person (Jesus) from death indicated that punishment from God can be averted. This came to take a very special twist, however, which again is best illuminated by a reference to Buddhism.

In the Hindu teachings, and certainly in the teaching of the Buddha, individual liberation can be achieved only by individuals. In other words, my karma is mine alone, you have your own distinctive karma. Consequently no one—neither priest nor teacher—can relieve us of our karma, only we can do that for ourselves. And since liberation from karma cannot be taught because it is not a technique, one person's liberation from karma might be strikingly different from another person's. Paradoxically, Buddhism, which stresses the ultimate nonexistence of individual souls, states that only individuals can experience liberation. Philosophically there may be a great deal to be said about the logic or the lack of logic in the Buddhist claim. For Buddhism this does not matter, because it is the experience of liberation which counts, and philosophical logic is a part of the wheel of existence from which we long to escape.

In contrast, almost from the start Christianity saw guilt and death as collective, rather than personal. Death is punishment from God, but not necessarily punishment for your own personal actions. The whole of humanity is ridden with guilt. Humanity (which is the literal meaning of the word Adam) has disobeyed God from the start and, consequently, has been sentenced to death, as told in the story of the Garden of Eden at the start of the Bible. For this reason death is universal. Humanity, by its own innate nature is disobedient to God; humanity is sinful. Christianity inherited this belief from the Judaism of its time, but it was not limited to Judaism because the Mystery Religions and the philosophical traditions of Greece and Rome for the most part held a similar view, thus reinforcing the convictions of the Christians.

It was an attractive idea to early Christian converts to assume that freedom from guilt and therefore from death can arise from carefully obeying God's laws, which in turn were to be found in the Jewish sacred writings as well as in inspiration claimed by the early Apostles. But some of the most influential Christians, in particular the Apostle Paul whose writings comprise a substantial part of the New Testament, claimed to have kept strictly to the letter of God's laws, yet continued to feel guilt and consequently to fear death. Their conclusion: it is not possible by yourself to free yourself from partaking of humanity's collective guilt. Eventually this too became a doctrine of the Church, the doctrine of Original Sin. But in the earliest years it seems clear that it was not a philosophically based doctrine, but an agonized response to the perfectionism demanded by many Christian teachers and also said to have been demanded by Jesus in many of the teachings attributed to him.

How to reconcile the traditionally gentle, forgiving nature of Jesus, who according to tradition actually restored some people to life, with the image of a furious God who brings death upon every living thing because of universal guilt? Paul, whose writings are the only ones we have that discuss this issue in the very early period, resorted not to logic but to personal experience. He had himself, he wrote, seen Jesus as a supernatural being. Paul is noted for his claim to direct revelation from Jesus as God's supernatural agent. Jesus had succeeded in evading death, though not totally because he did die physically, and returned to life—he experienced death but his death was not final. If we can share in the same Spirit of God which filled Jesus, we can, like Jesus, be free of humanity's universal guilt. It is a matter of accepting the Spirit of God which is being offered to everyone.

This is the key to the divergence of Buddhism and Christianity. In Christianity, a God-focused religion, God's Spirit is constantly searching out anyone willing to accept it. Salvation is the result of an active readiness of God to find and to accept whoever is willing. In Buddhism, an atheistic religion, liberation is not the act of anyone. It occurs, when it occurs, at the time when the person involved has lost all craving for existence and is therefore ready for liberation.

According to both Buddhist and Christian premises, we are, under normal circumstances, condemned to whatever we can make of life here on earth. The solution differs: lose all craving for life, or accept the Divine Spirit which is being extended to you. Despite first appearances, these two solutions are not as far from each other as might be thought. They both operate with the same underlying assumption: that liberation/salvation requires submission of your own will to an experience that is not under your control and that cannot be taught.

The similarity is enough to make a bridging of the two religions possible, and this has occurred among mystics, including Muslim mystics, fairly frequently. But, as we will see in the chapter on Mysticism, mystics as a whole tend to ignore doctrine and belief in favor of direct personal experience.

In the very early writings of the first Christians, as found in the New Testament, belief has very little to do with what they taught. Translation difficulties make this point unclear to most English-speaking Bible readers. In

English we distinguish between the words *belief, faith*, and *trust*. In the Greek texts, from which the English language New Testament was translated, only one word, *pistis* is used. "If you trust God that ... " has a very different connotation from "If you believe that God will ... " The one is a statement of religious emotion, the other a statement of religious intellectualism. The practical consequence is that acceptance of particular intellectually worded doctrines came to dominate in Christianity over individual experience which dominates in Buddhism.

Perhaps the ultimate origin of the divergence of these two religions is that the originator of Christianity, Jesus, was a practicing Jew, as were his followers, for a number of years. Neither he nor they repudiated Judaism, but as they understood it, they were purifying and expanding Judaism. In contrast, the founder of Buddhism, Gautama, was rejecting as best he could his Hindu religious background in favor of a completely new beginning. Had, let us say, the Spirit of Vishnu filled Gautama and worked through him, Buddhism could well have been a sister religion to Christianity, as Islam is—for Islam proclaims that God spoke through Muhammad the same eternal truths that Jesus taught.[8]

In this respect we can see the emphasis on belief in both Christianity and Islam, in contrast with Buddhism. What makes Islam distinct in the modern world is not only its traditional rituals and rules for the conduct of life, but assent to its essential religious slogan, "There is only one God, His messenger is Muhammad." This means, in particular, that God spoke—through Muhammad—verses which were eventually collected in written form as the Koran as well as other teachings which are not found in the Koran but which satisfy Muslim religious historians as tracing back to Muhammad through verifiable oral tradition. Unlike Buddhism, in which an appeal to the statements of the Buddha Gautama have little place, the sister religions of Judaism, Christianity and Islam require that all religious statements go back to their scriptures or, by an unbroken chain of tradition, to the originators of the religion.

To pass judgment on the historical truth of the physical or spiritual resurrection of Jesus is beyond the scope of a neutral interpreter of Christianity. All that I can do is to point out that historical material relating to first century Palestine is so scanty that the only records on which to base a conclusion are the texts in the New Testament. Christianity is a system based first and foremost on belief. You believe—or you do not believe—the New

Testament statements. Or perhaps you believe some but not others. In any event, belief becomes uppermost.

THE HOLY RITUALS

Although formal Christian services of worship followed the traditional pattern of worship in the Jewish synagogues, one all-important addition was made. By the time historical records come upon the scene, Christian worship centered on a special ritual called the Eucharist (from a Greek word meaning gratitude), but more popularly called by the simpler term Holy Communion. This focuses on the New Testament tradition of the last meal eaten by Jesus before his execution. The account states that Jesus and his twelve closest male disciples ate the traditional Jewish Passover meal, perhaps Judaism's most important ritual. The Apostle Paul, who was the author of the earliest written record of the event, wrote about this:

> For I have it from the Lord, and you have it from me, that Lord Jesus, the night that he was betrayed, took bread and after expressing thankfulness broke off some with the statement: "This is my body which is for your benefit. Do this as a memorial for me." After eating he acted similarly with the goblet, stating "This goblet is the new compact through my blood. Whenever you drink, do it as a memorial for me." Consequently, whenever you eat this bread and drink from this goblet you are proclaiming the Lord's death until he comes.
> (Bible: 1 Cor. 11:23–26)

As already mentioned, the Roman authorities tended to view Christianity as a Jewish sect, and to apply the same restrictions to them as to those who practiced Judaism. Once Judaism was outlawed, in principle this meant religious gatherings of Christians were also illegal. But in most parts of the Empire problems were easily avoided. Held in a private home, the Christians' meal of bread and wine hardly gave Roman authorities the impression of a Jewish religious ritual.[9] Also the ceremony of the bread and the wine could be incorporated in the context of a regular meal, or could be separated out and held on its own, which meant that the amount of time required for the ritual could be varied. It also became customary for news and letters from eminent Christians to be read out during the ritual. Bible readings, prayers and singing, following the custom in the synagogue, were included when feasible. The collection of donations for the support of fellow Christians in poverty also became a standard and necessary part of the gatherings.

The communal participation in the ritual of bread and wine remained the focal point for Christian worship, and eventually became the only worship ritual actually required of all Christians, though they were encouraged to take part in prayers and other religious activities as well. As a formal priesthood developed, the leader of the Eucharist meeting came to be exclusively a priest.

By the time Church councils were debating a formal definition of the relationship of Jesus to God, they were also debating the supernatural significance of the ritual of the bread and the wine. A literal understanding of the words said to have been used by Jesus in his last meal was eventually adopted and Christian doctrine stated that, though still appearing to be ordinary bread and wine, the bread and wine as used in the Eucharist became transformed into Jesus' body and blood. Thus participation in the Eucharist meant that the worshipper was actually eating Jesus' body and blood, and thus taking into her/himself God itself. We are reminded again of the divergence of Buddhism and Christianity, with Christianity moving in an extroverted manner to an emphasis on sacred people, objects and rituals as all-important. Jung summarized the central concept of the Eucharist penetratingly:

The ritual ... has a dual aspect, human and divine. From the human point of view, gifts are offered to God at the altar . . . The ritual act consecrates both the gifts and the givers. It commemorates and represents the Last Supper which our Lord took with his disciples, the ... death and resurrection of Christ. But from the divine point of view this ... is only the outer shell or husk in which what is really happening is not a human action at all but a divine event. For an instant the life of Christ, eternally existent outside time, becomes visible ...
(Jung, C.W. vol. 11, paragraph 378)

The Christian Church was never a completely unified religous movement, and by the eleventh century a major split between the Western and Eastern parts took place. Eastern Christianity came to consist of the "Orthodox Churches," a name still in use. Western Christianity was centered in Rome. Small breakaway movements soon became common in Europe, however, and by the sixteenth century there had emerged a variety of organized Christian Churches unrelated to each other except in so far as they sprang originally from a common heritage. Because many of the new Churches began as a protest against beliefs or practices in the traditional Church, they came to be given the vague, general title of Protestants. The traditional Western Church, in contrast, came to be known as the Catholic Church ("catholic" is a Greek word meaning "general, found everywhere") which over the centuries split into several branches, frequently due to political demands. In the West the principal Catholic Church is the Roman Catholic Church, so named because its administrative and theological centers are in Rome. The Catholic and Orthodox Churches together account for about two thirds of Christians at present. Protestant Churches continue the traditional beliefs and rituals to varying degrees—ranging from the Lutheran and Anglican churches, which are Catholic Churches in all but name, to the Unitarian Church which has abandoned virtually all the traditional beliefs, though retaining much of the general pattern of worship services.

One other ritual of equal importance to the Eucharist must be mentioned: baptism (a Greek word meaning "dipping"). Originally a Jewish ritual of self-rededication, it came to be a Christian ritual embedded in theological doctrine and having supernatural significance. In form it consists of a threefold application of water (the method used varies greatly among the Churches) while the sacred phrase "I baptize you in the name of the Father, and of the Son, and of the Holy Spirit" is recited by the person administering the ritual.

Virtually from the beginning, Christians attributed a supernatural value to the ritual of baptism. In the New Testament, the Apostle Paul wrote of its significance, and his interpretation became the basis of standard Christian doctrine. The gist is that in the ritual of baptism the person involved symbolically drowns and then is restored to life, in this manner participating in the death of Jesus and his resurrection. "Symbolically" in this context means supernaturally. Though the baptized person's body eventually dies, their personal spirit is granted eternal life (Bible: Rom. 6:3–4). Christian tradition holds that this ritual is necessary in order for a person to be granted life in heaven after death, or in the resurrection of true believers at the end of the world.

Thus baptism is understood in Christian theology not only as a ritual of purification but as a sacrament (Latin for "obligation," especially "oath of allegiance") of sacred import. Although, apparently, originally applied only to adults, within a very short time baptism was administered to new born babies, and so it has remained among virtually all Christian Churches. In the Catholic traditions it is the time at which a baby receives a name, in other words becomes a true individual, parallel to the time when, at Jesus' baptism, God's Spirit came to him and his identity was, so to speak, declared:

> *Jesus came from Nazareth in Galilee, and was baptized in the*
> *Jordan by John. As soon as he came up out of the water he*
> *saw the sky split open and the Spirit came down upon him*
> *like a dove. There was a voice from the sky, "You are my*
> *very dear son, my favor rests upon you."*
>
> (Bible: Mark 1:9–11)

Folk-belief once held that a baby has no soul until baptism and the receipt of a name, for—so it was said—that which has no name does not exist.

Baptism can also be felt as a rebirth, or a spiritual birth accompanying physical birth. As in dreams, birth images are frequent as indications of a major change in the direction or character of life, so emergence from the sea is also an image for a new kind of living. It has been suggested that the ultimate origin of this imagery traces as far back as the emergence of life from the sea in evolutionary terms. Less fanciful, perhaps, is the observation that each of us is born from a liquid environment, the amniotic fluid, which may persevere as an early memory embedded in the neurone system and thus be a basic unconscious source for the religious/spiritual imagery.

EXCLUSIVE ALLEGIANCE

Quite apart from rituals, one of the strongest features of Christianity in contrast to Buddhism is its exclusivity. In Buddhism, beliefs and participation in rituals are generally left to the discretion of the individual, and participation in other religious traditions such as Shinto or Taoism is accepted and often encouraged. The Christian Church, ever since it separated from Judaism as an independent system, has regularly demanded exclusive obedience and total dedication, with very strong emphasis on beliefs and participation in strictly standardized rituals. It appears that this situation had come into being before the last pages of the New Testament were written. Of the major religions, three stand out as demanding total and exclusive allegiance and have systems by which members may be deprived of membership by the religion: Judaism, Islam and Christianity. This exclusivity goes along with the teaching by each of them that it alone has absolute and total divine truth and divinely instituted rules for life.

There is a definite emotional advantage for a participant in a religion to feel that there can be no reasonable doubt about the details of the prevailing system. There is a clear-cut division between right and wrong, and truth and error in every aspect of life. This advantage is shared by the rulers of society who eventually come to double as the authoritative heads of the religious system. Few political regimes are totally divorced from the prevalent religious system. The historically recent experiment of true multireligious pluralism, totally divorced from the prevailing political regime in a handful of countries, mostly English speaking, is a daringly bold innovation whose long-term effects are yet to be known.

According to the "Acts of the Apostles" (one of the new Testament texts), Paul and the other earliest Christian missionaries at first confined their teaching mission to Jews and the many devout friends of Judaism. Judaism had spread throughout the whole of the Roman Empire because of a series of deportations which had taken place in earlier centuries. Judaism's emphatic monotheism, coupled with a stringent ethical code and the simplest of theologies, held an almost magnetic attraction for many Greeks and Romans, whose cultural views had spread also throughout Turkey. But Judaism's very detailed regulations for social and personal conduct and its closely prescribed daily religious rituals prevented it from becoming as fully accepted as it might have been. The result was that there were a good many religiously devout "friends of Judaism," but, in comparison, very few actual converts to Judaism. To these people the teachings of the early Christian missionaries were a welcome message: while the thoroughgoing monotheism and ethics of Judaism were kept intact, the entire ritual framework was discarded, replaced by a simple, friendly but brief gathering together to commemorate the founder's death through the sharing of bread and wine. That this new form of Judaism emphasized the forthcoming end of the world and stressed personal readiness was neither novel nor unwelcome.

RELIGION AND SOCIAL REFORM

For at least a thousand years Judaism had been closely linked with political reform in Palestine. In recent centuries Judaism had been teaching that God would soon intervene to purify the entire world and set all of society right with a totally new social system through divinely inspired political revolution. The new Christians were understood as stating that this process had now begun. Disillusionment with the growing corruption and social degeneration of the Roman Empire had already set in and it was clear that the rot would continue to spread unless something radical were done. The new Christians, as seen by outsiders and particularly the imperial authorities, provided a social network for this "something radical." This may be the reason why Christians emphasized that Jesus insisted upon political stability and the legitimacy of Roman rule, and that his words were against corruption and misuse of power which if not reformed would inevitably lead to catastrophic upheavals. This echoed the sentiments of a great many of the Roman intelligentsia as well as of the working classes. One of the most remarkable aspects of the growth of the early Christian Church was its success in penetrating into the highest circles of government and the military. This in turn was probably one of the reasons that an almost endless series of official edicts against Christians had virtually no lasting effect at all.

Buddhism, too, began as a system of both religious and social reform. It met no serious resistance in its country of origin (that was to come centuries later, with the resurgence of Hindu tradition and the Muslim conquests) and its spread to the East was, from the perspective of twenty-five centuries later, as smooth and successful as that of Christianity to the West. If in the space of three centuries Christians had succeeded in converting the official rulers of the Roman Empire, so Buddhism had equal success on both the political and social scene in the East. Buddhism appealed to the masses as well as to the intelligentsia because it was a new, fresh system. Gone were the clashes between castes. Gone was the greedy priesthood which, as Plato put it, promised that the more you filled their pockets, the more certain you were to rise in the Gods' esteem. (*The Republic*, 564b-c.) Gone were elaborate rituals and theologies. The impact of Buddhism in the East was equally as strong as the impact of Christianity in the West, so much so that we speak as easily of "Buddhist nations" as we do of "Christian nations."

But why was it that the peoples to the West were so easy to persuade that Jesus was God, while the peoples to the East were rapidly converted to the conviction that there is no God? Why, for two thousand years, has there been no substantial change in the relative position of the two religious systems? For although in the modern day many Westerners are quite anxious to learn the ways and teachings of the Buddha, their number is but a tiny spark in the population explosion, as is the number of Christian converts in the East.

Both populations, those in the West as much as those in the East, were equally aware of the moral bankruptcy of society and the never-ending tale of the rich getting fewer and richer while the poor became always more numerous and poorer. Despair was in the hearts of all but the rich throughout the world. It is as if people as a whole were ready to embrace any ideology that promised relief. And that is precisely what both Buddhism and Christianity promised. "It is easier for a camel to pass through the hole in a needle than for a rich person to enter heaven," taught Jesus (Bible: Mark 10:25). The more you oppress the poor, the more miserable will your life become, for all eternity, taught Gautama. Both were teaching much the same hope. And both were emphasizing that social reform was prerequisite for any true religious outlook.

The West was already largely convinced that the old Gods were pretty useless, if indeed they existed at all. And the West had a remarkably well organized and administered political system—one which required an ideology to give it unshakeable legitimacy. In the West the government's need was for a raison d'être, for some ideology that could hold it together in the face of separatist movements. Government and religious ideology had always gone hand in hand. Rome required a religious ideology that would keep its peoples under its administrative and economic thumb.

A single God who is the supreme ruler had for centuries been the basic belief in Palestine, and that the Supreme Ruler of The Empire is divine was the catch-cry of Rome, even if the meaning of "divine" had to be stretched almost to breaking point. The theme of oneness—one God, one Ruler—found immediate recognition throughout the West. Marx's emphasis that governments have regularly used religion as a means of control of the people was well-based. Christianity became, in particular, the system of control for the later Roman Empire and its descendants. The peoples of the West knew far too well that revolt brought only Roman revenge, not freedom. Better to acknowledge the existing social order, and try to reform it from within; to be comforted by the conviction that, though you died young, ill and poor, you went to live with God and at the end of time would live again on earth in God's paradise—while those who oppressed you spend the rest of eternity in intolerable suffering as recompense for their misdeeds. The net effect of this teaching is not greatly different from the Buddhist.

In the East governments were no less oppressive and corrupt. But the lack of cohesion was felt everywhere. The universal system of writing brought to all of the West by the Romans contrasted with a different system of writing in every society in the East, a situation which persists to the present day. The promise of peace made by the Romans to the peoples they conquered contrasted with an ever increasing internecine policy of extermination in the East. If anything, what the East felt the need for was not one government, but no government. The message of full and equal brotherhood taught by Buddhism was something that could be grasped and struggled for. The message of the Buddha did not have to be introduced and enforced by the sword, as was the case with Christianity in the West as the Roman Empire continually attempted to expand its boundaries. Buddhism was welcomed with outstretched hands. And though Buddhists suffered just as much as their Western cousins from corrupt governments and the insatiable greed of the rich, they too knew that they would in the end receive their just rewards. Every kindness done to help another fellow creature in time of misery was another step towards liberation. And so it was that the One All-Loving God of the early years of Christianity brought, in effect, the same promise of hope as did the All-Compassionate Buddha. If there was any difference at all in this respect, it was that the Buddha extended compassion to all living creatures, human and animal. But perhaps even this difference was not truly missing at the start, for it is said of Jesus that he taught, "Sparrows are sold two for a pittance, yet not one of them falls to the ground without your Father." (Bible: Matt. 10:29)

Women's role

From the social point of view, Christian ideology had as little place for universal equality and freedom as Buddhism. Slavery and the subjection of women were unquestioned in both religions.

The Gospels are clear that Jesus' following consisted of women and slaves as much as it did of free men, and many anecdotes take care to portray him as concerned with women. According to the accounts, he was frequently chided for this even by his disciples, particularly when it concerned prostitutes and others similarly held in low esteem by society. Yet in Paul's writings preserved in the New Testament, it is made clear that women were to be given second place, even to the point of not being allowed to speak or ask questions in Church gatherings, unlike the men. This attitude persisted.

Despite the fact that women converts were often the wedge which opened influential Roman households to Christian teaching, they were excluded from positions of authority and tended in Church organization, as in society at large, to be relegated to the status of servants.

Similarly, though slaves came eventually to form a very large proportion of Christians in the Roman Empire, the Church never condemned the practice of slavery, even into modern times. One of the oddities of the movements tracing back to Gautama and to Jesus is that male slaves were allowed positions of authority in the Church while even free women were not admitted to such positions. In the same vein, the elaboration of religious doctrine was, and continues to be, kept firmly in the hands of men. This seems paradoxical in the light of the fact that usually 80 percent or more of the people present at a Christian religious meeting are female. That the actual practice of religion is a "women's concern" has held sway in Christianity since shortly after its beginning. Consequently we have the situation that organization and doctrine are prescribed by men while active participation is by tradition allocated to women.

UNCONDITIONAL LOVE *VERSUS* ETERNAL PUNISHMENT

Whether it is a cause or effect of the place relegated to women in the Church, the lack of traditional "motherly values and concern" is very noticeable in early Church doctrine. The tradition, inherited by early Christianity from Judaism, that God is Father leaves a gaping emotional void. The social tradition that father equals rule, authority and discipline, while mother equals tender concern and personal care combined with unconditional love and forgiveness, brings difficulties when God is defined using human terms. This is particularly true when it is stated that there is only One God, who consequently must be the spiritual embodiment of all loving virtues and values, but at the same time of arbitrary discipline, judgment and eternal punishment. (Arbitrary because natural catastrophes were understood to be the action of God, even though no specific human misdeeds seemed severe enough to warrant them.) The concept that the One God combines unconditional love with unlimited vengeance is self-contradictory.

To judge by what little material we have from the period, it appears that Christianity inherited a solution to this dilemma from one part of Judaism: the concept of a supernatural evil being called Satan, alternatively called the

Devil, who coexists with God in an uneasy state of eternal battle. To understand the background of this doctrine and the way it developed in early Christianity, a short step backwards in time to the influence of Zoroastrianism is necessary.

As already pointed out, Zoroastrianism was a religion which originated in Persia (modern Iran) some five to six centuries BC. It began as a series of revelations to the prophet Zarathustra, whose name in Greek came to be spelled Zoroaster. Zarathustra's revelations focused on an eternal battle between two Gods, Ahura Mazda (the God of Light, the Good God) and Angra Mainyu, also called Ahriman (the Evil God). There is some evidence that both Gods were understood to be the children of one God who is morally neutral. Although as a formally organized religion Zoroastrianism was largely confined to the Persian Empire, it survived the collapse of the Empire and its teachings were widely known throughout the Middle East and western Asia. Zarathustra's teaching of the conflict between Good and Evil entered Jewish theology, in which Ahriman became known as Satan. The first major references to this new doctrine in Jewish theology appear in the Book of Job, a part of the Old Testament in the Bible.

Jesus is portrayed in the Gospels as fully accepting the reality of the Devil, or Satan, in eternal conflict with God. It seems that very early Christian thinkers came to modify the doctrine so as to conceive of Jesus Christ as the equivalent of Ahura Mazda, the personification of divine Goodness and Love, and kept the concept of Satan without much change except to complete the symmetry by the addition of a figure called the Anti-Christ, so that Jesus' relation to God was paralleled by the Anti-Christ's relation to Satan. The relation between the Trinity as a whole and Satan (and/or Anti-Christ) has never been satisfactorily defined in formal Christian theology, although much Christian folklore about the Devil and the Devil's angels/demons has become widely known through such major works of literature as John Milton's *Paradise Lost*.

It appears that virtually all religious cultures have found a need for "evil" beings in their belief-systems. These may vary from ghosts or malevolent spirits of the dead to formally recognized and endowed antigods. Many, perhaps most, religious systems also include the phenomenon of demon-possession in which, it is held, an evil spirit or demon abruptly takes control of a previously normal person. Many of the reported occasions of this give rise to the thought that the "demon-possessed" are persons suffering schizophrenia or other psychiatric illness. There is also sometimes a hint of multiple personality. It is possible, in fact probable, that frequently the concept of evil demons arose in order to explain mental illness.

"Demon possession" is not the only phenomenon attributed to "evil spirits" or a devil. They are also called in to explain apparently unconscious impulses which influence a person to undertake actions that would usually have been considered morally wrong. In this regard, the Devil is conceived to be something of an antisuperego, Freud's frequent conceptualization of the id. "Temptation by the Devil" is, especially in the monotheist religious cultures, the name given to any impulse or desire which runs contrary to the accepted mores of the culture or of the subculture. This fits in with Freud's general view that instinctual impulses are always anticultural, or socially subversive.

Following Jung's concept of complexes, however, it is more generally helpful to see "demonic" inspiration as an incomplete separation of splinter personalities from the conscious processes which we traditionally call mind. One major reason why splinter personalities remain cut off from conscious recognition is that we are unwilling to acknowledge that what are possibly quite acceptable ideas, doubts, feelings and desires exist in us. Instead, for one reason or another we do not want to admit, even to ourselves, that they exist and are legitimate.

A spiritual location conventionally called "hell" in English (it may have a number of other names in other cultures) is supposed to be the spiritual realm in which the Devil and demons exist, and is often considered to be a counterpart to heaven. Its main characteristics are that it is a place of eternal fire, misery, and, in monotheist traditions, total absence of any influence of God. For non-monotheist traditions, such as Buddhism, the term "hells" is used in English to refer to an area in the spirit world in which living conditions are vastly poorer than in this world.

In Christian thought the concept of hell poses a very difficult question which has never been satisfactorily resolved by theologians. In the Gospels, Jesus is represented as teaching that all evildoers will suffer eternally in hell. Virtually from the beginning of organized Christianity, Christian teachers assumed that only believing Christians could be acceptable to God, and hell was conceived to be a place for all those who are not or, if dead, were not believing Christians. For quite some time nonbelievers and evildoers were lumped together in the same category, as is still the case in some Christian theologies today, based on the proposition that all human beings are inherently evil and must accept God's grace and forgiveness by becoming

Christians in order to avoid being assigned to hell after their death. To counter this extreme Christian chauvinism, the Catholic Churches and some Protestant Churches have in their theological conceptions added one or sometimes two further spiritual realms: Purgatory, a spiritual realm of punishment to which Christian souls go in order to be purified sufficiently to enter heaven and be with God; and Limbo, a spiritual realm occupied by persons who are not so evil as to warrant punishment in Hell, but are not Christian believers and therefore cannot enter heaven.

A reference is made in the New Testament (Bible: 1 Peter 3:18–20) and was later taken over into "The Apostles' Creed" (a formal statement of basic Christian beliefs) that Jesus descended into the underworld of the spirits of the dead during the period between his execution and his return to life. Many early theologians interpreted this to mean that he did so in order to convert and rescue those of the dead who had died before his time on earth, thus extending the possibility of salvation to all those who would have been believers if they had had the opportunity. But as for people alive on earth, it was made clear in the New Testament that during the interim between Jesus' lifetime on earth and the end of the world, his work is limited to bringing only God's laws, love and guidance to believers or potential believers, while Satan attempts to subvert this by tempting all persons into absolute evil.

The danger in the doctrine of Satan is that it implies the independent existence of an antigod, and it may be well for us to remember that in Zoroastrianism, in which the concept of Satan first appeared, there does seem to have been an original bi-theism of two Gods, one evil and one good, in eternal conflict with one another. Christian theology eventually attempted to avoid this movement away from monotheism by teaching that Satan was created by God in order to represent and instigate evil in the world, a part of the necessity for humanity to have some degree of free will in choosing their course of actions. Nevertheless Christian theologians through the centuries have never quite been able to come to agreement on the nature of the origin of Satan and Satan's relationship to God in the supernatural realm. Adding to the confusion in the early stages of the development of Christian doctrine, both Christ and Satan are portrayed as having rather similar roles in bringing, at the end of the world, unlimited terror and eternal misery in hell to all who deviate from the worship of God or, simply, are not believers in the doctrines about Christ. Although the gospels represent Jesus as teaching God's totally unconditional love, care, and unlimited forgiveness, in seeming contradiction he also teaches eternal divine punishment. The overall picture presented is that evildoers are handed over to Satan at the time of the Last Judgment which is to take place at the time of the end of the world. Early Christian theology came to stress the threat of ensuing eternal punishment at the behest of God to the virtual total neglect of the teachings of unconditional love, care, and forgiveness—values which do not permit the concept of eternal terror and punishment. While such teachings of eternal punishment might be useful in enforcing obedience to political regimes which claimed to have been established by God, they were of no comfort to the poor who lived in misery; that is, the people who constituted the vast majority of Christian Church members. The imbalance between teachings of punishment and lip service to the values of unconditional love, unlimited care and unconditional forgiveness inevitably brought a counterreaction.

The obvious candidate to represent these values was the Holy Spirit, which was unique in name as well as nature. In Greek the word "Spirit" is neuter; that is, it has no gender. (The Greek language distinguishes between masculine, feminine, and neuter nouns.) But in Syriac (the language in which a great many of the early theologians wrote, and in which all nouns are designated either masculine or feminine) the custom was in religious writing to assign a feminine gender to Spirit. The Holy Spirit was, then, for them a "she." For several centuries Syriac-speaking theologians assigned feminine qualities to the Holy Spirit, and some even went so far as to use the family analogy of Father+Mother+Son to explain the meaning of the Trinity, with the Holy Spirit playing the role of the divine motherhood of God.

With the eventual adoption of the Latin language for Christian theology, and the center of theological discussion moving westwards, the mother analogy for the Holy Spirit was dropped, but something of the motherly qualities persisted in the theological descriptions of the nature and activity of the Holy Spirit. In Christian theology as a whole, the Holy Spirit is considered to be the divine activity which inspires, teaches, guides, and—in general—cares for the individual, both believer and nonbeliever alike. While for many centuries the assumption that only Christian believers are eligible for salvation, continued officially to go virtually unquestioned, there have always been tendencies among theologians to allow for persons who are not Christians to be eligible for salvation by virtue of the activity of the Holy Spirit. The motherly nature of the Holy Spirit has been perpetuated also by statements, attributed to Jesus in the Gospel of Saint John in the New Testament, that after Jesus' death God would send a "Comforter" to be with the faithful. This "Comforter" in turn was understood by early theologians as the Holy Spirit.

Nevertheless, for an ordinary reader of the New Testament, the anecdotes attributed to Jesus show God as highly ambivalent. At times "He" is an all-loving parent who will do everything in his power for the sake of his child, regardless of what the child has done; no crime is too great, no misdeed too serious to be beyond repair by a simple "I'm sorry," and even the "I'm sorry" may not be required. But in other anecdotes God is the terrible ultimate judge who shows no mercy, takes no account of mitigating circumstances, and demands absolute obedience with no deviation tolerated. This is not the image of Love but of a Tyrant determined to have his own way at any cost. A compensatory figure who can intercede with God is then an emotional necessity for believers, and emotionally the rather abstract "Holy Spirit" is not really adequate, no matter how much theologians might argue in their attempt to make a philosophical system out of the grand mixture of anecdotes and essays that go to make up the New Testament.

The possibility for Christian theology to be expanded to accommodate still further supernatural figures was always present. Long before Christianity came onto the scene, Judaism had included the belief in angels as a part of its traditions. Angels were conceived to be supernatural, nonhuman beings, subordinate to God and—in general—acting as intermediaries between God and human beings. Eventually the concept of supernatural beings subordinate to Satan—the demons—was added. Both angels and demons were taken for granted by the earliest Christians, apparently including Jesus, as part and parcel of the Jewish cultural heritage which formed the basis of religious thought. But Graeco-Roman culture also had a tradition of bestowing divine honors on venerable persons whose lives were models of virtue and piety. It soon became customary in the Christian Church to adopt this custom, though only for the dead, calling such persons "saints." (In the New Testament all Christians, alive or dead are called "holy," for which the Latin word is *sanctus* from which our word "saint" derives. But quite early on tradition came to limit the use of this word to only those persons pure enough to reside with God in heaven immediately they died.)

The spiritual "family"

The allocation of individual supernatural figures to be patrons of cities, professions, and ordinary people is one that reaches far back into history.

Thousands of years before Christianity came along, the Sumerian-Babylonian religious beliefs in Iraq included patron gods to represent the interests of individual persons as well as of cities and so on.[10] The need for individual supernatural protection and representation continued in Christianity and continues up to the present. Guardian angels, one assigned to each Christian, and patron saints are very much in vogue in the Catholic Church. Saints are popularly regarded as being able to help individuals on earth, and also to intercede with God on behalf of those who petition them. But although there are as many female saints as male, and no saint is superior to another, they are not in any sense gods, and they cannot fill the need for a superordinate maternal divine quality. Nevertheless, they fill the emotional gap which is inevitable when a person feels isolated, without roots and connections with the world, especially the world of nature but also with fellow human beings. As a patron saint, after whom a newborn baby is named, the saint constitutes a direct link with the whole of Reality, both material and spiritual, and could psychologically be seen as personifying that link. Like the bodhisattvas, saints are, so to speak, charged with overseeing the welfare of those on earth and giving them guidance, especially in moments of distress or need. The difference in practice between a saint and a bodhisattva is very narrow, and perhaps consists simply in the subtle distinction which says that a bodhisattva is a buddha for all practical purposes, while a saint is not a god nor is conceived as acting as one.

As we have seen, the more theology officially promulgated doctrines about God, the more it described God in patriarchal terms. The void created by the gradual elimination of all maternal qualities from the concept of God was keenly felt. It could not have been otherwise. A reaction was inevitable.

Most of the religious cultures of the ancient world were familiar with the concept of a Mother Goddess, either as an everyday part of their own beliefs or as a part of the beliefs of neighboring peoples. Certainly in Turkey, Greece, and Rome, the three centers where Christianity first became established, a mother goddess was not only an integral part of religious tradition, but frequently the actual center of focus for religious faith.

The very male-centered development of Christian organization and theology quite early on led to the feeling of a need for a genuinely female figure on a par with the figure of Jesus, who is represented in the Bible as definitely male. (In fact, some of the requirements demanded of Christians in the writings of the Apostle Paul depend on his assumption that Jesus Christ is specifically male.) The need for a female divine representative was felt fully as much by men as by women.

The Virgin Mary

Jesus' mother Mary plays very little role in the New Testament. She is rarely mentioned. But by the time official Church doctrines were being made, that "little role" had been enormously expanded in both popular and official belief. Once the formal conclusion was reached that Jesus was/is God, then his mother Mary inevitably acquired the title of "Mother of God" and this title was formally incorporated into Christian doctrine by a Church Council in the year 431. Since Jesus Christ is, according to official doctrine, "fully God and fully human," it was almost inevitable that his mother Mary would be considered as having some sort of divine status, though short of being part of God.

Here again we are faced with the fact that early Christian doctrine was based primarily on feeling, and theologians were confronted with the task of finding a philosophical basis for what had already become common belief. For many centuries, theologians have argued about the precise meaning of the term "Mother of God," and Protestant theologians in particular have been disturbed by its apparent illogicality. Logic would say that "Mother of God" means the Mother who "gave birth to" God, and therefore preceded the existence of God. If Jesus were to be regarded as a simple human being who eventually became the Christ, and therefore God, the statement is within the range of reasonable definition. But with the official proclamation of the doctrine that Christ is eternal, without beginning or end, and in no sense chronologically subsequent to God the Father, then problems begin. But we must be mindful that in Jewish and Christian belief, time does not relate to God. Time is a creation by God. There is no "before" and "after" in respect of God. God is the eternal Is, experienced as Ultimate Being. From this perspective, Mary represents the "hidden" mother-quality within God, supplementing the traditional father-character. She does, however, pose a logical dilemma for theologians attempting to work in terms of the human perception of space and time. For us in the space-time continuum, Mary gave birth to the space-time manifestation of God as Jesus. What this means in terms of the realm of the absolute Is which knows neither past, present, nor future but is extra-temporal, the human mind is unable to apprehend. Again religious feeling has triumphed over philosophical attempts to apply human logic to the divine realm.

An intriguing passage in the "Gospel According to Saint John" reads: "The Jews said to him, 'You are not even fifty years old, yet you have seen Abraham?' Jesus said to them, 'I tell you that beyond any doubt, before there was an Abraham I am.'" Abraham was a holy man held to have lived and died nearly two thousand years previously. The mysterious "I am" has meaning for those familiar with the Old Testament in Hebrew, for God is reputed to have told Moses (some twelve hundred years BC) when Moses asked his name, "Tell them that I Am has sent you."

Christians of the early centuries were for the most part converts, many of them influenced by religious backgrounds in which a mother goddess was the center of worship. The "Mystery Religions," groups which, usually after payment of large fees, initiated members into (sometimes) secret knowledge and experience, largely focused on encounter with a mother goddess. These religious movements were widespread among peasants and aristocracy alike. For Christians with such backgrounds, the feeling of emotional loss when converting to Christianity was very great. When the centers of Christianity came to be in Turkey, Greece, and eventually Italy, the feeling that something essential was missing, in the patriarchal teachings of the Palestinian Jewish Bible (both Old and New Testaments) and in early Christian dogma, was overpowering. Convinced, as many early Christians were, that their previous faiths were not false, merely incomplete, it was hardly surprizing that they should look for something in Christianity to correspond with their earlier experience of a mother goddess. Who could fill this role better than the mother of Jesus?

By the fifth century the Church had come to hold—and, generally speaking, the Catholic Churches continue to hold—that religious truth is not confined to the Bible and that Christian Church tradition holds equal sway. It is not surprising that this should be so, for many points of religious belief require explanation, and there must be some objective basis on which to rest the official explanation. Tradition in this sense means beliefs which can be documented to trace back to quite early centuries of Christianity, and for which the case can be made that they trace back to the teachings of the original disciples of Jesus. Although it might seem difficult to support the view that a particular teaching goes back to the original disciples, in practice it is not so difficult, for many early Church writers claimed that what they were saying came from those disciples, or from students of those disciples. Also, a formally organized priesthood is known to have been in existence within only a few decades of Jesus' death, and it is claimed that it is only reasonable to suppose that older priests taught new aspirants to the priesthood many details long before they came to be written down. (Precisely the same situation obtains also in Islam, where teachings that can be demonstrated to trace back without a break in oral tradition to God's messenger Muhammad hold equal authority with the written text of the Koran.)

Although Jesus' mother Mary is only sporadically mentioned in the Bible, what *is* said of her early became incorporated in a doctrine which has come to play a dominant role in popular Catholic Christian faith. There are two references to the birth of Jesus in the New Testament, which read:

> The angel said "... you will become pregnant and give birth to
> a son whom you will name Jesus ... " Mariam [alternative
> spelling of the name Mary] said to the angel, "How can that
> be, since I have not known a man?" The angel answered her,
> "Holy Spirit will come upon you, and power of [the] Highest
> will overshadow you. Therefore the holy baby will be called
> God's son." (Bible: Luke 1:30–35)

> Jesus' birth was as follows: while his mother Mary was engaged
> to Joseph, before they came together she was found to be
> pregnant by Holy Spirit. (Bible: Matt. 1:18)

The entire tradition relating to the Virgin Mary (in AD 451 she was officially declared to have remained a virgin eternally) is quite extensive. Although many of the key beliefs can be traced back many centuries, there was a long hiatus before others of the more vital points were formally proclaimed as dogma; that is, as coming from tradition the truth of which is beyond doubt. In 1854 she was proclaimed to be sinless, sharing with Jesus Christ himself this unique distinction, for the inherited guilt which extends to all humanity is not applicable to Mary and Jesus. The formal name of her freedom from original sin (i.e., participation in universal guilt) is the Immaculate Conception, meaning that though Mary was born by the natural processes of sexual reproduction, hereditary guilt did not apply to her. As her birth was unique, so was her death. In 1950 it was proclaimed that she entered heaven in her body, which is also said of Jesus in the Bible. Despite the length of time over which various parts of the teachings about the Virgin

Mary were proclaimed as certain truth—from 431 to 1950—historical records show that these were not new beliefs entering into Christianity at various times in history, but were under discussion as early as the fourth century.

One other aspect of the Virgin Mary that has not yet been formally promulgated as certain truth, but which enjoys the status of a permitted teaching and in practice is quite universally held by the Catholic Churches, is her role as comediator.

In the Bible only Christ and perhaps the Holy Spirit intercede with God on behalf of individual persons. Put into theological jargon, two "persons" of God intercede with the third "person" of God. This is not a case of two Gods interceding with a third, we must remember the origins of the concept of the Trinity: the holy drama in which the single actor, God, is seen by the audience as being simultaneously three persons. In drama there would be no difficulty in two of the persons interceding with the third. Outside the Bible, Church tradition states that alongside these persons, who are the single actor God, is a separate figure, the Virgin Mary, who may also intercede directly with God. In a very real way, it may be said that the Virgin Mary incorporates those very attributes which had gradually been lost from popular teachings, and in some instances from theological discussions about God. For Mary neither deals out punishment, nor discriminates between believers and non-believers. She is the embodiment of unconditional love, forgiveness, and grace. Yet she too is but a human being, albeit a very special human being, and not God.

Christianity is one of the very few modern religious traditions which continue to hold that God and other divine figures may appear on earth in human form, though usually these appearances are termed visions, which generally means being visible to some people but not to all. Jesus is said to have appeared to many people over the centuries, but the Virgin Mary is probably better known for her appearances on earth. Such appearances may be limited to one person, or a small group, rarely to a large group. The appearance to Marie Soubirous, better known as Saint Bernadette, in 1844 when Marie was fourteen, led to the establishment of the shrine at Lourdes. Another well-known appearance was to three children in the Portuguese village of Fatima in 1917, which also led to the building of a shrine. While seen by only the three children, in Fatima, the appearance of the Virgin Mary was reported to have been accompanied on one occasion by a vision of the sun spinning and then rushing towards the earth. This is reported to have been seen by a number of people.

Just what is happening in such an event? What is it that is being seen? Is anything being seen at all, and if so, how? Arguments about these questions have gone on for many years, but they generally get bogged down in the assumption that for something to be seen it must be external to the viewer. Some have argued that the "spiritual body" is allowing itself to be seen by the children. Since Jesus is held by all Christian Churches to have entered heaven in bodily form, and the Catholic teaching is that Mary did also, there is nothing, theoretically, to prevent them from reappearing on earth in bodily form, although this does not answer the question of why only a tiny few see it, even though there may be hundreds of people present.

Very little research has been done on the mechanisms of inner vision—that is, just how the brain formulates a "picture" from the neuronic impulses it receives, and particularly how it is that pictures are formulated by the brain when the impulses come from within the nervous system (for example during the visual aspect of dreams, of hallucinations, perhaps in some instances ESP, and possibly religious visions). We must be cautious at this point. That the visual processes of the brain cannot distinguish between an image coming from the eyes, from whatever processes are at work in forming dreams, from hallucinations brought on by chemicals, hallucinations associated with mental disease, and visions/apparitions, does not necessarily mean that the origins of these pictures must always be the same. A similar visual response to a variety of processes, those of internal origin as well as those originating from external stimuli, is both possible and highly probable.

Many believers will, of course, assume that in the instance of a religious vision or "apparition" the spiritual body of the supernatural Being is truly present before their eyes, and by some as yet unknown means is made visible only to them. This is not, however, the only possible religious conclusion. We are not faced with a simple either/or situation—either that a spiritual body is present outside of the bodies of the viewers, and seen like any other external object, or that we are dealing with pure delusion. There are other possibilities.

Because we are awake, we tend to assume that everything we "see" must be being seen with our eyes, therefore the Virgin Mary, or whoever, "really" is standing in front of us or we are being deluded. Psychological research has shown that images coming from within our nervous system can, in appropriate situations, appear to the visual centers of the brain, and the brain is unable to distinguish between images coming through our eyes and those coming from within the nervous system. Consequently, it is a general psychological tenet that visions and hallucinations are dream-type imagery experienced while we are awake.

If a person sees a "vision" or "apparition" of the Virgin Mary, it may well be that because of that person's cultural conditioning an image of a presumed "supernatural" woman seen with the "inner eye," so to speak, must be the Virgin Mary because the only "supernatural" woman claimed in that culture to become visible is the Virgin Mary. It does not particularly matter whether the person seeing the vision believes in the reality of the Virgin Mary or not. If the conviction is strong that the vision must be of a supernatural figure, the assumption will inevitably be that it is of the Virgin Mary simply because no other possibility is presumed to exist. If the person has already seen paintings of what the Virgin Mary is presumed to look like, the visual centers of the brain will adapt the appropriate details of the image to fit.

Were the person seeing the vision acquainted with Buddhist beliefs, the image might be interpreted by the brain centers to be of Kwan-Yin. The conscious beliefs of the person involved are of little importance, because we are all aware that some part, at least, of our cultural milieu believes in the reality of the supernatural figure, and we are unconsciously prepared to make the identification accordingly.

The increasing official Christian recognition of the nature and appearances of the Virgin Mary may very well have a sociological background. The patriarchal nature of society past and present has meant a repression of "feminine" values among both men and women alike, as both sexes attempt to emulate a particular image of the "ideal" person. This ideal stresses emphasis on objectivity as against subjectivity, and impersonal judgments against the personal needs and character of individual persons. In general, it opposes all the qualities which the Virgin Mary represents. Despite a series of feminist movements throughout history, the overall patriarchal nature of society and social ideals has been steadily increasing in strength, partly because of a tendency among feminists to adopt masculine stereotypes as a goal for themselves. Such steadily increasing repression of "feminine" emotional needs determines the nature of feminine figures in our dreams, which try to redress the situation by emphasizing precisely those needs, so that "anima" figures (feminine imagery) have, as James Hillman has frequently pointed out, become familiar in the dreams and fantasies of women as well as men.[11] It may well be that the same repression is responsible for the waking visions or "apparitions" of the Virgin Mary and the decision barely forty years ago to re-emphasize her objective reality.

Once it is recognized that an "inner image" is experienced by the brain exactly as is an image from the "outside" world, then the truth of the vision/apparition is no longer in dispute. What is in dispute is merely whether the original source of the image is supernatural, or whether the image is created by the same emotional processes within us which result in dream formation when we are asleep. There is another possibility also, that emotional "readiness" enables the unblocking of the perception of non-normal imagery. (I am leaving aside the question of charlatanism, which must be considered in any specific case.)

The situation is again, then, that psychological investigation cannot determine the "truth" or "fictitiousness" of supernatural claims for a vision/apparition, nor can it determine whether a claimed image is due purely to repressed (or perhaps merely suppressed) characteristics within the person making the claims, or partly or wholly to non-natural factors. At the time of writing this chapter, an "apparition" of the Virgin Mary to three children is claimed to be taking place at Medjugorje in the former Yugoslavia. These apparitions began in 1981. Numerous pilgrimages to Medjugorje have taken place, and a frequently updated publication reports on the progression of the appearances. One statement is of special interest in explaining the role of the Virgin Mary in the Catholic Churches: when the children asked at the request of a priest if people should pray to Jesus or to Mary, her answer was:

> "Please pray to Jesus. I am his Mother and I intercede for you
> with Him. But all prayer goes to Jesus. I will help. I will
> pray, but everything does not depend only on me. It depends
> also on your strength, the strength of those who pray."[12]

As we have seen, the place of the Virgin Mary in the divine world is becoming more defined as the centuries pass. We might ask just what is happening to bring this about. The answer might be addressed by examining another question: why is the Virgin Mary lacking from the Protestant Churches? Why is it that in the major share of Christianity, the Virgin Mary's status is increasingly being incorporated into official dogma, while in the smaller yet very influential Protestant branch of Christianity her very existence is denied, with no indication of any likelihood of her inclusion into popular belief or theology?

There may be a clue to the answer to this in the sociological observation that religious belief and participation are strongly on the wane in the Western countries. A very large proportion of the one-time "Christian" population is finding it continually more difficult to see the relevance of the Christian tradition to what is commonly accepted as scientific fact. Still others are discovering in other religious traditions (such as the Buddhist) an attraction which, for one reason or another, the Christian tradition no longer holds for them. When a traditional belief-system is felt to be under attack, there is usually a tendency for its adherents to split into two opposing groups, those who attempt to reinterpret tradition in terms of the newly emerging world views, and those who hold all the more tenaciously to the details of the tradition in defiance of the new views. Virtually everywhere in the Christian world, an increasing part of the population—often well over 50 percent—have no link with any religious group. Generally the explanation for this is laid at the doorstep of science. Among Christians, one difficulty in the strong reliance on detailed teachings and historical events, is that the details and history are open to re-examination and possible total rejection. As secular, non-religious views of the world take hold in the West, the tendency is for religious belief and activity to move towards two extremes—an increasingly more belligerent emphasis on traditional beliefs on the one hand, and growing skepticism on the other. The Catholic response has been to modernize in the field of liturgy and external appearances, while holding all the more firmly to religious traditional beliefs. Among Protestants, the relatively new (i.e., in the past two centuries) "fundamentalist" or "evangelical" teachings re-emphasize a literal understanding of biblical texts, while the "liberal" Churches, in an attempt to make it possible for religious traditions to coexist with modern science, increasingly reinterpret the biblical texts and the traditions in metaphorical fashion.

It could be said that the Catholic Churches are searching for a sense of security by increasing emotional fervor about and stress on intimate relationship with the supernatural figures. This is also true of the evangelical Protestant Churches, where intimate encounter with Jesus is emphasized, sometimes to the exclusion of all else. The liberal Protestant Churches, in turn, are looking for security by blending scientific discoveries with reinterpretation of traditional teachings. Yet all three sides are, seen as a whole, more or less only just holding their ground. Most Christian "converts" in the present day are persons converting from one form of Christianity to another, rather than a substantial extension of the Christian sphere of influence.

THE MYSTICAL CHORUS
98

The reason for the resurgence of emotionalism may not be difficult to understand. Particularly in the modern West, links with nature are being severed, and Christian teachings which originated in an unindustrialized, agrarian environment have less relevance. If the function of religion is to express and further the evolutionary tie between human beings and the natural environment in which they live, then the Christian religious tradition appears increasingly less relevant. The two strongest groups among Christians at the present day, the Catholic and the evangelical, have been most able to survive because they have adopted an emotional approach to a religious tradition which, as Toynbee described it, is traditionally an extroverted thinking (i.e., intellectual) tradition.

The evangelical movement stresses personal communion with Jesus, who, being God, is able to bring emotional reassurance, sense of direction, and inner stability. At the same time, the growing feeling of terror and despair as the world moves more and more into an age of nuclear threat and scientific manipulation of life, can be personified as the workings of the devil, Satan. The New Testament teaching that the end of the world is near retains more emotional reality and value than Browning's naively optimistic "God's in his heaven, / All's right with the world!"

The Catholic traditions rely on their concept that a spiritual family (God the Father, Jesus Christ the Son, Mary the Mother) is eternally available. The increasingly chaotic nature of human relationships on earth and the breakdown of the nuclear family are compensated by the Holy Family, whose intervention can give comfort and promise.

What we are seeing is a shift in popular Christianity from intellectualism to a new, emotion-based allegiance—an allegiance that is, in reality, not all that different from the nature of Christian teaching back in its earliest years before the philosophers and theologians took it over.

I left the Holy Spirit out of the discussion in the last few paragraphs for special consideration. At several points the possibility of a bridge between Buddhism and Christianity has been mooted. In the light of the changing nature of society and the understanding of religious traditions, might there be a place for suggesting that the "Holy Spirit" and the "Buddha nature" have something in common? Both the Holy Spirit and Gautama appear to have originally been seen as performing the function of a guru to the individual, guiding her or him along the path to freedom. Gautama Siddhartha no longer exists, for Gautama is a Buddha and totally outside the realm of existence. But the Buddha nature, indefinable as it may be, is akin to Gautama and allows for the hope of ultimate liberation. If, as I suggest, we look at these beliefs and traditions, not in the light of intellectual content but in the light of how they portray and also guide our emotional participation in the world around us, the difference between Buddhism and Christianity begins to wane and even to disappear.

KARMA AND PREDESTINATION

There is one more major item in Christian tradition which I have not yet discussed, yet which is strangely parallel to the concept of karma in Buddhism. That is the doctrine of predestination. A few centuries ago predestination was a burning issue in Christian thought, and while the public controversy has all but disappeared in the present day, the concept remains firmly ingrained in popular Christian belief and technical theology alike.

"Predestination" is a word made from *pre-* (equals before) and *destination*. In its simplest form, it means that God has foreknown and predetermined the course of every person's life and death. In personal belief it is found most vividly as the conviction that God has predetermined when each individual is to die. In this respect, it is virtually universal in Christian conviction. Along with this conviction is the belief that there is a right course of life unique to each person, and that, as many people put it, God has a plan for your life. In this simple form it looks like there is a major difference between predestination and karma, for predestination appears to be an active intervention in the world by God, while karma is in its simplest presentation merely the principle of cause and effect carried over more than one lifetime, an inherited destiny rather than one created for the individual.

Further reflection, however, brings out a more basic point. In Christian ideology, God is outside of time. Time was created by God. Time and space are two aspects of one reality, and that reality is of God's creation. Consequently, in Christian speech, it cannot be said that "before," "during," and "after" have any meaning which refers to God. I have referred to this point before, in discussing the eternal nature of the Christ according to Christian belief. In regard to predestination, the relevance is that, for God, an individual's life is a single, finite reality—not a series of events but, rather, the completed manuscript of a play, in which all events are present from first word to last. We saw an analogy to this in Plato's parable, in which each soul after death chooses for itself the course of a new life, having free choice but committed to the details once the choice is made.

Just as "beginning" is not applicable to God, neither is "end." As an early Church council hammered out in detail, there never was a time when Christ did not exist, nor can there ever be a time when Christ will not exist, for existence in time and space is created by God (of whom Christ is a "person") whose reality transcends existence beyond comprehension.

The consequence is, many Christian theologians argued, that there is not really any such thing as free will at all, for the entire course of your life is present, so to speak, in manuscript throughout all eternity. God foreknows every detail of your life, as if God were a playgoer who has read the script, the difference being that God is the author of the script as well.

Does this then apply also to salvation; that is, to liberation from sin and punishment? Is the spiritual outcome of your life preordained; that is, foreknown by God before you are even born? Theologians went in two separate directions when trying to answer this question.

One direction was to say that the predestined fate of the individual means that the script, so to speak, has been written and will be played out to its inevitable end unless the individual takes active steps to change it. God is willing to permit a change, and the receptiveness of the individual to damnation or salvation, to the Devil or to the Holy Spirit, decides the final outcome. Though this view is logically difficult to defend, in emotional terms it poses no difficulty. As an evangelical preacher would say, it is up to you to open your heart to Christ.

The other direction which Christian theologians (and, in general, those in any monotheist religious belief-system, such as Islam) argued as a possibility is that logically there is no escape from your predestined fate. It is meaningless to say that you can change the script, because the script is, in reality, the totality of your life as it actually takes place and thus includes any change of heart. The difference between the two schools of thought might be linked to different forms of drama: The first interpretation might be represented by the type of drama which assigns a basic character and role to each of the actors, yet requires the actor to improvize the precise details; the second interpretation is like the traditional drama which follows a set script from which no deviation is possible.

Even the traditional form of scripted drama incorporates a considerable amount of improvization, for two highly skilled actors will bring quite different interpretations of their roles when enacting the play on stage, and even the same actor will make small or large changes of interpretation between one performance and the next. The emotional impact consequently differs greatly.

The same is to be said even more of music. The score of a particular musical piece indicates the notes to be played and to some degree the timing of each note, but each individual musician is required to input a personal interpretation simply because the printed score does not indicate with any precision exactly how it is to be played. Since we have come to associate emotion with music more than drama, by and large, we need to take this musical analogy quite seriously, for it is this analogy which in practice represents the conclusion ultimately reached in Christian theology, and which is also the best analogy for the Buddhist concept of karma.

Another way of putting the same point is to make a comparison with the age-old game of chess and the quest to make a computer program which can invariably win when playing against any human opponent at any time. Every move made on a chessboard is subject to pre-established rules, yet every move makes an infinite variety of subsequent moves possible. The computer, no matter how complex, has a finite ability to foresee possible moves, it cannot deal with an infinite possibility of choices as, apparently, a human brain can. The ability to make unpredictable choices or decisions appears to be a human quality. How this can be has been the supreme dilemma for philosophers and psychologists alike throughout the centuries.

The form of predestination as finally accepted in most Christian thought and karma involve the belief that at the time of birth the broad outline of the life that is to be lived already exists, just as a musical score for a violin sonata already exists when the musician takes up a violin to perform the sonata. However, just as the individual interpretation of the music by the violinist determines whether what results evokes the emotions of a dirge or of an expression of hope, and the final notes of the music receive their meaning from the way the previous notes have been played, so the individual interpretation of the drama of life depends to a great extent on how that individual understands and expresses a personal interpretation.

Although the intellectual presentation of God and Buddha, of predestination and karma, may emphasize enormous gulfs between the two belief-systems, the essence of the gulfs consists of the presuppositions about the origins of the reality of the item in question. God is the ultimate author of your life, in the Christian belief-system; past lives are responsible for the nature of your life, in the Buddhist belief-system. Presented this way the two belief-systems are worlds apart.

Yet presented in terms of the actual experience of the individual person, the two belief-systems merge and become one. Every one of us is born with the essential outline and details of life already determined, though how we deal with that outline and those details affects what happens after our death. If we limit our view to the way we see our life take its course and to the results of our active intervention in that course, our experience becomes identical whether we operate in a Christian or a Buddhist conceptual framework.

We are, of course, faced still with the ardent conviction of many millions of people over a period of at least two and a half thousand years, that we have lived before and that this previous life is the basis on which our present life begins. Not only Buddhists and Hindus hold to this, but a great many Christians as well (though not in any of the orthodox theologies) and perhaps the majority of other religious systems. What experience—apart from the possible reality of reincarnation—could cause such a conviction which continues fully as much among highly educated, scientifically minded people as among uneducated peasants? From the point of view which I have been suggesting in this book, the conviction stems from a generally ignored yet obvious truth: that none of us is in fact born completely new. Each of us began with the merger of two living cells from our parents, and on the cellular level there has been an unbroken chain of existence since life first began some billions of years ago. The genetic link from the hypothetical first living cell to each of us today is unbroken, though mutation of genes has led to an endless series of changes. Is the sense of karma, or of predestination, anything different from the unconscious feeling of tracing back over endless generations into the past? Is the unconscious "knowledge" of our body anything other than characteristics carried by the genes which have been passed on to us and existed before we as separate individuals came into being? Is this the basis behind the problem of determinism and free will, that each of us inherits two karmas, as it were, by coming from a merger of the genetic structure of two parents and by having the ability to decide, to a limited extent, whether to develop and merge some of the genetically inherited psychological traits, or to suppress them in favor of other traits? Do we then simply reify this unconscious "knowledge"? Or is this a gross oversimplification? As the other half of our dialog, your answer will help determine how you relate to and agree or disagree with the chapters that follow.

When we identify psychology with the way in which life is felt and responded to, then the religious dimension takes on a new form, and with it a new understanding. The next chapter will deal with religion not as a series of systems, but as variations on a common theme through mysticism. Then, in Chapters 5 and 6, we are going to turn to what will be, for most readers, quite new territory—the religious experience among North American Indians and among Australian Aboriginal people. What we will discover is not, as early anthropologists and also early psychologists thought, a primitive level in the evolutionary ladder of the development of thinking, but what for us may be a completely new and most definitely a very highly sophisticated way of perceiving the world and relating to it.

REFERENCES

The historical material presented in this chapter is common property in Western history, and it is difficult to single out individual references for individual items. In general, for the theological concepts and their evolution, see:

Martin Werner, *The Formation of Christian Dogma*, Adam & Charles Black, London, 1957. Also Evaldo Pauli, *Mil Jaroj de Kristana Filozofio*, Eldonejo Simpozio, Florianópolis, Brazil, 1985.

and for references to Zoroastrianism, see:

R.C. Zaehner, *The Dawn and Twilight of Zoroastrianism*, Weidenfeld & Nicolson, London, 1961.

For discussion of biblical points, see:

The Interpreter's Dictionary of the Bible, 4 vol., Abingdon Press, New York and Nashville, 1962.

NOTES

All biblical quotations and all material from the Greek are my own translation.

1. Morris West, in an interview published in the Australian magazine *Elle*, vol.1, no.1, March 1990, p.216.

2. In a few passages in the Old Testament and several in the New Testament, the phrase "God's spirit" is used in a manner that seems to require that it be understood in some other way than as a simple synonym for God. Since popular belief in Jesus' time held that a living person consists of body and spirit, it seemed obvious that God could be thought of in a similar way, for virtually all religious persons conceived of God as some kind of person, even if not a human person. The Jewish scriptures of the time frequently spoke of God's appearance in human bodily form, which would therefore presumably encase a spirit just as in ordinary human beings as popular thought held.

However, for most Christians, God's "spirit" was not a problem, for in the Bible it is never portrayed as if acting of its own volition in the way that Jesus is portrayed. It remained a loose end in theology, however, and eventually Church councils tidied up the doctrine of God by including God's spirit, now officially termed the Holy Spirit, as a third "person" of God, making a neat Trinity. In popular thought the Holy Spirit was usually conceived of as divine inspiration, though theologians worked out a much more sophisticated view.

3. Sigmund Freud, *Moses and Monotheism*, Hogarth Press, London, 1939.

4. In *C.W.* ll. 1958.

5. Sigmund Freud, *The Ego and the Id* (1923), Hogarth Press, London, 1952.

6. William McGuire and R.F.C. Hull, (eds) *C.G. Jung Speaking*, Princeton University Press, Princeton, 1977, p. 424.

7. McGuire and Hull, *C.G. Jung Speaking*, pp. 377–8.

8. Islam may justly be considered a sister religion to Christianity in its goal of purifying Christian teachings of the accretions of doctrine formulated after the New Testament was written. Much of the Koran consists of retelling biblical events. The principal differences between the two religions are due to the social backgrounds in which they originated.

9. This is not to deny that many Christians were tortured and killed by Roman authorities during the second century. But in the Empire as a whole, Christian meetings were tolerated if held in private. Secret meetings such as those held in the catacombs, were the exception rather than the rule.

10. Henri Frankfort, *Kingship and the Gods*, University of Chicago Press, Chicago, 1948. In particular chapter 16.

11. James Hillman, series of articles in *Spring*, Spring Publishers, Zürich and Dallas.

12. *Miracle at Medjugorje*, no place or original date given. Quotation on p.3, dated Dec. 11, 1985. This publication is currently replaced by *The Medjurgorje Sentinel*, Drummoyne NSW (Australia).

CHAPTER FOUR

MYSTICISM

I was going on a bus tour with a number of other persons. The
bus stopped and we all got out. After a bit of walking we came
to a restaurant where we were to eat. We entered. Inside there
were many rows of tables, each of which seated six persons,
two on each of the long sides and one at each end. When we
sat down the restaurant was full. The tables were filled starting
with the back row so that when I came to sit down it was at
the last table in the front. As we ate, an announcement was
made, apparently over a loud speaker, which I could not hear
clearly or else paid little attention to. All I caught was the
final admonition to "shake hands." We continued eating. I
noticed that gradually, table by table, starting at the back,
people began to disappear, until finally all that were left was
the fellow to my left and me. He turned to me and said
"Remember: Shake hands" and he disappeared. Then as I
wondered at this I also disappeared. Now I discovered that we
were all still in the restaurant but all the tables were gone,
music was playing and people were all dancing. Bewildered I
could only think "shake hands." The nearest person was a
fellow a fair distance from me. I went over to him and he held
out his hand. I held out mine and our hands just barely
touched. But apparently that was enough. Suddenly I found I
was also dancing. We formed into two lines, as in some square
dances, and I found myself at the head of one of the lines. As
we danced the lines slowly moved along out of the dining hall
into a long corridor at the end of which a bright light was
shining. A woman in the opposite line said that I had led my
line long enough and someone else should have a go now. But
a woman in my line said I should remain at the head of our

line. We continued dancing without stop, and I had the feeling
of pure ecstasy.

[Author's dream]

Probably no other words have been more misused than "mystical" and "mysticism." Mystical has almost become a swear word. In popular usage, if someone disagrees with an author and cannot think of any good arguments to use to support the disagreement, they finally resort to calling the author's ideas "mystical," and in Western society this seems to be the final condemnation. The reason for this may lie in the tendency of mystics to be a rather hidden minority among the highly organized and highly extroverted religious systems of the West. Also, since most mystics have tended to dethrone reason in favor of emotional experience, the modern West has largely come to demote mysticism to an "unscientific" and therefore unacceptable status.

"Mysticism" is a difficult word to define, although it is a type of experience fairly easy to describe. Mysticism cuts across all religious boundaries. It is an attitude towards a type of experience. In religious terms, the closest mystics have been able to come to a description is to say that it is a direct encounter with God—an encounter without anything or anyone intervening, neither prayers, rituals, doctrines, priests nor teachers. It may be found among "orthodox" believers in a religious system as much as among persons who would be considered "unorthodox" or indeed outside any religious system at all.

Immediately "encounter with God" is said, serious problems arise. There are mystics, some of them quite well-known, among Buddhists, Taoists, American Indians, Australian Aborigines, and other groups—despite the fact that none of these groups holds to a belief in God. As an example, if we move away from the attempt to make definitions and limit ourselves to descriptions of experience, mainstream Buddhism is one of the prime examples of a religion founded on mysticism. In the West there are, of course, many people within and outside of the organized religions who are important examples of mystics, some of whom believe in God and others who do not. In the Christian tradition the Quakers rank as mystics, as do the Sufis in Islam and at one time members of the Hasidic movement in Judaism, represented in this century by Martin Buber, whose personal writings have bec/me classics in their own right, and whose spiritual attitude is well described in the chapter on American Indian Religion.

Generally speaking, God-focused systems—whether highly organized movements like Islam or loose groupings of separate traditions as in Hinduism—are based on the idea of a relationship between human beings and God. For the most part, these religious systems, in contrast to individuals' personal approaches to religion, hold that such relating must be of a closely prescribed kind. It is not expected to be a total two-way encounter, as would occur between two ordinary persons in which God is affected and involved in precisely the same way as the human individual. This is because, in part, it is usual for God-focused religious systems to stress that God is so far from humankind in nature and quality that a direct meeting can take place only on a very special level. The encounter is held to take the form of worship services, prayers, and in many cases sacraments and special holy actions. These may range from baptism and the Eucharist (Holy Communion) among Christians to pilgrimage, as in Islam, or ritual re-enactment of sacred events (Jewish Passover), and other special actions by which the human individual and God draw close together. Usually there is a formal ceremony or at least a formal gathering. The importance of being a group is emphasized, as in the statement attributed to Jesus in the Bible: "Wherever two or three meet together in my name I am there among them." (Bible: Matthew 18: 20) Toynbee's description of the mainstream Western religions as being highly extroverted[1] is very applicable here. Although individual worship may be encouraged, it is held to be subservient to group meetings and, most especially, to group sanctioned beliefs and actions.

A God-focused mystic, in contrast, holds to an individualist approach. Mystics may or may not shun religious organizations and meetings, but tend to consider them a hindrance or at least not essential. For the mystic, a person-to-person two way meeting on an equal footing with God, and often a merger with God, is the most important aspect of religion.

All formally organized God-focused religious movements hold that direct meeting of the individual worshipper with God is all important, and make provision for such a direct meeting, claiming that it takes place during organized ritual meetings. As well, personal prayer and meditation are generally emphasized as particularly valuable, but this as a rule is neither the only concern nor the primary concern. If you become a member of an organized religion, it will be necessary to undertake and undergo group prescribed activities. If an individual feels that there is a choice to be made between direct individual experience and the religion's teachings and traditions, it is the teachings and traditions which must prevail. In all organized religious systems, whether general social tradition or (as is usual in the West) legally incorporated institutions, the group prescriptions must prevail.

In such a situation, the pure mystic who follows only personal experience leads a very precarious and uncertain existence. Religious organizations usually find it impossible to deny the validity of mystical experience on the one hand, but feel that such an approach is fraught with danger on the other hand. A working compromise has been tacitly made in Christian tradition: mysticism is allowed but discouraged from becoming too intense, and what the mystic experiences is subjected to scrutiny and authentication by Church authority. Much the same can be said of other organized religious traditions. In Islam the mystics have had a very checkered career. At one point in Muslim history mysticism was held to be a serious enough aberration to warrant an inquisition and to be stamped out by force. But mystics survived, and at present mystical experience holds an important, though somewhat suspect place, in Islam. Jewish religious leaders in the Jewish and Christian Bible, such as Moses, King Solomon, Jeremiah, Ezekiel and others have frequently been characterized as mystics. Albert Schweitzer made a strong case for characterizing the Christian apostle Paul as a mystic.[2]

Let us look at several brief excerpts from mystical writers of several religious traditions to see the type of expression which marks the mystical experience as a type of experience which transcends the boundaries between religious systems.

> *For granting that the soul could not be happy without it [that is, being conscious of its own processes], still its happiness does not consist in that; for the foundation of spiritual blessing is this: that the soul look at God without anything between; here it receives its being and life and draws its essence from the core [grund] of God, unconscious of the knowledge-process, or love or anything else. Then it is quite still in the essence of God, not knowing at all where it is, knowing nothing but God.*
> *(Eckhart, Christian, about AD 1300, as quoted in Suzuki,*
> *Introduction, p. 82. Bracketed comments by Suzuki.)*

> *The Tao that can be told is not the eternal Tao.*
> *The name that can be named is not the eternal name.*
> *The nameless is the beginning of heaven and earth.*
> *The named is the mother of ten thousand things.*

Ever desireless, one can see the mystery.
Ever desiring, one can see the manifestations.
These two spring from the same source but differ in name; this
appears as darkness.
Darkness within darkness.
The gate to all mystery.
                    (Taoist, attributed to Lao Tsu, about 500 BC.)[3]

In the market, in the cloister—only God I saw.
In the valley and on the mountain—only God I saw.
Him I have seen beside me oft in tribulation
In favor and in fortune—only God I saw.
In prayer and fasting, in praise and contemplation,
In the religion of the Prophet—only God I saw.
I oped mine eyes and by the light of His face around me
In all the eye discovered—only God I saw.
Like a candle I was melting in His fire:
Amidst the flames outflanking only God I saw.
Myself with mine own eyes I saw most clearly.
But when I looked with God's eyes—only God I saw.
I passed away into nothingness, I vanished,
and lo, I was the All-living—only God I saw.
                    (Baba Kubi of Shiraz, Muslim, about AD 1050,
                              as quoted in Happold, p. 220.)

You know always in your heart that you need God more than
everything: but do you not know too that God needs you—in
the fullness of His eternity needs you? How would man be,
how would you be, if God did not need him, did not need
you? You need God, in order to be—and God needs you, for
the very meaning of your life. In instruction and in poems men
are at pains to say more, and they say too much—what turgid
and presumptuous talk that is about the "God who becomes";
but we know unshakably in our hearts that there is a becoming
of the God who is. The world is not divine sport, it is divine
destiny. There is divine meaning in the life of the world, of
man, of human persons, of you and of me.
                    (Martin Buber, Jewish, 1923)[4]

Into this Dark, beyond all light, we pray
    to come and,
        unseeing and unknowing,
    to see and
    to know
        Him that is
            beyond seeing and
        beyond knowing
    precisely by not seeing,
        by not knowing.
For that is truly to see and
            to know and
            to hymn transcendently
                Him that transcends all.
That is, negating, to do as sculptors do,
    drawing [from marble]
        the statue latent there,
    removing all that
            hinders or
            hides
        the pure spectacle of the hidden form and
    displaying, with this mere removal,
        the beauty hidden there.
One must, I think, hymn in
        negating and
        affirming
    for affirmations proceed
        from the topmost
        through the middlemost
        to the lowest.
But here
        from the lowest
        to the topmost,
    one denies them all, thus
        to lay bare the Unknowable who is
            by all known beings veiled,
        to see the transcendent Dark that is
            by the light of beings hid.
                (Pseudo-Dionysius the Areopagite, Christian
        about the fifth century AD, as quoted in O'Brien, pp. 72–3)

"UNION" AND "COMMUNION"

It is a long standing tradition to distinguish two different sorts of mysticism, "union" and "communion." This refers to what the mystic claims to have experienced during the mystical encounter; that is, either an actual merger with God or Supreme Reality, or a face-to-face, person-to-person meeting with God or Supreme Reality, during which each keeps a separate identity.

Many mystics hold that they merge or unite with God. They often call this the unitive experience. In the God-focused religious traditions, this is taken to mean that there is a total union between God and person so that they are no longer two, but one. This is beautifully expressed in a passage from a major Christian mystic, Johannes Eckhart (c. AD 1300) who speaks of the feeling during the mystical experience, what he calls the "breaking through," when he and God literally unite. He contrasts this with his feeling during ordinary life among the multiplicity of things that make up our daily existence, when he feels himself to be merely one of countless creatures made by and subordinate to God:

> When I came out of the Godhead into multiplicity, then all things proclaimed, "There is a God." Now this cannot make me blessed, for hereby I realize myself as creature. But in the breaking through I am more than all creatures. I am neither God nor creature. I am that which I was and shall remain now and for ever more. There I receive a thrust which carries me above all angels. By this thrust I become so rich that God is not sufficient for me, in so far as He is only God in his divine works. For in thus breaking through, I perceive what God and I are in common. There I am what I was. There I neither increase nor decrease. For there I am the immovable which moves all things. Here man has won again what he is eternally and ever shall be. Here God is received into the soul.
>
> (Happold, p. 238)

In short, during the unitive experience Eckhart feels what Jesus seems to have felt when he spoke of being the "I am" who pre-existed all of creation. (This was discussed in Chapter 3 on Christianity.) This experience is by no means limited to Christianity. A Muslim mystic of a few centuries earlier (c. AD 922), Husayn ibn Mausur al-Hallaj, identified himself with the Christ by repeating of himself what Jesus had said: "I am Truth" (Jesus as quoted in the Bible: John 14:6). We must remember that Islam as well as Christianity accepts the nature and role of Jesus as described in the New Testament in the Bible, and al-Hallaj was familiar with the text of the Gospel of Saint John. Al-Hallaj goes on to speak of his unity with God by elaborating on a passage from the same gospel:

> *Betwixt me and Thee there lingers an "it is I" that torments me.*
> *Ah, of Thy grace, take this "I" from between us!*
>
> *I am He whom I love, and He whom I love is I,*
> *We are two spirits dwelling in one body.*
> *If thou seest Him, thou seest us both. (Eliade, p. 524)*

The gospel passage underlying this poem reads:

> *Thomas asked him: "Master, we do not know where you are*
> *going. How can we know the path?"*
>
> *Jesus answered him: "I am Path, Truth, Life. If you knew*
> *me, you would know my Father. From now on you know*
> *Him and see Him."*
>
> *Philip said to him: "Master, show us the Father and we will*
> *be content."*
>
> *Jesus answered him: "I have been with you for such a long*
> *time and you still do not know me, Philip? A person who has*
> *seen me has seen the Father. How can you say 'Show us the*
> *Father'? Don't you believe that I am in the Father and the*
> *Father is in me?" (Bible: John 14: 5–10, author's translation)*

For Christians, Jesus' identification of himself with the Father is no problem because Christian theology teaches that Jesus is one of the "persons" of God. But for traditional Christians and Muslims alike, al-Hallaj's application of this claim to himself is pure blasphemy, while most rationalists would simply take it to be lunacy. Yet it is a self-identification which "union" mystics have made consistently through the centuries, and is not a personal aberration on the part of al-Hallaj. For this reason mystics have frequently undergone persecution from "orthodox" believers, regardless of which God-focused tradition they are a part. Yet if we were to transfer this into a Buddhist context, where there is no God but there is a potentially endless number of Buddhas, we would feel no unease. It would merely reflect a momentary glimpse of nirvana, and the sense of being torn from one's real nature when this glimpse of nirvana fades into the past. Remembering what was said of the "negative theology" approach of Pseudo-Dionysius and of the "negating description" of nirvana, both discussed in Chapter 3 on Buddhism, it comes as no great shock for us to discover that one of the greatest mystics of all time, Jalil al-Din Rumi (c. AD 1250) could write:

> What is to be done, O Muslims? For I do not recognize myself.
> I am neither Christian nor Jew nor Zoroastrian nor Muslim.
> I am not of the East, nor of the West, nor of the land, nor of the sea;
> I am not of Nature's mint, nor of the circling heavens.
> I am not of earth, nor of water, nor of air, nor of fire;
> I am not of the empyrean, nor of the dust, nor of existence, nor of entity.
> I am not of India, nor of China, nor of Bulgaria, nor of Saqsin;
> I am not of the Kingdom of 'Iraquain, nor of the country of Khora-san.
> I am not of this world, nor of the next, nor of Paradise nor of Hell.
> I am not of Adam, nor of Eve, nor of Eden and Rizwan.
> My place is the Placeless, my trace is the Traceless;
> 'Tis neither body nor soul, for I belong to the soul of the Beloved.
> I have put duality away. I have seen that the two worlds are one;
> One I seek, One I know, One I see, One I call.
> He is the first, He is the last, He is the outward, He is the inward.

I know none other except "Ya Hu"* and "Ya man Hu."
I am intoxicated with Love's cup, the two worlds have passed
out of my ken.
I have no business save in carouse and revelry.
If once in my life I spent a moment without thee,
From that time and from that hour I repent of my life.
If once in this world I win a moment with thee,
I will trample on both worlds, I will dance in triumph forever.
Oh Shamsi Tabriz [Rumi's martyred teacher], I am drunken
in this world,
That except of drunkenness and revelry I have no tale to tell.
(Eliade, pp. 526–7, spelling and wording somewhat
modernized.)

* These letters in Arabic spell the Hebrew name of God.

The similarities in expression and feeling of this passage are so close to those of the Christian Pseudo-Dionysius and of the description of nirvana to King Milinda, that it is easy to understand that all three are describing very much the same experience. It is not suggested that the three were completely independent of each other. On the contrary, it is probable that Pseudo-Dionysius was familiar with Buddhist claims, and Rumi was well acquainted with the gospel traditions both from the Koran and from earlier writers including those of the New Testament. What is important is that each in the context of her/his particular religious culture found it possible and necessary to express the same experience in such similar form. These mystics felt the experience to be of oneness with God, each interpenetrating the other so that no clear line of distinction could be made during the experience. There is, of course, one important distinction: in the Buddhist concept, existence and nonexistence cease altogether, never again to take place, when nirvana is fully experienced. The God-focused mystic does not merge into God in such a way that God swallows up the individual and brings about annihilation. Rather, God and the individual become one and the same for a time. As mentioned already, most theologians in God-focused religions have felt very uncomfortable with this idea. For this reason union mystics claiming to have had the unitive experience have always trod a very fine line between heresy and sainthood, and many have perished at the hand of the religious orthodox.

Communion mysticism is rather different from the unitive experience. In communion mysticism the mystic feels that the personality meets God person-to-person, in the same way that two persons meet but do not merge. The communion mystic will often see visions. A Jewish writer in the Bible, Isaiah, described a visionary experience he had in about 740 BC (roughly the legendary date of the founding of Rome, and the time of the Chou dynasty in China):

> I saw the Lord sitting on an elevated throne. His skirts filled
> the temple. Seraphs* stood above him, each with six wings.
> Each covered its face with two, covered its feet with two, and
> with two it flew. They called out to each other: "Holy, holy,
> holy is Yahweh Sabaoth.** His glory fills the entire earth."
> The hinges of the gates shook at the sound of their shouting.
> The room was filled with incense.
>   I said: "Woe is me! I may not speak for my lips are
> profane and I live among people whose lips are profane, yet my
> eyes have seen the King, Yahweh Sabaoth."
>   Then one of the seraphs flew to me, holding in its hands
> a burning coal which it had taken from the altar with tongs. It
> touched my mouth and said: "Now that this has touched your
> lips, your misdeeds have gone and your sins have been
> buried."
>   Then I heard the Lord's voice say: "Who shall I send?
> Who will go for us?"
>   I said: "Here I am, send me."
>   Then he said: "Go and tell the people this ... "
>   (Bible: Isaiah 6: 1–9, author's translation)

*Mythological winged animals, frequent in ornamentation of religious buildings.
**Yahweh = the Hebrew name of God. Sabaoth was a title perhaps meaning "of the Constellations."

This is an account which contains all the typical aspects of mysticism. The individual sees a vision, sees God. There is a feeling of inadequacy, shame and despair. Then comes purification and a mission to take to the world. Unlike the unitive experience, there is no urge to leave the world behind. Often a mission of a practical kind is given. So it is that we find that a large share of social reformers in the history of religion have been communion mystics. In contrast, the union mystic, having merged with God, returns from the experience with the feeling of disillusion and despair at having to return to everyday life. Such a person strives to re-enter the united state again with God, to lose individuality once more.

The distinction in reality is far from so clear-cut. Few or no mystics consistently fall into one category or another, and frequently it can be argued that a particular experience belongs to either or both types. If, as I have been suggesting, the basic religious experience is one of being flooded with the sense of being at one with all of Reality, an individual yet an indispensable link in the whole, both viewpoints about mysticism are simultaneously valid. A comparison could be made with a link in a chain: it is individual and can be removed, yet at the same time also forms the chain and without it the chain would not be what it is. As a less mechanical image we might use John Donne's phrase: "any man's death diminishes me, because I am involved in Mankind." Or, as Buber was quoted earlier in this chapter as saying, in divine terms: "… do you not know too that God needs you—in the fullness of His eternity needs you?" These, as I have repeatedly stressed, are not philosophical statements subject to logical analysis. They are feeling statements, rational not according to logic but according to experience.

Extroverted religions (following Toynbee's analysis) tend to stress communion mysticism as the only acceptable form of mysticism, for communion mystics appear to claim that God has objective reality outside of the person having the experience. To many in the modern West, this is the only way of putting it that has any meaning. For, in the West, we have largely come to the conclusion that "objective" and "real" are synonyms. To say that someone's conclusion is "subjective" is to imply that it is not "really" real.

Only a small minority in the West insist that there are degrees of reality. That which happens is real, regardless of whether it is "verifiable" (i.e., objective) or not (i.e., subjective). Writing in the seventeenth century, George Fox, one of the most influential Western mystics of modern times, went strongly against the tide of religious opinion in his claim that only if an experience is subjective can it be real. (He was, for example, indifferent about the historical truth of accounts in the Bible. For him it was irrelevant, because only in so far as the biblical accounts are understood as describing what goes on inside the individual's own personal self are they significant.) Thus he could experience among the American Indians, when he journeyed in America, a religious understanding which he could not find among the orthodox whites. In his *Journal* of 1672, Fox recounts numerous such occurrences. We may take one account as typical:

> And there was a doctor [= teacher of doctrine] that did dispute
> with us, which was of great service and occasion of opening
> much [= making clear] to the people concerning the Light and
> the Spirit. And he so opposed it [denied it to be] in every one,
> that I called [for] an Indian, because he [the teacher] denied it
> to be in them. And I asked him [the Indian] if that he did lie
> and do that to another which he would not have them do the
> same to him, and when he was wrong was not there something
> in him that did tell him of it, that he should not do so, but
> did reprove him. And he said that there was such a thing in
> him when he did any such thing that he was ashamed of them.
> So we made the doctor ashamed in the sight of the governor
> and the people. (Fox, p. 642)

Among introverted religious viewpoints, such as predominate in Buddhism, in which an "objective" God (i.e., separate, external to the cosmos) is denied, union mysticism tends to be the dominant type. The hope is to be merged with nirvana, to participate in the dharma (True Reality), and thus to end the illusion of independent existence. Such at least is the situation in the Hinayana form of Buddhism. In the Mahayana, in which the bodhisattvas represent a more personalized form of potential buddhahood, union with the Buddha—in a very wide sense which includes all the Buddhas and in effect ultimately all beings—is the ultimate aim, but the bodhisattva is very much the model of a communion mystic: a person who has glimpsed Ultimate Reality yet has come back from it with a sense of mission, much as did Isaiah in the previous biblical quotation. From this perspective Gautama himself was, during his life on earth, a communion mystic and a bodhisattva, for despite his enlightenment he did not enter nirvana directly, but returned from his experience to bring his message to the people of the world for the rest of his natural lifetime before he entered nirvana at the time of his death.

Such considerations bring up the interesting possibility that communion mysticism is a preparatory stage leading to union mysticism. In other words, in a God-focused religious context, the mystic might first reach a state of communion with God, meeting It person-to-person, and only later on, after repeated experiences, merge with It. This seems to be a fair description of the process elaborated as the ideal in the Christian classic *The Imitation of Christ* (first known in its present form in AD 1427). Near the end of the book the Disciple meditates in an inner conversation with Christ, who is called The Beloved:

Disciple:

How I long and pray to separate my heart from all that is created and be wholly joined to you, and by means of the Holy Communion and frequent celebration to grow more and more to love the heavenly and the eternal. O Lord God, when shall I be one with you, absorbed in you, with no more thought of self? You in me, and I in you—O make us one for ever ...

The Beloved:

If a man in all sincerity directs his whole intention up to God, if he empties himself of every undisciplined dislike or love for any created thing, then he will be fit to receive the gift of grace and will be worthy of the blessing of devotion. For God pours out his blessing into vessels he finds empty. It is when a man renounces all that is base, scorns the claims of self, and dies to all that self involves, that grace can come to him quickly and in abundance, and bear his heart unhindered to the heights.[5]

Nevertheless, although most mystics do express both forms of mysticism, usually one form or the other tends to predominate. It should also be noted that a person who is a mystic at one moment is not necessarily so throughout life. This may be behind some of the vigorous disputes among religious historians as to whether some particular individual was a mystic. To be a mystic does not generally mean that all of life is filled with mystical experiences, but only that on occasion—sometimes perhaps only one occasion—a mystical experience takes place. It then becomes a pointless controversy to debate whether the person involved deserves the "title" of mystic. Thus the ancient world's Gautama Siddhartha and Isaiah expressed mystical experiences in their teachings, yet also expressed much that is nonmystical. The same is true of the modern world. George Fox (seventeenth century) and Teilhard de Chardin (twentieth century) both expressed themselves in mystical writings, while carrying on social-political reform and scientific research respectively.

The fact that mystics do tend to be classified as union or communion mystics leads to the unfortunate result that all too frequently they do not acknowledge the others' claims to mystical experience. This is also the situation in many studies of mysticism, in which the author often chooses one type as genuine mysticism and quite dismisses the other type.

Similarly, individual religious cultures generally tend to endorse one type of mysticism and to reject the other. The tendency is that religious traditions which emphasize a sharp distinction between God and the universe are relatively happy with communion mysticism but not with union mysticism. Judaism, Christianity, and Islam in their main streams have at times during their history persecuted union mystics as heretics who deny the essential division between humanity and God, reserving the possible full union of human and divine for only one person (Jesus, in Christianity) or denying it altogether (as in Judaism and Islam). A philosopher-mystic of great renown, Spinoza (Jewish, seventeenth century) was ultimately rejected by the Judaism of his time because of his union-oriented teaching. But communion mystics, too, have had hard going at the hands of orthodox believers from time to time, the prime example being the Roman Catholic Christian Joan of Arc who was executed for heresy in 1431, though five centuries later (1920) formally proclaimed to be a saint. The persecution of communion mystics generally was based on their tendency to spread, and sometimes to instigate, social and political reform. In modern times they have met with much greater though not always untroubled success, as the popular acceptance of Martin Buber (Jewish) and Teilhard de Chardin (Roman Catholic Christian) testifies.

It is intriguing, and perhaps indicative of the cultural history of the societies in which they flourish, that two religious systems which appear to be very close in nature and concept, Hinduism and Quakerism, maintain radically opposing views on the nature of the desired and acceptable mystical experience. In the West it has been the Quakers who, for over three centuries, have kept alive the active practice of communion mysticism as a relatively organized religious movement. Those Quakers who tend to a belief in God hold that God appears and speaks exclusively in the "center" of the individual, but at no point does God become the individual nor does the individual become God, though God is to be found within each person and nowhere else. Quakerism originated and grew in the Christian culture of seventeenth century England, where the complete identification of Christ (or, as it is more commonly expressed in the modern day, the Inward Light) with the individual was taboo—because that status is traditionally held for Jesus alone. Although this point has never, to my knowledge, been argued explic-itly, it became firmly established during the lifetime of George Fox, founder of the Religious Society of Friends (Quakers), when a well-known Quaker named James Naylor was understood to actually claim to be Christ. Naylor's claim was rejected by Fox and by the Quakers generally, and Naylor was prosecuted by the civil authorities as well. In summary, then, active commu-nion with God within the center of oneself is the goal and active practice of Quakers, while with Hindus it goes further to full union and identification of God and the center of oneself.

There are Quakers who do not consider themselves to be believers in God, yet still hold that the Inward Light, "Christ" in a symbolic sense, is to be met through the same communion mysticism. My own experience, as one of this latter group, is that there is very little of substantial difference between Quaker communion mysticism and Zen Buddhist experience, the principal differences being superficial and due to the cultural underlay of Christian tra-dition in those areas where Quakerism originated and spread, and the cultural underlay of Indian, Chinese and Japanese Buddhism which gave rise to Zen. There is a definite tendency in both groups to say that the use of such terms as "God" and "Buddha" is more misleading than helpful in describing the basic mystical experience.

Individuals quite unconnected with belief in any formal religious tradi-tion frequently report mystical experiences. As an example, Carl Jung's description of his childhood experience:

> In our garden there was an old wall built of large blocks of
> stone ... In front of this wall was a slope in which was
> embedded a stone that jutted out—my stone. Often, when I
> was alone, I sat down on this stone, and then began an
> imaginary game that went something like this: "I am sitting on
> top of this stone and it is underneath." But the stone also
> could say "I" and think: "I am lying here on this slope and
> he is sitting on top of me." The question then arose: "Am I
> the one who is sitting on the stone, or am I the stone on which
> he is sitting?" This question always perplexed me, and I
> would stand up, wondering who was what now. The answer
> remained totally unclear, and my uncertainty was accompanied
> by a feeling of curious and fascinating darkness ...

*Thirty years later I again stood on that slope ... and
suddenly I was again the child who had kindled a fire full of
secret significance and sat down on a stone without knowing
whether it was I or I was it. I thought suddenly of my life in
Zürich, and it seemed alien to me, like news from some remote
world and time. This was frightening, for the world of my
childhood in which I had just become absorbed was eternal,
and I had been wrenched away from it and had fallen into a
time that continued to roll onwards, moving farther and farther
away. The pull of that other world was so strong that I had to
tear myself violently from the spot in order not to lose hold of
my future.[6]*

Many people find that this type of unitive experience comes easily. If
you just sit on the grass, on a warm spring day, and listen to the birds chirp-
ing, let your mind drift and stop thinking consciously, the sounds move in
upon you and soon you lose all sense of I-ness, and feel just a part of nature,
an experience that is so refreshing that to "come back to reality" seems a
shock. Some people experience this more easily than others. Some find it
impossible to do at all.

Religious mystics, too, may experience similar union with the universe.
For example, from George Fox (1648):

*Now was I come up in spirit through the flaming sword into
the paradise of God. All things were new, and all the creation
gave another smell unto me than before, beyond what words
can utter. I knew nothing but pureness, and innocency, and
righteousness, being renewed up into the image of God by
Christ Jesus, so that I saw I was come up to the state of
Adam which he was in before he fell. The creation was opened
to me, and it was showed me how all things had their names
given them according to their nature and virtue. (Fox, p. 27)*

When we look at mysticism in general and consider its place as a religious experience, it becomes clear that there is nothing unaccountable about
mysticism. It is not in itself mysterious or magical. As a religious form it
simply means feeling that God is present, and the degree to which this feeling engulfs you determines whether you feel an onlooker, a participant, or

actually merged into and with God. Those who do not believe in a God may prefer to state, simply, that their experience is of Oneness, being "at one" with or being merged with all of reality. This way of considering mysticism inevitably presumes that between communion and union mysticism the difference is one of type or degree of participation, rather than a totally different experience.

Thus a communion mystic may have visions, or may not. Often it is just a feeling, a sense that God is near, nothing more. This sense, of course, may change the course of one's actions. Let us consider a situation in which a university student one Sunday was walking from his room near campus to the student canteen to buy a snack for his evening meal.

He was aware that a student religious group was about to gather in a nearby church for a meeting which included a shared meal along with religious activities. He had decided not to go to that meeting. The concrete paths across campus leading, respectively, in the direction of the canteen and towards the church in which the group was meeting intersected at about the middle of campus. On reaching that intersection, the student found it impossible to move in the direction of the canteen, it felt as though something was restraining his legs so that they would move in one direction only: along the path towards the church. He was unable, despite strenuous efforts to move in any but the one direction. The sensation was one of finding it physically impossible to turn his feet in any but that one way. After a time he resigned himself to this fact and went to the church meeting.

A religiously minded person reared in a God-focused religion would be likely, as this youth did, to see in this the action of God. It reminds us of an account of a somewhat similar event described in the Bible, of a Jewish traveler walking along the road to the city of Damascus, the famous conversion of Saul (who later preferred to spell his name Paul) to Christianity:

As he neared Damascus suddenly a light from the sky encircled him. He fell to the ground and heard a voice say to him: "Saul, Saul, why do you persecute me?"

He answered: "Who are you, master?"

The voice said: "I am Jesus who you are persecuting. Now get up and enter the city. You will be told what you are to do."

The men accompanying him stood in confusion—they heard the voice but they saw nothing. Saul got up from the ground, but when he opened his eyes he could not see. They

> *led him by the hand into Damascus. He could not see for three*
> *days and he did not eat or drink.*
>
> *(Bible: The Acts of the Apostles, 9:3–9, author's translation)*

Given the context of the situations, it was only reasonable that both the university student and Saul should conclude that God had directly intervened in their lives and literally changed their direction. There are, of course, other ways of interpreting what happened. Jung commented on Saul's experience that Saul had already absorbed so much of Christianity's beliefs unconsciously that a complex had formed in him. It might be termed a "Jesus complex" which eventually broke through into his conscious awareness, taking on visual/auditory form. In its psychological nature such a waking "vision" is not substantially different from a dream. It is, as Jung put it, unconscious passive fantasy which has gathered enough energy to break through into awareness without the need for the body to be asleep, whereas dreams consist of the same material but it is too weak to break through directly while the body is awake. (Jung, *C.W.*, vol. 6, paragraph 714)

The student's experience can be described in much the same fashion, except that no visual or auditory form emerged. It did however, manifest in hysterical form. Hysteria is essentially the conversion of an emotional or psychological experience into a physical symptom that is not caused by an underlying physical malfunction. In Saul's case the symptom was first the experience of a light and then of the inability to see, a condition which cleared up after Saul contacted a Christian leader in Damascus. In the student's case the symptom was a malfunction of the voluntary nervous system, so that normal conscious control of his legs was temporarily taken over by an unconscious complex. Let us look briefly at a third experience of a similar nature, George Fox's first visionary experience.

Fox had originally considered entering the priesthood, but was dissuaded from this by his relatives. For a number of years during his late teens and early twenties he was plagued by severe psychiatric problems which appear to have been symptoms of a manic-depressive cycle.[7] In 1647, at the age of 23 he had exhausted all the therapeutic resources available:

> *And when all my hopes in them and in all men were gone, so*
> *that I had nothing outwardly to help me, nor could tell what*
> *to do, then, Oh then, I heard a voice which said "There is*
> *one, even Christ Jesus, that can speak to thy condition," and*

when I heard it my heart did leap for joy. Then the Lord did
let me see why there was none upon the earth that could speak
to my condition, namely, that I might give him all the glory;
for all are concluded under sin and shut up in unbelief as I had
been, that Jesus Christ might have the pre-eminence, who
enlightens, and gives grace, and faith, and power. Thus, when
God doth work who shall let [=hinder] it? And this I knew
experimentally [=by experience] ... For though I read the
Scriptures that spoke of Christ and God, yet I knew him not
but by revelation, as he who hath the key did open, and as the
Father of life drew me to his Son by his spirit. (Fox, p. 11)

In all three examples—Saul/Paul, the student, and Fox—there was no temptation by the person involved to identify with God, which in religious terms would be a unitive experience. Saul and Fox considered themselves as having encountered God through hearing God's voice. The student's experience was exclusively a brief hysterical symptom in a religious context. Fox appears not to have undergone a hysterical symptom in this his initial experience, though he mentions an abundance of such symptoms as consequences of later visions which he discusses in his *Journal.*

The form which these experiences take relies heavily upon the cultural belief-system in which the experiencer is immersed. As the Western world has become progressively more secular, and as Hindu and Buddhist thought have made an impact on the West, mysticism—which emphasizes encounter with the unnameable innermost experiences inside oneself—has become a dominating theme among those who are mystically inclined. In line with the more introverted religious philosophies of the East to which many Westerners are turning, "God" has come to be understood more and more as an inner experience and less and less as an identifiable "object" existing apart from the individual. In an unexpected turn about, sophisticated Western thought has again begun to understand "God" in terms of process rather than as a distinguishable being, thus bringing about a Westernized religious conception that shares more with the Native American traditions than with rationalist philosophy which has largely dominated Western religious thought for well over twenty centuries.

In the context of the now widely popularized Hindu belief systems, such experience tends to be understood as finding the divine "spark" that actually is the kernel around which individual personality is formed, and this kernel is the same kernel around which all other individuals' personalities are formed, so that all persons are manifestations of a single extracosmic God:

> These rivers flow, the eastern towards the West and the western towards the East; from ocean to ocean they flow. They actually become the ocean. And as they do not know which one they are, so all these creatures here, though they have come forth from Being, do not know that they have come forth from Being. Whatever they are, whether tiger, lion, wolf, boar, worm, fly, gnat, or mosquito, they all become That—That which is the subtlest of the subtle. The whole world has it as itself. That is reality. That is the self. And That art thou.
>
> (Zaehner, p. 139)

MYSTICISM AND BIOCHEMISTRY

The types of statements which we have been looking at in this chapter are by no means always spontaneous, nor are they always limited to people whom we acknowledge as mystics. Many mystics are known to have induced their visions by using special practices and, often, also by smoking or ingesting special substances. In modern times the use of drugs has also been documented in the foundation of some religious groups. One notable example is a twentieth century Winnebago religious movement. A first hand account of this by the founder of the cult has been preserved. An extract is as follows:

> On the following night preparations were again made to eat peyote. Then I thought to myself, "Last night I almost injured myself." Yet when those (gathered around) said, "Let us do it again," then I answered, "Good, I'll try it too!" So there we all ate seven peyote apiece.
>
> Suddenly I saw a large snake. I was very much frightened. Then another snake (appeared) and came crawling over me. "Oh my! Where are these coming from?" Then I felt something behind me and I looked around and I saw a snake about to swallow me completely. It had legs and arms and a long tail and the end of its tail was like a spear.
>
> "Oh my, Oh my! Now I am surely going to die," I thought.

Then I looked around again and there in a different place I saw a man with horns and long claws and with a spear in his hand. He jumped toward me so I threw myself on the ground. He missed me. Then I looked back at him and he appeared to be going back. Yet it seemed to me nevertheless that he was directing his spear at me again. Again I threw myself on the ground and again he missed me. Yet there seemed to be no possible escape for me.

Then suddenly the thought ran through me as "Perhaps—yes, it is this peyote that is doing this to me?"

"Help me, o medicine, help me! It is you who are doing this! You are holy. It is not these fear-inspiring visions that are causing this!"

"I should have known that you were doing this! Help me!"

"Then my suffering stopped."

"As long as the earth shall last, so long will I make use of you!"

This (i.e., these sufferings and the release from them) had lasted a night and a day. For one whole night I had not slept at all.

Then we all breakfasted. When we were through, it was I who said "Let us eat peyote again tonight."

That evening I ate eight peyote.

In the middle of the night I saw God. To God, living above, our father, to him I prayed. "Have mercy upon me! Give me knowledge that I may not say or do evil things. Do thou, O Son of God, help me too.

"This religion let me know! Help me, O grandfather, help me! Let me know this religion."

Thus I spoke and sat very quiet.

Soon I beheld the morning star and it was good to look upon. The light was good to look upon. Indeed, as the light appeared, it seemed to me that nothing would be invisible to me. I seemed to see everything clearly ...

"O medicine, grandfather, most assuredly you are holy. All that is connected with you, that I would like to know and that I would like to understand!"

"Help me! I give myself to you completely!"

For three days and three nights I had not slept.

Throughout all the years that I had lived on earth, I now realized that I had never known anything holy. Now, for the first time, I knew something holy.

"O, would that some of the other Winnebago might also learn about it!" ...

Today the Winnebago say that only God is holy. One of the Winnebago said to me, "Truly the life I used to lead was a very evil one. Never again will I lead such a life. This medicine is good and I will always use it." ...

Before (eating the peyote) I thought I had knowledge but I really had none. It is only now that I have acquired it. In my former life I was like one blind and deaf. My heart ached when I thought of what I had been doing. Never again will I do it. This medicine alone is holy and has made me good and rid me of all evil.

The one whom they call God has given me this (knowledge). I know this positively.[8]

This account by an American Indian, John Rave, was dictated to the anthropologist Paul Radin in 1911 in Rave's native language. The above is part of Radin's English translation of the original dictation.

Since John Rave's time, the visionary experiences and religious feelings evoked by drugs have become well-known and, indeed, a cult in many parts of the world. A considerable literature has grown up about the correctness or not of including such drug-induced experiences under the heading of mysticism. The case for regarding these as true mysticism was put by Aldous Huxley, already famous for his studies of religious mysticism, in *The Doors of Perception* in 1954. The case against was argued very persuasively by a highly renowned and respected historian of religion, R.C. Zaehner in 1957 in *Mysticism, Sacred and Profane*. Both relied to a large extent on their own experiments with the use of mescalin, the drug extracted from peyote.

Aldous Huxley experienced what appears to have been a fairly profound mystical experience, to judge by his own evaluation and by his reports of the content of the experience. R.C. Zaehner, on the other hand, reprints a transcript of his own report while under the influence of the drug; he appears to have had an experience quite similar to that familiar to many of us when drunk—different from sober thought, to be sure, but in no way profound or suggesting religious insight.

That two such experts on religious experience should differ so dramatically in their conclusions about the religious nature of the effect brought about by mescalin is certainly bewildering. Both scholars' experiences differed quite greatly from John Rave's. It should be added that many other American Indians have found the religious use of peyote to be a path to divine experience, and Rave is but one of the Indian leaders who have combined traditional rituals with the use of peyote as a sacrament in the formation of genuine religious systems.

The use of drugs to evoke religious experiences has a very long history. Centuries ago, in the first millennium BC or possibly earlier, a plant known as soma was in use in India. Its liquid was pressed out, filtered, mixed with milk and water, and drunk in a sacrificial ritual. In the Rig-Veda, a sacred Hindu text, Soma was identified as a god. Although Zaehner, the major specialist of the history of Zoroastrianism, states that Zoroastrianism is "the one major religion that never developed mysticism," (Zaehner, p. xii) he does make it clear that a Haoma ritual similar to the Soma ritual was practiced in Zoroastrianism. Haoma is the Persian form of the Sanskrit word Soma. Zaehner's comments about this are quite interesting for our study:

> ... it would seem that there was more sense of a "real presence" in the sacrament of the plant-god. Haoma, like the fire, is the son of Ahura Mazda, ordained by his father to be an eternal priest who, as son of God, offers himself up in the form of a plant to his father on high. The earthly sacrifice as performed by human priests is merely the re-presentation of the eternal sacrifice which the god Haoma offers "on the highest peak of high Hara" where heaven and earth meet. The Haoma sacrifice and sacrament, then, is in every sense one of communion. The plant is identical with the son of God: he is bruised and mangled in the mortar so that the life-giving fluid that proceeds from his body may give new life in body and soul to the worshipper.[9]

IS MYSTICISM TRULY RELIGIOUS?

The question has been asked many times: if it is possible with the use of drugs to produce experiences which are indistinguishable from those of traditionally acknowledged mystics, and if we also acknowledge that psychological factors and physiological processes sometimes account for experiences that otherwise appear to be mystical, are we justified in claiming that mysticism is a genuinely religious approach at all? Zaehner, in his book *Mysticism, Sacred and Profane*, was at pains to distinguish between "natural" mysticism and genuinely religious "inspired" mysticism—the supposition being that natural mysticism is due to other factors than God, while inspired mysticism has a divine origin. Yet, as we have already seen, the more closely the question is examined, the more the distinction becomes blurred. Many acknowledged mystics have been known to use drugs as a preparation for their experiences, while it seems very difficult, if not impossible, to find a palpable difference between the utterances and descriptions given by some persons known to have been suffering from psychiatric disturbances and statements made by apparently psychiatrically healthy mystics, quite apart from the question of the use of drugs.

Huxley, however, wished to carry the matter a bit further. If we can have all the benefits of mysticism without having to accept the myths that traditionally have accompanied it—religious teachings about God, nirvana, and the like—then we can dispense with religious belief, which appears to be on the decline anyway, while retaining ecstatic experiences of great emotional value. As for insanity, the psychological health of religious founders and leaders has been in question for many centuries. Jesus was accused of being insane on several occasions, according to accounts in the Bible. A similar accusation against Muhammad is recorded in the Koran. Joan of Arc's own account of her experiences, which included the hearing of voices, according to the transcripts of her testimony during her trial, strikes the reader as distinctly pathological. And the apostle Paul was also bluntly told: "You are raving, Paul. All your study has driven you insane!" (Bible: Acts of the Apostles, 26:14)

To be sure, experiences brought on by drugs are by no means always pleasurable. But neither are mystic experiences. One striking feature of mystics is that they frequently find their experiences highly disturbing and frightening. The Apostle Paul qualified his experience of revelations by a reference to some type of highly unpleasant and apparently continual affliction, which he took to be Satan's work permitted by God so that he did not become too

THE MYSTICAL CHORUS
132

conceited. Many of George Fox's visions were highly unpalatable. For example:

> *About this time I had a fit of sickness, which brought me very*
> *low and weak in my body; and I continued so a pretty while,*
> *insomuch that some Friends began to doubt of my recovery. I*
> *seemed to myself to be amongst the graves and dead corpses;*
> *yet the invisible power did secretly support me, and conveyed*
> *refreshing strength into me, even when I was so weak that I*
> *was almost speechless. One night, as I was lying awake upon*
> *my bed in the glory of the Lord which was over all, it was said*
> *unto me that the Lord had a great deal more work for me to*
> *do for him before he took me to himself. (Fox, pp. 700–1)*
>
> *And I saw all the religions and people that lived in them,*
> *and the priests that held them up, as a company of man-eaters,*
> *and how they ate up the people like bread, gnawing the flesh*
> *off their bones. And great sufferings I was under at this time*
> *beyond words to declare, for I was come into the deep, and the*
> *man-eaters were about me and I warred with their spirits.*
>
> *(Fox, p. 571)*

Perhaps because of a wish to believe that encounter with God or some analogous experience will relieve the pains and burdens of life, there is a definite tendency of writers on mysticism to consider only the apparently blissful encounters, and to ignore the terrors, not to mention the "dark night of the soul" (a description attributed to the mystic Saint John of the Cross), which in reality is a period of great torment and intolerable depression.

PSYCHOLOGICAL FACTORS

An important aspect of the study of mysticism is the question of how psychiatric abnormality is related to mystical experience. William James brought the question to a head back in 1902, when he included mysticism as a special topic in his lectures published in book form as *The Varieties of Religious Experience*. He quotes a passage from J.A. Symonds as an illustration:

> *... I felt the approach of the mood. Irresistibly it took*
> *possession of my mind and will, lasted what seemed an*

eternity, and disappeared in a series of rapid sensations which resembled the awakening from anaesthetic influence. One reason why I disliked this kind of trance was that I could not describe it to myself. I cannot even now find words to render it intelligible. It consisted in a gradual but swiftly progressive obliteration of space, time, sensation, and the multitudinous factors of experience which seem to qualify what we are pleased to call our Self. In proportion as these conditions of ordinary consciousness were subtracted, the sense of an underlying or essential consciousness acquired intensity. At last nothing remained but a pure, absolute, abstract Self. The universe became without form and void of content ...

Often have I asked myself with anguish, on waking from that formless state of denuded, keenly sentient being, Which is the unreality—the trance of fiery, vacant apprehension, sceptical Self from which I issue, or these surrounding phenomena and habits which veil that inner Self and build a self of flesh-and-blood conventionality? (James, p. 371–2)

James also discusses the difficulty of distinguishing between what has generally been accepted as religious mysticism and experiences which sometimes occur under the influence of drugs. He quotes an instance of an experience while under the influence of an anaesthetic, apparently nitrous oxide:

Into this pervading genius ... we pass, forgetting and forgotten, and thenceforth each is all, in God. There is no higher, no deeper, no other, than the life in which we are founded. "The One remains, the many change and pass"; and each and every one of us is the One that remains ... This is the ultimatum ... As sure as being—whence is all our care—so sure is content, beyond duplicity, antithesis, or trouble, where I have triumphed in a solitude that God is not above. (James, p. 375)

About this experience, James comments: "This has the genuine religious mystic ring!"

James, like Zaehner, distinguished between authentic mysticism and psychiatric states which may look like mysticism. His comments on this are particularly important in view of the diagnosis which Carl Jung gave two decades later which was essentially a complement to James' discussion. James wrote:

> So much for religious mysticism proper. But more remains to be told, for religious mysticism is only one half of mysticism. The other half has no accumulated traditions except those which the text-books on insanity supply. Open any one of these, and you will find abundant cases in which "mystical ideas" are cited as characteristic systems of enfeebled or deluded states of mind. In delusional insanity, paranoia, as they sometimes call it, we may have a diabolical mysticism, a sort of ineffable importance in the smallest events, the same texts and words coming with new meanings, the same voices and visions and leading and missions, the same controlling by extraneous powers ... It is evident that from the point of view of their psychological mechanism, the classic mysticism and these lower mysticisms spring from the same mental level, from that great subliminal or transmarginal region of which science is beginning to admit the existence, but of which so little is really known. That region contains every kind of matter: "seraph and snake" abide there side by side. To come from thence is no infallible credential. What comes must be sifted and tested, and run the gauntlet of confrontation with the total context of experience, just like what comes from the outer world of sense. Its value must be ascertained by empirical methods, so long as we are not mystics ourselves. (James, p. 410–1)

At approximately the same time that William James was giving and publishing his lectures from which the quotations above have been taken, Carl Jung was formulating his theory of complexes, which had grown out of detailed observations of a young spiritualist medium. Jung found his theory of complexes to be of great value in application to many forms of unusual or abnormal experiences. James had earlier, in his *Varieties*, commented on the vision of Christ by St Paul:

> There is one form of sensory automatism which possibly deserves special notice on account of its frequency. I refer to

hallucinatory or pseudo-hallucinatory luminous phenomena,
photisms, to use the term of the psychologists. Saint Paul's
blinding heavenly vision seems to have been a phenomenon of
this sort ... (James, p. 251)

Picking up from the theme of the natural origins of visions, Jung in a lecture given in 1919, in generalizing about the topic of apparitions, dreams and visions went on to say:

Common to all three types of phenomena is the fact that the
psyche is not an indivisible unity but a divisible and more or
less divided whole. Although the separate parts are connected
with one another, they are relatively independent, so much so
that certain parts of the psyche never become associated with the
ego at all, or only very rarely. I have called these psychic
fragments "autonomous complexes," and I based my theory of
complexes on their existence. According to this theory the ego-
complex forms the center characteristic of our psyche. But it is
only one among several complexes. The others are more often
than not associated with the ego-complex and in this way
become conscious, but they can also exist for some time without
being associated with it. An excellent and very well-known
example of this is the conversion of Saint Paul.

Although the actual moment of conversion often seems
quite sudden and unexpected, we know from experience that
such a fundamental upheaval always requires a long period of
incubation. It is only when this preparation is complete, that is
to say when the individual is ripe for conversion, that the new
insight breaks through with violent emotion. Saul, as he was
then called, had unconsciously been a Christian for a long
time, and this would explain his fanatical hatred of the
Christians, because fanaticism is always found in those who
have to stifle a secret doubt. That is why converts are always
the worst fanatics. The vision of Christ on the road to
Damascus merely marks the moment when the unconscious
Christ complex associated itself with Paul's ego. The fact that
Christ appeared to him objectively, in the form of a vision, is
explained by the circumstance that Saul's Christianity was an

unconscious complex which appeared to him in projection [i.e.,
his brain interpreted it to be an external phenomenon seen via
the eyes, rather than the result of internal neuronic processes],
as if it did not belong to him. He could not see himself as a
Christian; therefore, from sheer resistance to Christ, he became
blind and could only be healed again by a Christian. We
know that psychogenic blindness is always an unconscious
unwillingness to see, which in Saul's case corresponds with his
fanatical resistance to Christianity. This resistance, as we know
it from the Epistles, was never entirely overcome, and
occasionally it broke out in the form of fits which are
erroneously explained as epileptic. The fits were a sudden
return of the old Saul complex which had been split off by his
conversion just as the Christ complex was before.

For reasons of intellectual morality [=doing intellectual
justice to a subject under discussion], we should not explain
Paul's conversion on metaphysical grounds, otherwise we should
have to explain all similar cases that occur among our patients
in the same metaphysical way. This would lead to quite absurd
conclusions repugnant to reason and feeling alike.

(Jung, C.W., vol. 8, paragraphs 582–3)

Jung's point here is that the descriptions of Paul's experience, whether
at second hand from the report in the Acts of the Apostles or at first hand
from Paul's own writings, are similar to reports given by many persons of all
times and places, including the present. As a psychiatrist Jung had examined
and treated a great many psychiatric patients who claimed similar experiences.
He felt there is no good reason to make a special exception for Paul, whose
experience was described in identical fashion. In other words that there is no
reason to make the arbitrary assumption that Paul's experience originated
from a supernatural ("metaphysical") source while psychiatric patients' experiences are explained as coming from much more mundane psychological and
biochemical processes.

Jung elaborated on the probable hysterical nature of Paul's temporary
blindness:

This blindness reminds us on the one hand of the blindness
which can be produced by suggestion [e.g., by hypnotism], and

*on the other hand of the blindness which occurs spontaneously
with certain hysterical patients and again disappears at a
suitable psychological moment. The best visions, and the ones
that are psychologically the most transparent, are found in the
legends of the saints, the visions being most colorful in the case
of female saints experiencing the heavenly marriage. An
outstanding visionary type was the Maid of Orleans [Joan of
Arc], who was unconsciously imitated by the devout dreamer
Thomas Ignaz Martin at the time of Louis XVI.*

(Jung, C.W., vol. 18, paragraph 713)

Jung's analysis of the mechanism of visions is important because it does
not require a resort to any special (e.g., supernatural or "metaphysical")
explanation. James' reference to *photisms* has since been taken up and investi-
gated at length under the name of *phosphenes*,[10] and their role in the eventual
production of "visions" has been demonstrated. That is, spontaneous hallucinations of sparks of light, more commonly induced by toxins or pressure on
the eyes, are linked together by the brain as best it can to produce the
impression of a recognizable image—not, in essence, much different from the
traditional custom of "seeing" imaginary shapes, the traditional constellations,
amidst the random pattern of stars in the night sky. Jung himself traced the
development of reports of a vision of light by a Swiss saint, Brother Klaus, to
its final theological formulation as a vision of the Trinity (Jung, *C.W.*, vol.
9/1, paragraphs 12–18). The basic point is that a vision, like a dream, consists
of a fantasy which has been in existence for some time. It has been rejected
in our conscious thinking until it so gathers in strength that it breaks through
and, because we consciously continue to refuse it status as our own fantasy,
the brain is forced to resort to an explanation of it as something alien. In consequence the visual centers of the brain record it as something seen by the
eyes.

All this is not to say that what is experienced should not be taken seriously, but that our understanding of the method whereby the experience
comes into being requires to be changed. An "unconscious" fantasy means a
blend of thought and imagery which we, via our conscious thinking
processes, for whatever reason refuse to accept as of our own making. Early
in his career Jung published the results of many laboratory experiments which
indicated that such blends of non-conscious thought processing and formation of imagery are normal. In psychoanalytic terms this came to be called the

"non-ego," or, as Jung preferred, the "unconscious." Though unfortunate terms in that they imply mental structures rather than neuronic processes, they serve as catch-all titles to refer to the ways in which we produce and experience the thought-imagery blend which turns up in dreaming, visions, hallucinations, and drug-induced states.

The perplexing problem which has plagued the study of the inter-play of psychology and religion for a long time is that brought up by Jung in his discussion of Paul's vision: is there any universally reliable method by which an "authentically religious" experience and a hysterical or toxin-induced hallucination can be distinguished? As we shall see shortly, I consider this to be an illegitimate question because it implies some kind of sharp division between the "spiritual" or religious and the customary functioning of the human psyche. (Let us remember that I use the term "psyche" to refer to the psychological/neurological/biological functioning of the human individual considered as a unit, rather than the old yet still familiar custom of dividing the individual into a mind + body, or spirit/soul + body.)

The subjective difference between the experience felt by a hysteric and that felt by a mystic is usually that the hysteric is involuntarily overpowered by spontaneous experiences which cannot be controlled—such as the university student previously mentioned, who could not control the direction in which his feet walked. The mystic as a rule voluntarily seeks and induces, as well as to some extent controls, the religious experiences. To be sure, the observer finds that there is something of a continuum between the hysteric and the mystic, making it impossible to pin-point where the one leaves off and the other begins. But as an overall observation it can be said that the communion mystic is a person who, in meditation, keeps a clear conscious separation throughout between what is experienced and his/her intentional thinking. A union mystic merges her/his conscious thinking processes with whatever is experienced and for a time experiences her/himself as being what is encountered. Jung expressed the essence of what the union mystic claims to take place as being a merger of the ego with the collective unconscious (the archetypes as a whole), a situation most commonly found in schizophrenia but also in partially or totally controlled meditation practices.

Because of our still traditional assumption that the human being is by nature separable from the sum total of the world of nature, we tend to assume that to speak of experiencing the "collective unconscious" means a totally subjective, "internal" experience, unconnected with the "outside world." The archetypes, however, which as a group are titled the "collective unconscious," constitute the natural patterns of relationship between the human being and the rest of the natural world—which includes, of course, all other persons as well. Because we are still far from knowing all that exists in the cosmos, much less the details of evolutionary development and the realm of instincts, the archetypes constitute for us largely still obscure aspects of human functioning. It is at this point that mystics, alongside speculative philosophers, may fairly claim a conviction that spiritual, parapsychological, or other as yet intuited forms of relationship make themselves felt. Union mystics generally claim that in the unitive experience they partake in much that is totally unknown to others—and even to themselves—in their normal state.

The Apostle Paul's experiences seem more akin to those of the communion mystics. He appears to have kept a clear distinction between himself and what he called Christ, throughout his writings, and this is true also in the report made by the writer of the Acts of the Apostles, whose account of Saul/Paul's vision on the way to Damascus was discussed earlier.

Paul, in his own writings, gives no direct reference to the vision on the road to Damascus, but he does discuss another ecstatic vision:

> I am obliged to boast, even though it is not fitting. I will discuss visions and revelations from the Lord. I know a person in Christ, who fourteen years ago was carried off to the third heaven—whether physically or out of the body I don't know, God knows. And I know that this person—whether physically or out of the body, I don't know, God knows—was carried off to paradise and heard inexpressible words which are impossible for a human being to repeat. I will boast about this person. But I will not boast about myself, except in regard to my weaknesses . . . As for the abundance of revelations: so that I would not be too proud, I was given a barb in the flesh, a messenger of Satan to buffet me about so that I would not be too proud. (Bible: 2 Cor. 12:1–7, author's translation)

Paul did repeat that what he had to say came directly from Christ:

> I want you to know, brothers, that the message I proclaim does not have a human origin. I did not receive it from any person,

nobody taught it to me. It came as a revelation from Jesus Christ. (Bible: Galatians 1:11–12, author's translation)

Muhammad reported a parallel experience:

Now when I was brought on my night journey to the Throne and drew near to it ... I besought my Lord to complete his favor to me by granting me the boon of having a steadfast vision of him with my heart. This my Lord did, giving me that favor, so I gazed at him with my heart till it was steady and I had a steady vision of him. There he was, when the veil had been lifted from him, seated on his throne, in his dignity, his might, his glory, his exaltedness ... Then after this he communicated to me matters which I am not permitted to tell you, and when he had made his covenant with me and had left me there such time as he willed, he took his seat again upon his throne ... Then I looked, and something passed between us and a veil of light was drawn in front of him.

(Eliade, p. 518–20)

The distinction between nature mysticism, communion mysticism, union mysticism, abnormal states due to drugs and as features of psychiatric disturbances is an artificial one, impossible to separate when the life and experiences of any specific mystic are examined. The various "types" are so intertwined that one utterance of a person must be attributed to one type and the next utterance of the same person to another type.

THE FUNCTION OF MYSTICAL EXPERIENCE

Let us lay aside as a possible red herring the entire question of whether or not there is a God, since mystics have proved to be as abundant among non-God-focused traditions and individuals as among the God-focused. Let us also set aside as another possible red herring the question of making a distinction between the religious values of experiences originating through purportedly natural/supernatural, drug-induced/insanity sources and so on and take the persons who report mystical experiences at face value. Is there something that can be said about the function that mysticism of whatever presumed origin plays in the lives of individuals and perhaps of communities as a whole?

The most thorough and equitable of the studies yet published on mysticism is, to my mind, Evelyn Underhill's book *Mysticism*, first published in 1911 and still going strong as it nears its thirtieth edition. In this exhaustive study Underhill outlines the "path of the mystic," a systematization of reports by mystics which has for our century laid down the foundations of discussion of mysticism. A major point which I must add and stress, however, is my conviction that there is no necessity to introduce the reality or non-reality of a God into the discussion. We may merely note that God-focused traditions tend to produce God-focused mystics, while those traditions which are not God-focused tend to produce mystics who are not God-focused, although it is certainly true to say that there are many individuals who do not fit into this simple generalization.

At various points in this book, as I pointed out previously, I have used the term "psyche," a neutral term because it does not assume a split between mind and body, or soul (and mind) and body, but refers to the whole of the mental and emotional processes within an individual, whatever their physiological, biochemical, or nonmaterial substratum might be. "Psyche" is particularly useful as a term in discussing the function of mysticism, in that many mystics themselves do not find it possible to make the common traditional distinction between mind and body. An example is the Apostle Paul, quoted above, who twice qualified his description of his experience with the words "whether physically or out of the body I don't know." I also term as mystical those statements which follow the traditional mystical forms of expression, regardless of the usual religious orientation of the person who made them. There is no reason to assume that every person who has reported a mystical experience is therefore throughout the whole of life a mystic—an assumption upon which many an argument about mysticism has foundered.

At the center of the psyche there is some organizing principle which is not acquired during life by the individual, but is there from the beginning. Various people have given many names to this principle. God-focused persons commonly use the word "God" or something akin to God such as the *atman* in Hindu teachings. A frequent term is also the "light of God," a phrase which in Christian tradition traces back to the Gospel of John in the Bible: "He was the true Light coming into the world to illuminate everyone." (Bible: John, 1:9) This image is beloved of mystics, and was taken up by George Fox and the Quaker movement as the name of that which is encountered by plumbing into one's own depths—the "inward light" or "the inner light." The "depths of the soul" is also a term preferred by many people. Jung used the term "self" as a neutral term—it neither implies nor rejects a religious connotation—to refer to what he takes to be the genetically inherited nucleus of the human psyche, a nucleus which he sometimes poetically speaks of as "the two-million-year-old person within us" emphasizing the point that at heart we are the product of many millions of years of evolution and are consequently a natural part of the natural world, from which we have only in relatively recent times become estranged. Some prefer to speak of reunion or communion with "Nature" with a capital N, to emphasize the so-to-speak interrelated oneness of humanity with all of existence, the theme which is central to the religious expression of both North American Indians and Australian Aborigines.

Regardless of how we may choose to imagine this nuclear self within us and its origins, mystics as a whole assume that there has been a split between it and what Underhill calls "surface consciousness"—at present the more usual term is "conscious ego" or just "consciousness." Particularly in recent centuries, we have become more and more preoccupied with the world around us and increasingly more interested in identifying ourselves with ego-consciousness, to the point that the existence of any processes in the psyche apart from those of which we are conscious is frequently denied. The more we identify ourselves with ego-consciousness, the less we are aware of, or in communion with, the depths within ourselves. The mystic is, in short, a person who is in communion with her/his inner depths. Whether this communion reaches at times the stage of total immersion into the inner depths or merely momentary sporadic intuitions of their existence is a matter of degree of experience, not of kind.

The "Mystical Path" or the "Way of the Mystic" is the process by which any person can discover their inner depths and reunite with them in one way or another.

THE MYSTICAL JOURNEY

The mystics often speak of themselves as starting out on a long and hazardous journey. It should be noted, in view of Jung's comments quoted in this chapter, that the experience of apparitions, dreams, visions, and hallucinations has a common base in the internal experiences of the psyche. It is also particularly intriguing that the theme of the long, hazardous journey is also very frequent in dreams, as also in mythology and literature, where it is a frequent image for the "journey" of the "soul" through life.[11]

The mystic's journey is usually spoken of as a response to a call of some sort, an invitation from another world which individual mystics may or may not recognize as their own inner world. The mystic then sets out on the envisioned journey and undergoes various difficulties (trials, problems, pains) during a gradual self-purification. There then comes a point of illumination, some experience which brings reassurance that the goal is near. This is followed by plunging into a dark valley of total blackness and despair where all hope seems to be lost, "the dark night of the soul." Mystics speak of being killed, crucified, and the like. An example from Muhammad:

> *While I was in al-Hijr, lying at rest, someone came to me,*
> *split me from here to here [from the hollow of his throat to his*
> *pubic hair], and drew out my heart. Then a golden basin,*
> *filled with faith, was brought. He washed my heart and*
> *intestines in it, and put them back in place. (Eliade, p. 154)*

Similar experiences are reported by many mystics, as well as shamans. The degree to which they take them literally or as a poetic description of their experience varies.

Following on the darkness and torment, the mystic eventually goes on to a glorious vision: the city of God, or a treasure, or a beautiful person. The mystic goes on to enter the city, take the treasure, or marry the person, only to discover that the city/treasure/person is God or, frequently, the mystic's own soul.

This theme of the mystic's journey has been written up in religious literature such as Dante's *Divine Comedy* and Bunyon's *Pilgrim's Progress*. It is interesting to note that the same journey was written up in the ancient Sumerian poem *The Epic of Gilgamesh*, written before 2,000 BC, in which it is a journey undertaken by Gilgamesh in his attempt to find immortality following upon the death of his divinely created counterpart Enkidu. Gilgamesh's adventures summarized in prose are as follows:

> *Bitterly Gilgamesh wept for his friend Enkidu; he wandered*
> *over the wilderness as a hunter, he roamed over the plains; in*
> *his bitterness he cried, "How can I rest, how can I be at peace?*

Despair is in my heart. What my brother is now, that shall I be when I am dead ... "

At night when he came to the mountain passes ... he lay down to sleep, until he was woken from out of a dream. He saw the lions round him glorying in life, then he took his axe in his hand, he drew his sword from his belt, and he fell upon them like an arrow from the string, and struck and destroyed and scattered them ...

[With considerable effort Gilgamesh obtains permission to pass through a mountain guarded by a couple who are half-scorpion and half-human]

He followed the sun's road to [its] rising, through the mountain. When he had gone one league the darkness became thick around him, for there was no light, he could see nothing ahead and nothing behind him. After two leagues the darkness was thick and there was no light, he could see nothing ahead and nothing behind him. [and so on, for three, four, five, six, seven and eight leagues.] After nine leagues the dawn light appeared. At the end of twelve leagues the sun streamed out.

There was the garden of the Gods ... by the edge of the sea. [However Gilgamesh could only learn there that his journey was in vain, there was no hope of finding immortality there in the garden of the Gods. He persevered with his journey, however, and came to Siduri, the maker of wine ...] with the golden bowl and the golden vats that the Gods gave her. She is covered with a veil; and where she sits she sees Gilgamesh coming towards her wearing skins, the flesh of the Gods in his body but despair in his heart ... and she barred her gate against him with the cross-bar and shot home the bolt. [Eventually he managed to talk with her and she told him his quest was impossible and she advised him thus:]

"When the Gods created man they allotted to him death, but life they retained in their own keeping. As for you, Gilgamesh, fill your belly with good things ... dance and be merry, feast and rejoice. Let your clothes be fresh, bathe yourself in water, cherish the little child that holds your hand, and make your wife happy in your embrace; for this too is the lot of man."

[Gilgamesh, however, would not be put off, and learned
that he must cross the Ocean in his quest, the Ocean filled
with the waters of death. With much difficulty he did manage
to cross the Ocean and on the other side was able to gain the
herb of immortality, which, however, he lost on his return
journey.][12]

This epic served as a religious text for the Sumerians and Babylonians for some thousands of years, presumably as a guide and a warning for any human being who wishes not only to arrive in the paradise of the Gods but even to obtain immortality. When the mystic makes use of such imagery to describe the path that has been taken, it is usually made clear that the imagery is intended to be metaphorical, a spiritual experience taking place within the mystics themselves. This is not always clear, however, either to the mystic or to the reader. We have already seen the Apostle Paul's uncertainty whether his experience was "physical or out of the body." George Fox made it clear that his vision of the divine City was a vision and not a physical journey:

> *Whilst I was in my travails and sufferings I saw the state of*
> *the city New Jerusalem which comes out of heaven. And I and*
> *Richard Richardson and John Stubbs cast it up according to the*
> *account as it is written in Revelations. According to the world's*
> *account of the measure of the earth, it was ten times bigger*
> *than the earth.*
>
> *Oh, this blessed city is appeared. Oh, glorious things will*
> *come to pass. You will see glorious things will come. I desire, I*
> *wish that these outward powers of the earth were given up. I*
> *can tell what to say to them. Oh, hypocrisy! It makes me sick*
> *to think of them. I have given them a visitation and as faithful*
> *a warning as ever was. There is an ugly a slubbering hound,*
> *an ugly hound, an ugly slubbering hound. But the Lord forgive*
> *them—destruction, destruction. We have given them indeed a*
> *visitation and salutation and they will not hear, but refuse it*
> *and reject the Lord. But we shall be clear of all their blood.*
>
> (Fox, pp. 575–6)

Here, as with many persons caught up into an ecstatic vision, for a time it is unclear whether it is the mystic or God who is speaking—for a moment the two are one. But only for a moment. The identification is not elaborated, the mystic is only briefly speaking as God.

Fox, as was his wont with all the biblical texts, understood the New Jerusalem as an inner spiritual state rather than something external and, as we would say, supernatural. Perhaps we could say that this is a feature typical of many mystics, although by no means all. It appears that Muhammad's account of his ascension to heaven was understood by his followers much more literally. The traditions record a description of Muhammad's ascent into the presence of God. God's dazzling glory was so bright that Muhammad feared going blind, and by God's direction he looked at God through his heart instead of his eyes. Then at his request he was granted a steady vision of God:

> *Then I was filled with joy, my eyes were refreshed, and such*
> *delight and happiness took hold of me that I began to bend*
> *and sway to right and left like one overcome by slumber.*
> *Indeed, it seemed to me as though everyone in heaven and*
> *earth had died, for I heard no voices of angels, nor during the*
> *vision of my Lord did I see any dark bodies. My Lord left me*
> *there such times as He willed, then brought me back to my*
> *senses, and it was as though I had been asleep and had*
> *awakened. My mind returned to me and I was tranquil,*
> *realizing where I was and how I was enjoying surpassing favor*
> *and being shown manifest preference ... Then after this He*
> *communicated to me matters which I am not permitted to tell*
> *you, and when He had made his covenant with me and had*
> *left me there such time as He willed, He took his seat again*
> *upon his throne. (Eliade, pp. 519–20)*

THE PSYCHOLOGICAL MECHANISM IN MYSTICISM

A somewhat different way of looking at mysticism should be carefully distinguished from the symbolism of the journey, since it concerns an appraisal of what is happening in the mystic's psyche—something that the mystics themselves do not always address. Mystics in describing their experiences often describe the process of discovering and directly encountering their inner depths by speaking of states of being. In this they begin by speaking of everyday conscious life, joys, thoughts, memories, and interests. They then begin to contemplate and turn their attention away from the external world and to look inside, into the "unknowing" as it has popularly been called, which appears to be largely what depth psychologists mean by the term "the unconscious." There they look into the depths of darkness and eventually encounter an inspiration or a ray of light, seeing with "the eyes of the soul." As Underhill points out, the mystic rarely mistakes these visions for events seen with the physical eyes. There follows a period of disorientation when the mystic is unable to pay attention to and understand the external world, ending with a return to full everyday consciousness, sometimes with a feeling of having been reborn.

Underhill makes a good case for identifying the mystical path with what we would now call integration or, in Jung's terminology, individuation. From a psychological point of view I think that there are some seven stages to be identified:

1. The mystic begins as a normal human being, something far more complex than we usually assume. I have already discussed at length that various personality "functions" may occur simultaneously, giving the impression to the onlooker that they are separate, even though partial and incomplete, personalities in competition with each other. It is important to re-emphasize here that we are not talking about "things" but about processes, which are in the final analysis functions of the nervous system. The everyday word "personality" refers to a coordinated grouping of complicated and largely still only vaguely understood functions of the nervous system—primarily, but not exclusively, the brain. "Mental disturbances" and other abnormal states would more accurately be called a conflict between neuronic processes which have failed for some reason to coordinate in normal fashion. When functioning normally, they produce harmonious interaction with the world around us. It is this coordinated capacity for interaction which is what depth psychology means by the term "ego." "Ego-consciousness" means awareness that this is taking place. As both Jung and Freud have pointed out at length, there is much interaction with the environment which we are generally unaware of, and this, in depth psychology, has come to be termed unconscious aspects of the ego.

2. The initial step in the mystical process is much the same as that found in systems of meditation, in the act of dreaming, and in the outbreak of a neurosis or even a more severe psychiatric disturbance. There is a definite tendency for the psychiatrically ill to say that they have

undergone an illumination, or even encountered God, when these "subpersonalities" emerge; that is, when they take temporary or continuous control of the thinking, visual, and auditory systems of the brain. Some mystics present this initial encounter with the functions competing for "surface consciousness" in vivid, visionary terms. They may hear a voice speaking to them, or see a vision—as seems to have been the situation with the Apostle Paul, George Fox, and Joan of Arc. More often, as Underhill points out, the encounter is vague and general, impossible to specify, a deep sense of anxiety, fear, terror, or depression, that cannot be explained or even expressed clearly in words but is persistent and, for the person suffering, quite alarming. A quick reading through of the initial parts of Fox's *Journal* indicates the desperation which he had reached. At this point there is little or nothing to distinguish the mystic's experience from an ordinary neurosis or incipient psychosis. Indeed, in the final analysis we may have to conclude, as William James did, that the difference between the mystical and neurotic/psychotic states is "the value for knowledge of the consciousness they induce. To pass a spiritual judgment upon these states, we must not content ourselves with superficial medical talk, but inquire into their fruits for life." (James, p. 398)

3. The conscious ego allows itself to be depotentiated. In other words, the mystics, like persons in meditation, intentionally create for themselves as far as is possible a shutting off of attention to stimuli coming from around them in order to strengthen the "break-through" of the subpersonalities. Underhill devotes two substantial chapters to introversion of attention, seeing this as the key to the mystical path. The mystic introverts by various procedures; such as by an internal quietening down and relaxation of the mind and turning away from preoccupations and thoughts about life. Meditation may then occur by fixing attention on one thing, an object such as a crucifix or string of beads, a thought, a word or name (mantra), or by tuning the senses to a fine degree, increasing awareness of sounds or fixing the gaze upon something so that sensations flow in without being named or contemplated. The effect of all these is the same: relaxation of conscious thought in order to allow inner imagery and fantasy to enter into conscious awareness— a process closely related to that of inducing a waking dream. The same result may be obtained by drugs, and can occur spontaneously. At this

point there is little to say about any attempt to distinguish between kinds of experience.

4. Imagery begins to appear to the visual centers of the brain. Underhill terms this phase "Active Imaginary Vision," a name which Jung later simplified to "Active Imagination" for the high point of this stage. At this point there is a sort of waking dream, the "dreamer" being neither fully awake nor fully asleep. This is an experience most normal people also have during the last brief period before falling asleep or at the moment of waking, the "hypnogogic" state, which often can be cultivated and intentionally prolonged. The term "active" in the name for this phase means that the individual is still capable of manipulating the process and interacting with the imagery. Much use of this state is also found in some therapeutic procedures stressing "guided imagery," which is made possible by the individual's ability, at the onset of the phase, to exercise some voluntary choice over what initial images are to be visualized. Drug-induced or spontaneous falling into such states generally allow for very little voluntary interaction with the "inner imagery," though this varies considerably from time to time.

5. Temporarily the involuntary imagery becomes so powerful that it takes control. The person may begin to write with paper and pen while quite unaware of what is being written ("automatic writing"), or to speak without consciously controlling what is said. From a neurological point of view, it would seem that the usually coordinated centers of the brain are in a state of non-coordination, a matter which has received much attention in recent years through research on persons in whom the link between the two hemispheres of the brain has been severed. What is of considerable interest is that an apparently similar state can be induced via hypnosis, except that in the hypnotic state the individual receives the stimulus for "mental" activity (visual, auditory, and memory manipulation etc.) not from something within but from an outside person, the hypnotist. Self-hypnosis, such as that attained by the procedure outlined by the Australian psychiatrist Ainslie Meares in his book *Relief Without Drugs* can also lead to a state which is nearly or totally indistinguishable from this state of "Active Imaginary Vision."

    When this stage ceases to be temporary and continues beyond the control of the person experiencing it, a psychotic state closely resembling schizophrenia or manic-depressive disorder may be diagnosed. It is not clear whether intentional cultivation of the "Active Imagination" state brings on a state of psychosis in prone individuals, or whether a latent psychosis is merely made more manifest and, perhaps—again in prone individuals—may have led the individual concerned to experiment with the induction of the state. The answer to this uncertainty may lead to an answer to the vexing question of the difference, if any, between the mystical sounding descriptions given by mystics and those given by the insane. Occasionally, brain lesions and early forms of grand mal epilepsy also give the initial impression of visions, which appears to be behind the popular diagnosis of the Apostle Paul's condition as epilepsy by psychiatrists in the late 1800s and early 1900s.

It is often at this stage that experiences occur which correspond to the "dark night of the soul" in the terminology of mystics and it may become difficult to distinguish between the mystic's experience and the depressive pole of a manic-depressive disorder, particularly if the psychotic episodes are sporadic. The practical difficulty in making a distinction is particularly obvious in the case of George Fox, who's *Journal* stresses not only severe depressive states but also apparent swings into a manic phase, if it is fair to thus interpret his statement of at times receiving an insight "into the nature of all things." Again we may ask ourselves whether the differential diagnosis of psychotic as opposed to religiously mystical is justified, or whether we may possibly be considering the entire matter from the wrong direction—a point I shall pick up on shortly.

6. The unconscious processes of the psyche are not as chaotic and disorganized as researchers (including Freud) originally assumed. The same organizing principle which operates to integrate the physical functioning of the body, seems also to maintain a reasonable state of integration of the mental and emotional functions as well. Similarly, the attempts made by the functioning of bodily organs to return to homeostasis are paralleled by apparent attempts to return to homeostasis in the "mental" sphere. It has frequently been pointed out that the delusions of the insane can be viewed as abortive attempts to organize their inner experiences into a system they can understand and deal with. If, in fact, we are going to hold to the view that there is no clear dividing line between mind and body, it becomes clear that the "center" of the inner depths of a person is the same, regardless of whether we are considering physical or mental functioning. God-oriented beliefs generally consider this "center" to be God or the work of God. Thus the God-oriented

mystics without exception call it God. There is good reason for this, since the God-focused religious traditions affirm that God is at the root of all existence and of all events. "Isn't a pair of sparrows sold for a pittance? Yet not one of them falls to the ground without your Father." (Bible: Matthew 10:29) "We created man. We know the promptings of his soul, and are closer to him than the vein of his neck." (Koran: sura 50) It is impossible to find a basis for distinguishing between the statements of a God-focused mystic and those of a non-God-focused mystic. Non-God-oriented language can express the experience of the "center" as both numinous and natural. In such language, the center of the inner depths is felt as the organizing principle of the entire personality—which we may take as the evolutionary development of human personality functions as transmitted by the same genetic make-up which determines the development of the physical body. The content of ultimate mystical experience is experience of the evolutionary content of the collective unconscious, what Jung called the "self." Whether we wish to introduce a concept of God into the process seems an arbitrary decision. Some have the conviction that this concept is necessary, while others reject it, to use Jung's phrase, "on the grounds of intellectual morality."

7.   Underhill found use for the mystics' appropriation of the Gnostic idea of the soul as a spark from the flame which is God. In this conception there is a divine spark at the center of the personality. When the ego meets this spark and returns enriched by the encounter, it turns again to the world with what various mystics have called "enlarged consciousness," "expanded consciousness," and "super-consciousness," meaning that there are no longer unexperienced deep mysteries. Such encounter is called *satori* in Zen, in which, of course, it is not God but the ineffable that is meant.

CONTRASTING VIEWPOINTS

It probably causes no difficulty by now to realize that the frequent statement "Now I know all things" as used by mystics, persons undergoing a manic episode, or under the influence of a drug, is a feeling statement rather than a content statement. In other words, although the conviction is strong that all things really are known to the speaker, nevertheless any specific facts "known" are difficult or impossible to elicit. The mystic's statement of "knowing all things" is basically a statement that "I have encountered the true nature of all things." This same claim is also made by the manic and during the drug-induced experience. It can be understood as a simple statement: "Now I have encountered the depths wherein all of Reality resides." In the West it seems virtually axiomatic that these "depths" must be real, must exist, that there must be some "center", whether in the individual psyche, the external world, or a nonmaterial world. Our science is convinced as much as our religions that the universe is an ordered whole, a "cosmos," with a coherent unitary pattern throughout, originating from some specific original core. We find it difficult to accept that this "center" might be a purely imaginary construct which originated as an explanation for our already formed religious, psychological and scientific beliefs rather than being the basis of those beliefs.

In the West, most religious philosophy and theology assume the existence of a "center" of some kind, so that the usual controversy is between whether (a) this "center" is a single entity which directs the sum total of all individual lives, in other words a sort of universal soul, whether personified or taken in the abstract as an all-pervading "energy" which both permeates and links all of existence and all events, or (b) it is an individual "center" which is specific to each living thing, each of us having been formed and stamped in the same mould, so to speak. In Western psychology the concept of a center is almost universally assumed, though it was most explicitly expressed in Jung's hypothesis of the "self" and the collective unconscious. Jung's own view appears to have been midway between the sides of the controversy, agreeing with (a) that there is a universal pattern of events (this view was most clearly formulated in his theory of synchronicity, a nonreligious application of his concept of a universal pattern to ESP phenomena), but also (b) holding the opinion that the collective unconscious and self are to be considered the principle of individuality in a person by virtue of genetic inheritance (Jung, C.W., vol. 8, paragraphs 266–77, 342), thus existing independently in each living person. Although he devoted considerable discussion to the Hindu concept of the Self as the Atman and Brahman (Jung, C.W., vol. 6, paragraphs 327–57), it does not appear that he adopted the Hindu viewpoint as his own.

There is, however, an alternative viewpoint which does not require the concept of a "center." In its simplest form this viewpoint would be that the original zygote (the cell which began the existence of each of us) split and the splitting continued an unknown number of billions of times to form the individual living thing, without any controller directing and maintaining the overall functioning which we call life. The illusion of there being a "controller" would simply be a reflection of the presence within each cell of an identical genetic make-up, identical because each cell is a split-off from a previous cell back to the original zygote.

The hypothesis of "no-center" finds its proponents in the Eastern religious sphere. If there is anything in the Buddhist tradition that is most difficult for the Westerner to understand, it is the Buddhist insistence that there is no center, neither for the individual nor for the cosmos. This aspect of the Buddhist viewpoint is frequently missed by Westerners, because Buddhist writers in English usually speak of there being no "ego," a phrase bound to be misunderstood because of the many meanings of the word "ego" in English usage. In particular, in Western psychology "ego" has acquired a special meaning which is far from what the Buddhist is attempting to express. The Buddhist statement that there is no "ego," no "I," is intended to mean that there is neither a metaphorical nor a literal center within us. This point is discussed at length by Suzuki in his chapter "The basis of Buddhist philosophy," in his discussion of Buddhist mysticism (Suzuki, *Mysticism*, Chap. 2). Is it possible for us in the West to set aside our age-old convictions and accept the possibility that each of us is a highly coordinated mass of billions of differentiated cells functioning without any administrating center, as Buddhism claims? And equally that the universe is not necessarily a cosmos (=an ordered whole) but randomness which we assume to have a coordinated or coordinating center by forcing our own preconceptions onto it, much as the ancients saw imaginary constellations in the sky?

Let us pick up on this question and discuss the mystics' experiences in the framework of the concept of "no-center." Suppose that what the mystic is expressing is not that she/he has experienced a "Suprapersonal" Center of some kind, but merely an awareness that there is a pattern throughout her individual being which actually is simply the genetic unity which pervades each of that individual's cells because each living being began as a single zygote which was replicated over and over again. Naturally I am not suggesting that the mystic has had a conscious perception of this. I am suggesting that an existence of unity has indeed been experienced, but it is not a unity which comes from some directing, coordinating, unifying Center either "inside" or "outside" the individual. But tradition has unconsciously forced the mystic to clothe her experience in the wording and concepts familiar to the speaker.

If we continue with this line of discussion we can legitimately suggest that there is no need to distinguish between religious mysticism, non-religious mysticism, insane delusions and the effects of various drugs. We can conclude that the experience is one and the same, and has merely been clothed and elaborated by those who prefer to assume that the core of the experience of unity is to be found in God, or in the Atman, or in alteration of the functioning of the nervous system through drugs, or through meditation, or pathological processes, or complexes tracing back to archetypes developed through millions of years of evolution, or some other hypothesis. This type of consideration makes it impossible to sort out the various mystic experiences and classify them in categories of nature mysticism, divine mysticism, drug-induced hallucinations and psychiatric disorders. These categories properly have more to do with the value-judgments of the person making the classifications than the content or origin of the experiences.

I would very much like to leave the matter at this point of concluding that the mystical communion or unitive experience merely traces back to discovery that each of us originates as a zygote and intuitively personifies that zygote as a supernatural Creator, or the result of creative evolution, or some such explanation. I would prefer this not only because of Occam's Razor (don't use more hypotheses than you really have to) and my own personal feeling of what is simply common sense. Unfortunately I cannot. For one thing, though my intellect feels most satisfied with the suggestions I have just made, I simultaneously feel the tumult of rebelling emotions which remain totally unsatisfied. My psyche, which is as much emotion as reason, will not accept the topic as closed at this point. And I am only too well aware that throughout history what reason has from time to time proclaimed as unexceptionable truth has almost invariably later proved to be wrong.

Where discussions such as these go astray is their assumption that we know all the facts of the matters we are discussing.

Do we know of the existence of some "facts" which we have studiously been ignoring—not merely in our discussions in this book but in philosophy, theology, science, and even speculation as a whole? And can these facts bring out some hitherto obscured points which may revolutionize our view of the religious dimension as much as Albert Einstein's theories of relativity did physics? Strangely enough, the answer is yes. And it is to be found in the most unlikely places, among people whom we almost universally think of and call primitive and mentally somehow not up to scratch. The next two chapters are going to present two such peoples: North American Indians and

Australian Aborigines, who have (but just barely) managed to preserve their own unique way of understanding the world and themselves, despite all our attempts to wipe them out (both by genocide and education). The concluding chapter will make an attempt to integrate what they have to convey to us with what we have observed so far—not so as to provide us with the answers, but to give us the questions to start with.

REFERENCES

Mircea Eliade (ed.), *From Primitives to Zen*, Collins, London, 1967.

George Fox, *The Journal of George Fox*, (revised edn) Cambridge University Press, Cambridge, 1952.

F.C. Happold, *Mysticism*, Penguin Books, Harmondsworth, 1964.

William James, *The Varieties of Religious Experience*, (1901–2) Fontana Books, London and Glasgow, 1960.

Elmer O'Brien, *Varieties of Mystic Experience*, Mentor-Omega Books, New York, 1965.

Sidney Spencer, *Mysticism in World Religion*, Penguin Books, Harmondsworth, 1963.

Daisetsu T. Suzuki, *Mysticism Christian and Buddhist*, (1957) Allen & Unwin Ltd, London, 1970. (Referred to in the text as Suzuki, *Mysticism*.)

Daisetz Teitaro Suzuki, *Introduction to Zen Buddhism, Including A Manual of Zen Buddhism*, (1934) Causeway Books, New York, 1974. (Referred to in the text as Suzuki, *Introduction*.)

Evelyn Underhill, *Mysticism*, Methuen, London, 1911.

R. C. Zaehner, *Mysticism, Sacred and Profane*, Oxford Paperbacks, London, 1961.

NOTES

1. Arnold Toynbee, *A Study of History*, Oxford University Press, London, vol. 7: 1957.
2. Albert Schweitzer, *The Mysticism of Paul the Apostle*, A & C Black, London, 1931.
3. Lao Tsu, *Tao Te Ching* (tr. Gia-Fu Feng and Jane English). Vintage Books, New York, 1972, poem one.
4. Martin Buber, *I and Thou*, T. & T. Clark, Edinburgh, 1959, p. 82.
5. Thomas a Kempis, *The Imitation of Christ*, Fontana Books, London and Glasgow, 1963, pp. 241, 245.

6. C.G. Jung, *Memories, Dreams, Reflections*, Collins and Routledge & Kegan Paul, London, 1963, p. 33.

7. This diagnosis is my own, on the basis of a close reading of his *Journal* and other writings.

8. Paul Radin, "The religious experiences of an American Indian" in *Eranos Jahrbuch* vol. 18, Rascher Verlag, Zürich, 1950, pp. 259–62.

9. R.C. Zaehner, *The Dawn and Twilight of Zoroastrianism*, Weidenfeld and Nicolson, London, 1961, p. 91.

10. A detailed study of this process is to be found in Max Knoll, "Die Welt der inneren Lichterscheinungen" in *Eranos Jahrbuch* vol. 34,. Rascher Verlag, Zürich, 1966.

11. See Donald Broadribb, *The Dream Story*, Inner City Books, Toronto, 1990, p. 87; also: University of Western Australia Press, Perth, 1987. (Cygnet Books imprint.)

12. Summarized from N.K. Sanders, (tr.) *The Epic of Gilgamesh*, Penguin Books, Harmondsworth, 1960, pp. 94–115.

CHAPTER FIVE

A CHORUS OF POWERS

AMERICAN INDIAN BELIEF

MARILYN HOLLY

ORENDA

I am a Caucasian North American woman, professionally at work in the field of academic philosophy, born and raised in northern New York State which was once a central part of the Iroquois Indian territory, and I am a long-time student of Carl Jung's works. In 1971–72 I spent a year of post-doctoral study at the C.G. Jung Institute in Zürich, but I had already been reading Jung for a number of years before that.

Somewhere in the course of my Jung studies I realized that he had been keenly interested in and respectful toward American Indian culture and spirituality, had visited and conversed with several American Indian peoples, and had written about their culture and spirituality. As a result of studying Jung I became aware that, because the influx of non-indigenous white people onto the North American continent had been artificially superimposed on the far older red man's culture, it is imperative for non-Indians on the North American continent to try to understand more deeply the red man's cultures in order to get into a more authentic relationship with the deep and unique features of human life as shaped by and on that continent. Moreover, white culture has an enormous amount of value to learn from red culture.

But far earlier than my reading of Jung, early childhood experiences in the old, one-time Seneca Iroquois territory of northern New York State had left an ineradicable mark of awe and mystery on me that generated remarkable dreams years later and imprinted me for life with a sense of having been at that time in childhood in touch with a great mysterious

THE MYSTICAL CHORUS
160

something that later exposure to Protestant religious ideas left unexplained. For a number of years now I have been studying the red man's culture and belief, among other reasons in the hope of better understanding my childhood experiences on the Seneca Iroquois land as well as to live out what I took to be Jung's urgent directive to North American non-Indians to try to understand the red man's more authentic and far older rootedness on that continent.

Picture me now as a child of eight, living for a year in a house on Orenda Drive at the corner of Seneca Road, in a suburb of Rochester NY called Irondequoit. Just across Seneca Road there is a woods-covered hill sloping abruptly down to Irondequoit Bay which in turn opens onto Lake Ontario to the north. Behind the house where I live on Orenda Drive is a dense woods that looks as if it has always been there. When I walk east on Seneca Road I come to a steep sand bank and then to some red banks of clay on the road's south side.

For a year I live here, experiencing the change of seasons, picking my way over the dry, stubbled grass of November fields rimed with frost, studying individual snowflakes that land on my winter mittens, observing the "packing" qualities of the snow after different snowfalls ("good packing" snow is easily fashioned into snowballs and snowmen and snow forts, but "bad" packing snow won't hold together), making sundials out of an upright straight twig stuck in the ground circled round by pebbles, as springtime anguishes its way toward May through repeated thaws and mud and new light snowfalls. And now as summer comes on I am riding and rocking the tops of sturdy saplings so that they curve toward the ground and sometimes tumble me off onto the grass, leaping from the top of the steep sand bank with my three companions from next door or building sand castles with them, and in full summer climbing and reclimbing a very special tree—a big old maple—who lives back in the woods, studying from close up his sap that bubbles through his bark and watching all the bugs that climb up and down him and the squirrels and birds that live in his branches. There are berry bushes with their ripe black thimbles tempting

*my thievish fingers, and there are afternoons of splashing in the
warming waters of the Bay or sunning on rocks at its edge.*

*Every tree, every rock, every berry bush becomes a familiar
friend; a particular clump of Queen Anne's Lace near the top
of the sand bank becomes permanently imprinted on my
memory to turn up in dreams years later as just-so. Each of
the horizontal red clay veins in the clay banks east on Seneca
Road has its own personal shape, also to be remembered forever
after as just-so. Sometimes I am close even now to remembering
... just on the very brink of it ... the exact form of an
individual snowflake on my mitten.*

*I watch these friends changing with the seasons. My friend
the Grandfather maple gets his brilliant fall leaves of red and
yellow and then his leaves fall off, and then he gets icicles
among his branches, and still farther on in the spring he gets
buds and new tender green leaves. The lace at the top of the
Queen Anne's Lace stems goes and then comes back. I see a
dead squirrel, a dead bird, then new baby birds and squirrels.
There are changes every day; nothing stays quite the same,
there are so many processes going on, so many lives in process
to keep up with.*

*There comes a time of severe stress, to me as an eight-
year-old child, and one day in the summer, my heart fills with
an unexpected toxicity of bitterness that scares me and seems to
eat me up from the inside. I run into the woods behind the
house on Orenda Drive and seek out the big old maple tree,
my one most particular friend amongst all the trees, and I
climb up him into a place where his branches fork. There is a
place there into which I can squeeze and sit securely between
his branches. He holds me for a long, long time, this
Grandfather tree, and he stays with me as I long for some help
in my struggle to free myself from the frightening, strange, toxic
bitterness inside me. Bad things have been happening in my
world, but in a way this new thing is the worst of all, this
being eaten up from within by the alien bitter feelings. I feel
my familiar self disappearing.*

*As the Grandfather tree holds me, several hours go by
and I watch the familiar processions of little bugs going up and*

down him, I see and hear all the bird-people and squirrel-people who live in his branches, and at length it seems to me that the Grandfather tree and the bugs and the squirrel-people and the bird-people join forces together with me. After a while the life in all of us together proves stronger than the frightening bitter feelings that have been eating me up from the inside and threatening to turn me into an emotional alien. The Grandfather tree and the bugs and squirrels and birds and I have together won some sort of big fight, and I am once again who I am, though with a memory-continuum now forevermore stained through and through with this experience. I have been healed by the woods and its peoples; there is a great power for life here that I shall never forget.

Many years later I dreamed recurringly of a noble American Indian woman whom I thought of as Princess Orenda. The dreams of Princess Orenda came many years after my experience in the woods; they preceded a time of severe illness, and finally led to my going more deeply into studies of American Indian spirituality during the illness—with results most salutary to my healing. For the first time I discovered—or had I always sensed it?—that for the Iroquois peoples "orenda" was the name of the mysterious, potent life energy possessed in different ways by all of the entities and creatures of nature including ourselves, and which can indeed be channeled into healing processes. There is an Earth Woman of divine origin in the Creation myth; perhaps, says my imagination, she is the Princess Orenda of my one-time dreams.

I would not claim that my experiences in the woods off Orenda Drive were particularly unusual. On the contrary, I believe that most of us have had some such experiences. Perhaps it is only by a chance concatenation of events that these experiences of mine finally led to my personal mission to track down what it was all about, to the feeling that I must go back there in some sense, in order to find again something that seemed and seems of extraordinary beauty and significance.

My studies of Native American spirituality have therefore been for me a personal going back there and finding or refinding, on an adult level, something of what nature itself *was teaching me in the woods behind the house on Orenda Drive. I now ask the reader to remember, or else to seek, some sort of personal experience of the powerful life energies of nature as a point of orientation to refer back to again and again throughout the following discussion.*

In 1902, J.N.B. Hewitt published an important paper titled "Orenda and a definition of religion," which gives information of major importance about how the Iroquois actually used the term "Orenda" in everyday speech. Himself part Iroquois, Hewitt spoke four of the Iroquois dialects[1] as well as fluent English, and he was ethnologist to the Iroquois at the Smithsonian Institution. He worked for years in close collaboration with Chief John A. Gibson, a full blood Seneca chief who knew English and all the Iroquois dialects (Fenton, 1962). Hewitt translated the Iroquois word "orenda" as "mystic potence," and also used "orenda" to designate collectively the words "wakan" in the Siouan language, and "manitou" in the Algonquian. Several books written more recently than Hewitt's 1902 article emphasize the adjectival nature of these terms, translating them as "strange and wonderful," "sacred" and "possessing power" and "mysterious." In other words, Hewitt seems to have included in the meaning of "orenda" a reference to something which is understood to be mysterious or strange and wonderful or sacred or possessing power — namely, in his terminology, *potence*.

In 1920 Hewitt referred not to the potence attributed by the Iroquois to all things, but instead to their attribution of life to all bodies and objects and processes of the complex world of human experience, for to the early Iroquois, "life was omnipresent." The word that comes up time after time in subsequent writings to replace Hewitt's potence or life is the more modern term *energy*. *Power* or *power-in-action* are also used synonymously with energy. But this is not quite the modern physicists' energy, for orenda energy is seen as personal, and as intelligence or awareness. Yet this must not be construed as being, in non-human entities and creatures, either human or godlike intelligence or awareness (Allen p. 60). It is, rather, personal rather than impersonal natural energy, dwelling within a specific entity, and is seen as being causally effective (Hallowell).

The notion of a mysterious, strange and wonderful, powerful and sacred personal energy (actually, "sacred" to American Indians simply signified "powerful")[2] that is possessed by all the entities and creatures of nature as well as by humans, and by the beings of a people's pantheon as well, was so widespread among Indian peoples across the North American continent that I am treating it as the first of the four core themes in American Indian spirituality that this essay considers. Anthropologists may see in orenda the concept they are used to calling *mana*, but there is a problem in simply making this equation, since mana often gets translated as "supernatural power" in anthropological contexts and, for very important reasons that I shall presently set forth, it would be quite wrong to think of orenda as supernatural power. Let us for the time being simply think of orenda as energy, and then presently we shall be able to qualify it a little more.

Hewitt was not a philosopher, and he does not help us to understand more deeply how to think about orenda. I am going to follow his lead in calling the mysterious energy we're discussing here by the name orenda, to indicate the whole group of similar concepts called by various names among various Indian peoples. One does not find very much help with a philosophical elaboration of this concept in other contexts either, although Hallowell sees *manitou* (the Ojibwa name for orenda) as fundamental in Ojibwa ontology, and Native American writers give helpful leads.[3]

Let us start by looking at shortened examples of usage presented by Hewitt in translation of what he calls "sentence-words" from Iroquois languages to English, in which Hewitt indicates how the word orenda would typically be used:

> *A shaman has great, powerful orenda.*
> *A fine hunter has superior orenda.*
> *A successful hunter has thwarted the orenda of the game, but if*
> *he is unsuccessful then the game have outmatched his*
> *orenda.*
> *If someone defeats an opponent in a game of chance or skill, he*
> *has overcome the orenda of the opponent. Shamans*
> *reputed to possess powerful orenda can be hired to exercise*
> *their orenda to overcome that of the hirers' antagonists.*
> *When a storm is brewing, the "storm maker" is preparing its*
> *orenda.*
> *An angry bird, animal, or man is preparing its (his) orenda*
> *and when sufficiently aroused would put its (his) orenda*
> *to use.*
> *A prophet habitually puts forth his orenda to learn the future.*

A shy and hard to snare bird or animal has sensitive or acute orenda.

If someone's orenda has been instrumental in accomplishing some purpose, he is said to "possess orenda," implying that he has it in abundance (as a wealthy person is said "to have money").

Someone who exerts his orenda to accomplish some purpose is arrayed in (has put on) his orenda and has put forth his orenda (also meaning he is hoping for or expecting his goal).

To sing is to put forth one's orenda to execute one's will, whether the singer is bird, animal, man, or wind—and so the shaman when exerting his orenda chants or sings to imitate the entities or creatures of the environment. When the locust sings it exerts its orenda to bring on summer heat to ripen the corn.

Someone who habitually prays lays down his own orenda, indicating submission to, as well as a plea for, well-being from the prayed-to entity.

Plants, trees, rocks, mountains, birds, beasts, the water, the cloud, the sky, the darkness, and so on, all have their own orenda which man can persuade them to use in his behalf.[4]

To this we must add that a political entity such as the Iroquois League is said to possess orenda, and one's community has its own orenda too. As we shall see presently, a deity may also be said to have orenda.

Hewitt tells us that we must not interpret orenda as mind or soul; the Iroquoian languages use entirely different words to express these ideas. This point needs to be emphasized, because some writers earlier in this century misinterpreted the attribution of orenda to non-human entities as animism (the belief that all things have human-like minds or souls). But the prevailing present view of the meaning of "orenda," as expressed both in anthropological and Native American writings, is that it signifies the *personal energy* of an entity or creature, and also signifies that the bearer of this energy is considered to be a *person*, whether a human person or a person of the other-than-human class.[5]

Each entity is unique, but it has orenda suitable to its own kind. An individual shaman, though unique, has orenda suitable to shaman-kind, an individual bird, though unique, has orenda suitable to bird-kind, an individual rock, though unique, has orenda suitable to rock-kind, an individual deity, though unique, has orenda suitable to deity-kind. (Hewitt leaves deities out of his examples, but the Iroquois Creation myth, i.e., sacred account, to be presented later, shows at least two deities possessing respectively a good and a bad orenda; that is, their deity kind of orenda is being put to a good or bad use respectively. Since orenda is energy or power we should not be surprised to find claims that it is being put to evil use sometimes, as when someone is said to have died as the result of being struck by a bewitcher's evil orenda.)

When we look at Hewitt's presentation of usages of the term orenda, we may be struck by the fact that the list implies or suggests "Thous" (persons, or subjects-of-a-life) of the most diverse categories as possessing orenda: humans, animals, plants, inanimate objects, shamans, witches, and so on are all said to possess orenda. And we have added to this further "Thous" or persons consisting of putative deities and even of corporate, political entities such as the Iroquois League or one's community, as also possessing orenda. To a modern English speaker the list may seem to contain an incompatible mix of the animate and inanimate, natural and supernatural, sacred and secular, real and imaginary, factual and fictional, ordinary and extraordinary. How can entities of such incommensurable categories be understood all to be persons and all to possess orenda? And how are we to understand the idea that orenda possessed by other than humans or deities is personal energy as intelligence or awareness of a sort that is neither humanlike or godlike?

It is here that some philosophical elaboration and the providing of some points of contact in Western thought can perhaps make a contribution to our understanding. But let me start by harkening back to my experience of healing as an eight-year-old while sitting in the Grandfather tree in the woods behind the house on Orenda Drive. If I narrate this experience in terms of the usages Hewitt has provided from the Iroquois languages or in terms implied by these usages, I can stay pretty close to the original experience. In these terms, my narrative now goes as follows:

> At a time of trouble I went into the woods and I lay down my
> orenda and I prayed for help from the big Grandfather tree and
> from the birds and squirrels and all the other trees, and from

the Bay, wind, sand banks, veins of red clay, clumps of Queen Anne's Lace, and berry bushes. These responded to my plea for a restoration in my inner well-being by putting forth their orendas in my behalf; and the birds sang in order to put forth their orendas in response to my plea for help in my struggle. I felt their orendas all about me, most especially the orendas of the big old Grandfather maple who supported me in his boughs. I saw and heard a brotherhood of fellow Thous of whom I was one among others; I felt the presence of the creatures and entities around me as each the unique subject of an energy-life, and together the surrounding creatures and entities voiced a chorus of powers that each in its own ways spoke and acted and healed. Together their powers were mighty.

To extend the narrative a bit farther:

A noble Indian woman later came in my dreams and she was like the Earth Woman of whom the Iroquois speak. In my dreams she exerted majestic orenda that I acknowledged in according her the title of Princess.

And, extending the narrative now still farther:

I was, at the time of the Grandfather tree experience, acquainted with a young woman who practiced as a medium. I once saw her go into a trance during which she, for several moments, looked transformed into something like an unbreathing waxen effigy with closed eyes, until she finally came out of the trance. I experienced her exerting something like a shaman's energy as her appearance momentarily changed.

In the above narrative, I am in what Frankfort calls a mythopoeic consciousness in which there is no hard and fast line between the categories animate and inanimate, natural and supernatural, sacred and secular, real and imaginary, dream and non-dream, ordinary and extraordinary.[6] I am not saying that these categories do not come into the mythopoeic consciousness at all, but the special point here is that categories are not hard and fast in mythopoeic consciousness. Opposite categories can flow back and forth into each other rather than being dichotomous. For example, I may not think of that rock as alive (animate) right now, but presently in a vision it may communicate with me (become animate). In what I have just narrated, my stream of experience comfortably included relationships with a mix of what, in a consciousness that is *not* mythopoeic, would be thought of as entities of incommensurable categories: animate entities and inanimate entities, natural entities and supernatural entities, dreamed entities and non-dreamed entities, sacred entities and secular entities, and so on. Furthermore, metamorphosis is possible, as from an animal form to a human form or vice versa, with no loss of distinctive "personhood."

Everything I experience in the mythopoeic consciousness is equally validly experienced. I do not say to myself that I should throw out such-and-such a component of the experience as merely a dream or merely imaginary or merely superstitious. I keep the whole experience with all its components intact, experiencing all the components as in their own way important and in their own way real. Yet in doing this, I am not in danger of confusing with each other the different unique Thous with their different kinds of orendas, for I have some idea of what to expect from each Thou and my expectations differ with each unique Thou. However, the differing expectations are not based on the categories of animate and inanimate, natural and supernatural, and so on, but rather on my and my people's experiences with this particular Thou or other resembling Thous.

My experiencing life in the mythopoeic consciousness does not render me a fool who does not know how to get on in the world, even if in this consciousness I don't rigidly label what I experience in accord with the Western dichotomous, hard-and-fast categories of animate and inanimate, natural and supernatural. I can get on quite effectively with the various concerns of life without doing this. If later on I interpret my experience along the lines of these hard-and-fast dichotomous categories, I have entered the mode of "interpreting-as" and have left the mode of my mythopoeic experiencing. (Mythopoeic experiencing is just experiencing, period.) Western intellectual tradition insists on just this sort of "interpreting-as," but the orenda vocabulary and usages Hewitt presents to us stay close to original (mythopoeic) experience, avoiding the categories of the Western intellectual tradition. Western minds are taught to apply the dichotomous hard-and-fast categories as soon as possible, with the assumption that to do this is correct and true and the implication that to refrain from doing so is childish and/or primitive. But what if the unquestioned super-imposition of these dichotomous, fixed, hard-and-fast categories on what we experience originally (mythopoeic consciousness) obscures or even destroys very valuable ways of relating to life?

In Western thought, there have been, and are, some important thinkers and writers who have points of contact with the more mythopoeic experience and vocabulary of Native Americans. There were, and are, more such writers than I can include in this brief survey, and anything like a full exposition of the ideas of those included in what follows is not possible here. But even these admittedly brief, sketchy depictions will suggest some points of contact that may prove helpful.

The fourth century BC philosopher Aristotle argued that each thing in nature possesses its own "entelechy" or drive to completion, and can be seen as directing its behavior purposively. Similarly, American Indians see all entities and creatures as possessing orenda and hence as able to act purposively.

Baruch Spinoza, in his seventeenth century book *Ethics*, attributed what he called a "conatus" to each natural thing (i.e., nonmanufactured thing) or creature. The thing's conatus is its natural tendency or desire to persist in and maintain its own being—a tendency not only to continue to exist, but also to exist in as close to its own appropriate optimal condition as possible. Nowadays, we would put it that Spinoza viewed things and creatures as self-regulating or homeostatic systems. There is a hint here of the orendas of non-human things and creatures seen as energies that are intelligent and aware, though not in a human way. The homeostatic tendency of a thing to persist in and maintain its own being involves responsiveness to changes in the environment as well as to changes internal to the thing—a responsiveness that could be construed as a sort of nonhuman type of intelligence and awareness on the part of a nonhuman thing or creature. Spinoza can also be classified as a "process" philosopher; he emphasizes that, seen from one perspective, nature is a continual unfolding and continual changing — a process rather than an assemblage of static, unchanging things and creatures. This is not so different from seeing the orendas of things and creatures as their energies: energy is a process, it is not something static and unchanging.

Immanuel Kant in several works in the nineteenth century argued that human beings must be seen and treated as an end-in-itself, never merely as a means to an end (i.e., never merely as a tool for someone else's purposes). If we extend this way of thinking to animals and objects (Kant did not do so), we get a facet of orenda.

Henri Bergson in his nineteenth century book *Creative Evolution* emphasizes that change and process are fundamental to our experience of the world, and that human thought categories impose an artificially static and fixed superstructure on the flux of things that, to be known more truly, must be intuitively experienced. He, too, can be classed as a process philosopher, giving him a point of contact with the view of the orendas of things as their energy processes. He also can be seen to have a point of contact with the mythopoeic consciousness, in recommending a more intuitive mode of knowing reality.

The twentieth century philosopher, Alfred North Whitehead in his metaphysics presented in *Process and Reality* extrapolated from modern physics the idea that all things are energy processes that are aware and intelligent though not, in nonhumans, intelligent and aware in a human manner; he coined the term "prehension" to refer to the intelligence and awareness of nonhuman things. Prehension could be said to be their selective responsiveness to the environment in service to aims of their own. This has something in common with Spinoza's "conatus," and is even closer to a description of orenda. Whitehead charged that Aristotle's categories of substance (unchanging thing) and accident (property of a substance) falsify our actual experiences of change and process, and also falsify what physics tells us about the true nature of reality, making it hard for us to understand the ideas of modern physics about everything being fundamentally energy process.

Martin Buber, another twentieth-century philosopher, though focusing more on humans than on nonhuman creatures and things, in *I and Thou* emphasizes the importance of seeing other people, and even the cat or the tree, as Thou's—as each the unique, subject-of-a-life with each a good of his/her/its own, rather than as mere tools to our own purposes. We can have a mutual relationship with the cat or the tree as well as with other people, if we see each of these as Thou—but not otherwise. Failure to relate in the Thou mode also cuts us off from spiritual experience. These ideas make contact with the mythopoeic experience of each thing or creature as a Thou, deploying its own kind of orenda for its own benefit and also for ours, if we are in the right kind of interrelatedness with each Thou (i.e., if we perceive and respect each Thou as subject-of-a-life rather than as merely a tool for our own selfish use).

Native American parents told their children tales of selfish animals such as Mink who think only of themselves and who end up by getting into all sorts of messes because of this; an Indian child absorbed such lessons from the time he or she could listen to stories. The mythopoeic consciousness has an emphasis on getting into harmonious and cooperative and reciprocal relations with the Thous, the other orendas, in one's whole community, human and nonhuman, while at the same time not neglecting to assert one's own orenda toward the attainment of one's own well-being; hence, the mythopoeic consciousness fosters a balance between a responsive responsibility to the community, and personal self expression.

DEITY AND PANTHEON

Black Elk, an Oglala Sioux holy man, tells the myth of the White Buffalo Woman who brought the Sioux their sacred rites, as well as the sacred pipe which became for the Sioux their "portable alter" which was used in all holy rites ever after. At the start of the myth, two young Sioux hunters see approaching them in a sacred manner a very beautiful woman who is dressed in white buckskins and bears a bundle on her back. One of the hunters feels lust for the woman, but the other cautions him that she is surely "wakan," and he must put away such thoughts. The evil hunter ignores this advice and with unseemly intent approaches the woman; he and the woman are then enveloped by a great cloud which presently lifts to reveal the hunter reduced to bones, with snakes eating him. (Black Elk explains that he was too attached to ignorance and to his senses, and was consumed by his passions . . . the snakes.) The respectful hunter is then told by the wakan woman to return to his people and to instruct the Chief to prepare a big tipi in which the people are to gather, for she is coming to tell them something of great importance. The big tipi is prepared, the people gather, and the wakan woman enters and stands in front of the Chief and, taking from her back the bundle, holds it before him saying:

> Behold this and always love it! It is lela wakan [very sacred],
> and you must treat it as such. No impure man should ever be
> allowed to see it, for within this bundle there is a sacred pipe.
> With this you will, during winters to come, send your voices to
> Wakan Tanka, your Father and Grandfather.

She now takes a pipe and a small round stone from her bundle, and places the stone on the ground. She holds the pipe up with stem pointed to the heavens and says:

*With this sacred pipe you will walk upon the Earth; for the
Earth is your Grandmother and Mother, and She is sacred.
Every step that is taken upon her should be as a prayer. The
bowl of this pipe is of red stone; it is the Earth. Carved in the
stone and facing the center is this buffalo calf who represents all
the four-leggeds who live upon your Mother. The stem of the
pipe is of wood, and this represents all that grows upon the
Earth. And these twelve feathers which hang here where the
stem fits into the bowl are from* Wanbli Galeshka, *the
Spotted Eagle, and they represent the eagle and all the wingeds
of the air. All these peoples, and all the things of the universe,
are joined to you who smoke the pipe—all send their voices to*
Wakan Tanka, *the Great Spirit. When you pray with this
pipe, you pray for and with everything.*

She then touches the foot of the pipe to the stone she had put on the ground,
saying:

*With this pipe you will be bound to all your relatives; your
Grandfather and your Father [i.e.,* Wakan Tanka*], your
Grandmother and Mother [i.e., the Earth]. This round rock,
which is made of the same red stone as the bowl of the pipe,
your Father* Wakan Tanka *has also given to you. It is the
Earth, your Grandmother and Mother, and it is where you
will live and increase. This Earth which He has given to you
is red, and the two-leggeds who live upon the Earth are red;
and the Great Spirit has also given to you a red day, and a
red road. All of this is sacred and so do not forget! Every
dawn as it comes is a holy event, and every day is holy, for
the light comes from your Father,* Wakan Tanka; *and also
you must always remember that the two-leggeds and all the
other peoples who stand upon this Earth are sacred and should
be treated as such.*

This account is quoted from *The Sacred Pipe: Black Elk's Account of the
Seven Rites of the Oglala Sioux*, edited by Joseph Epes Brown (pp. 3–7; copyright © 1953 by the University of Oklahoma Press). The book is a verbatim
report of Black Elk's words *except* that Black Elk, who knew no English,
spoke in the Siouan language which was translated to Brown, who spoke no

Siouan, by Black Elk's bilingual son Benjamin Black Elk. I ask the reader to take note of this fact, because Brown in a later book indicates that the translation of *Wakan Tanka* into "Great Spirit" in English was misleadingly inaccurate, in a way that will be of very great importance for our discussion in this section. This point will be developed a little farther on. The expression "two-leggeds" in the myth refers to human beings; the other "peoples" are the four-leggeds (animals) and the wingeds (birds). The "red road," as a metaphor or symbol, signifies the traditional Sioux ideal way of spirituality, including unselfish concern for the good of one's people. The Sioux also spoke of a blue or black road, signifying a life ruled only by the senses and selfish lack of concern about the good of one's people.

The wakan woman now gives the Sioux seven sacred rites, and then she departs, turning into a brownish buffalo calf, then a full grown white buffalo, then into a black buffalo. After bowing to the four directions, she disappears over a hill. (Let us keep in mind that the buffalo were for the Sioux and other hunter peoples the source of food, winter warmth, and shelter, for the buffalo gave meat and sinews for sewing, and their hides made warm winter robes and blankets which when sewn together also made coverings for the tipis. Hence the buffalo people were very wakan, as providing humans with much of what they needed to live.) In some other renditions of this myth the woman turns simply into a white buffalo at the end. She really is a buffalo, manifesting in human form for the time being; in Sioux myth, animals take on human form at will.

In Brown's 1953 book, *The Sacred Pipe*, he added the comment in a footnote that Wakan Tanka is identical to the Christian Godhead and the Christian God (p. 5, note 6). But some years later, in his 1982 book *The Spiritual Legacy of the American Indian*, Brown—who had gone on to devote considerably more time to the study of Native American spirituality—admits that the Lakota word "wakan"

> ... *is not a noun with the implication of limit, but an adjective conveying a sense of mystery or the mysterious. This multiplicity of sacred mysteries tends to coalesce into an ultimate unity expressed through polysynthetic terms such as the Lakota Wakan Tanka, "Great Mysterious" ... The often-used translation "Great Spirit" employs a noun, and is undoubtedly the result of a Christian perspective that changes the original sense of the term.*
>
> (Brown 1982, p.15)

Let us note that Black Elk's son translated "Wakan Tanka" as "Great Spirit" in the myth of the White Buffalo Woman. I am bringing up this matter here because Brown's 1982 change of mind about the question of whether Wakan Tanka is or is not identical to the Christian God—with his decision in 1982 that a Christian perspective changes the original sense of Wakan Tanka, raises the question as to what, then, *was* the original sense of the term? Brown goes on to other concerns, and doesn't pursue this question.

In one's attempt to discover what Wakan Tanka, the Great Mysterious, meant to the Sioux people originally, before contact with the whites, one runs into problems. First of all, studies by white anthropologists of Sioux culture, traditions, and beliefs, only began after the Sioux culture had been broken up by whites and their traditional beliefs eroded by missionaries, when the Sioux were left only poor reservations on which to live under debilitating and artificial conditions. Much of the information collected under these conditions was, and is, of questionable accuracy with respect to the traditional, pre-white beliefs of the Sioux. Secondly, the few older medicine men, who retained knowledge of the oral tradition handed down from the pre-white period, were sworn to secrecy not to disclose it to outsiders. Thirdly, these older medicine men were dying off, and after their deaths the information they had imparted to anthropologists could not be verified by information from younger Sioux informants who either did not know the old traditions or who tended to present the Christianized versions that the whites often wanted to hear and who used the non-Siouan expression "Great Spirit" to translate "Wakan Tanka" because whites liked this expression. Fourthly, the earlier white anthropologists often assimilated and reworked what they heard, even from good Sioux sources, into their own western and Christian thought categories. Fifthly, these anthropologists did not necessarily have a good command of the Siouan language, and interpreters might enter in as middlemen and hence as further sources of inaccuracy.

Nevertheless, in spite of all these problems we are fortunate to have several independent sources of information that give enough of a view in common that we can see some themes emerging that are likely to have some accuracy with respect to the pre-white Sioux spiritual beliefs. Dr James R. Walker, a white man very sympathetic to the Sioux, was, during the years 1896–1914, the physician at the Pine Ridge Reservation in South Dakota where many members of the Oglala division of the Lakota Sioux lived. Desiring to help his Sioux patients as much as he could, Walker learned the Siouan language and he respectfully sought out the older Sioux medicine men with a great longing to learn from them. They finally accepted him as a trainee and gave him the traditional long training of a Sioux medicine man. During this time Walker was taught the old, pre-white Sioux oral traditions. He labored for years to put it all together in his mind and to render it into English and to publish some of it, and he was never entirely sure he'd got it all correctly put together, nor that his mentors had imparted one hundred percent of their secret knowledge to him (his notebooks disclose these concerns), but what he published about it in 1917 correlates well with other sources.

A little earlier, in the 1860s, a full blood Santee Sioux, Charles Eastman (his Sioux name was Ohiyesa), had grown up for his first fifteen years with no contact with whites. He was introduced to white culture at age fifteen and he later graduated from Dartmouth College and got his MD from Boston University. Dr Eastman was the physician at Pine Ridge reservation before Walker's time and there was no contact between the two. Eastman published books in English in the early 1900s about his Indian boyhood and about the spiritual beliefs he learned from the elders of his people.

In 1931, Black Elk, the Oglala Sioux holy man I mentioned earlier, dictated much of the tradition to a white man, John Neihardt, so that the tradition would not die with him. The dictation was done via Black Elk's bilingual son. (Neihardt's 1932 book *Black Elk Speaks*, an uninterpreted transcription of Black Elk's report which was read back to Black Elk in Siouan and approved by Black Elk himself, was what reached Carl Jung in Zürich.) At a later time, in 1947, Black Elk dictated to Joseph Epes Brown, once again via his bilingual son, further aspects of the secret tradition that he had withheld from Neihardt. Brown, who lived with Black Elk for a year, published the material in *The Sacred Pipe* in 1953. Black Elk was motivated in 1947 to disclose these previously withheld holy secrets because, now an aged man in his eighties, he was truly afraid that the old sacred traditions would die with him and he was hoping, among other things, that his broken and dispersed people might yet be reunited if they could learn and keep to the old traditions. Brown took Black Elk's report down accurately and with Black Elk's approval.

Another, younger, Sioux holy man, Lame Deer, who in his youth experienced the aimlessness, confusions, and bitterness of the younger generation of partially white-acculturated Sioux, in maturity returned to the traditions of his people and to his youthful vision. This had come during his Vision Quest at age sixteen, and had foretold that he would become a medicine man—which was for him as a youth his heart's dearest wish. Starting in 1967, Lame Deer imparted his people's traditions to his trusted white friend Richard Erdoes, who published the material in *Lame Deer Seeker of Visions* in 1972 with Lame Deer's full approval of the text. Again, this material correlates well with the earlier sources mentioned above as well as with James Walker's work.

As Walker struggled to understand and put together an integrated picture of the traditional Sioux conception of Wakan Tanka, the Great Mysterious, he found this conception centering in some way about Skan, also called Sky, construed as the invisible, fundamental force or energy underlying all visible natural creation.

Walker also found that the term Skan was used by shamans to mean a force or power or energy that moves everything that moves. He also found it to mean a distinct being or supreme spirit, though the latter is not to be construed as the Christian God. I suggest that whatever this "being" connoted to shamans, we westerners might do well to see it, in Buber's sense, as a saying of "Thou" to the cosmos. It can be interpreted as a refusal to regard the universe as a mere "It"—a mere mechanism or object or set of objects available for our manipulation with no *telos* (purpose) of its own. We must see the cosmos as a whole, as possessing awareness and understanding, and as a subject to be respected in its own right. It is person-like in this sense, rather than our object or tool to be used for our own purposes solely. This is all of a piece with our seeing the component creatures and entities of nature as Thou's, as persons to be respected in their own right.

The natural creation was conceptualized by the Sioux as having sixteen aspects, including Skan. Collectively, these sixteen aspects composed the one Great Mysterious known as Wakan Tanka, which I suggest be thought of as a *unified system*. The aspects included male and female entities, and good and evil entities, so that Wakan Tanka includes both male and female energy, as well as neuter energy, and includes both good and evil.

In Walker's final articulation of the Sioux Creation account, when the first-created, four natural powers (Rock, Earth, Waters, and Sky) came into being, they "assumed shape, [and] they said a voice spoke saying, 'I am the source of energy. I am *Skan*.'" Skan, Sky, is superior to all (Walker, 1983, pp. 207–8). The four superior powers of Rock, Earth, Waters, and Sky are recognized as one; Skan, at first known only as Sky, now is known as the superior underlying invisible force or energy that is the final arbiter of all things. Skan as energy is the underlying or most fundamental aspect of the oneness of everything. Skan then goes on to create the associate powers of Moon, Passion, Wind, Thunderstorm, and other entities including the buffalo people, growing things, birds and beasts and all that exists, to all of which Skan imparts vitality, or energy, or spirit. Each is wakan (mysterious, or sacred = possessing power).

Skan is the most fundamental aspect of Wakan Tanka, the Great Mysterious; Skan is the invisible, intelligent and aware energy underlying all the visible creation, an energy to be regarded with the respect accorded to a "Thou" rather than manipulated as a tool-like "It." All these aspects, whether visible material entities or underlying, fundamental, invisible energy, must, I suggest, be understood to be aspects of one unified system, Wakan Tanka. A modern way to put this might be to say that macroscopically discrete, visible, material entities can be construed as the aspect under which human beings see and relate to what, on the physicist's analysis, are more fundamentally and "really" knowable under the aspect of sub-macroscopic energy process, and all of this can be conceptualized as a unified system with a *telos* (purpose of its own) that must be respected. But on the Native American view, though not on the usual physicist's view, this energy is also (nonanthropomorphic) intelligence and awareness. Spirit, imparted by Skan to all that exists, seems in the Creation myth—as I read it to mean vital energy—as having in some sense the attributes of life though not in an anthropomorphic sense. In other words, it is orenda. The natural entities and creatures are bearers of spirit-as-vital-energy, and are "personal" forces of nature, or person-like "Thous."[7]

Walker's depiction of Wakan Tanka fits together well with Black Elk's independent formulation, for Black Elk addresses Wakan Tanka sometimes as Grandfather, when Wakan Tanka is being considered as the invisible potentiality for all creation which is by no means exhausted in the material creation now in existence, and at other times addresses Wakan Tanka as Father when Wakan Tanka is being considered as the totality of the various aspects of the visible creation. Thus as "Grandfather," Wakan Tanka is Skan, the underlying energy fundamental to everything that is now and that can become, and as "Father," Wakan Tanka is the totality of what has at present emerged from Skan as the material and visible aspects of the creation. Walker's account also correlates well with the other accounts I have mentioned. Nevertheless, it should be stressed that the meaning of the Walker materials is only just now beginning to be analyzed.

It must be mentioned that one of the medicine men, George Sword or Long Knife, who was Walker's central source, spoke of men doing things to please Wakan Tanka or avoiding things that might anger Wakan Tanka, and spoke of Wakan Tanka as having wishes. Eastman speaks similarly in his book *Indian Boyhood*. Long Knife had, before dictating his statement to Walker, renounced his membership in the Oglala Sioux order of medicine men to become a deacon of a Christian denomination; he taught Walker the Sioux holy traditions because he feared that his people's oral tradition might be lost as the older medicine men died off. His narratives need to be seen as mediating between Lakota and Christian beliefs. Eastman had also become a Christian before he wrote his books. Perhaps Long Knife's and Eastman's conversions lent an anthropomorphic flavor to their descriptions of Wakan Tanka as being pleased or angry or as having wishes. Wakan Tanka is so frequently described in the rest of the literature as *not* anthropomorphic that this must, I suggest, be taken as the truer view—and in this case I question whether it would make sense to think of Wakan Tanka as being pleased or angry or as having wishes. However, I think that Wakan Tanka construed as a unified system with a telos (purpose of its own) could be thought of as having its telos violated—a cautionary note to us humans not to tamper with nature.

The Lakota Sioux addressed prayer not only to Wakan Tanka but also to Mother Earth, to Father Sun, to the Four Winds, and to other entities referred to as spirit beings (spirit, as I take it, meaning a particular kind of vital energy, and a spirit being, as I take it, meaning a personified vital energy process).

The wakan energy of any natural entity or creature may be imaged as a spirit being and conceived as present in visions and dreams in one's personal Vision Quest (discussed later in this essay). In the dream or vision, such an imaged spirit being—experienced as actually present in the dream or vision—may communicate with one and bestow upon one some of its special kind of wakan energy. Other, later dreams and visions may come too, in which various energies may be imaged as spirit beings.

It is questionable whether one ought to speak of there being a genuine Sioux pantheon (hierarchy of deities). Sun, Moon, Sky, Earth, the winds, rock, the buffalo people, and the various natural entities and creatures with their respective wakan energies are simply components or aspects of the totality of the wakan powers or energies of everything and every entity in existence and that could come into existence. This stone is Wakan Tanka as one aspect, that bird is Wakan Tanka as another aspect, and likewise this tree, the sun, the moon, you, and I. A human being in his or her complexity is thought by Black Elk to reflect or to contain all of the aspects of Wakan Tanka, so that Black Elk speaks, at times, of Wakan Tanka being located within each person as well as being the totality of all that is in the cosmos (Brown, 1982, p. 21). In their interconnections, all existing entities and creatures form a network of brotherhood of beings which conjointly manifest Wakan Tanka's powers but do not exhaust them, for Wakan Tanka's powers or energies can, and will, manifest again and again in an ongoing creation. These powers and energies were considered beyond any human's ability to know fully, though holy men (wikasa wakan) shared in the energies and powers to some extent and could help mankind understand Wakan Tanka to an extent and also to impose some order on the energies and powers.

I submit that Wakan Tanka does not fit into the usual Western or Christian conceptions of deity. Usual Western and Christian views depict God as a divine *substance* (a divine *entity*, unchanging and existing independently of anything else), whereas the fundamental aspect of Wakan Tanka as a unified system is Skan, which is energy or *process*—energy as also in some sense intelligence and awareness along the lines earlier discussed. The English language uses substantives to denote God: Supreme Being, Creator, Heavenly Father. English is not well suited, except in its gerunds (words such as creating, ruling, thinking) to denote process. I suggest that Wakan Tanka might, awkwardly to be sure, be spoken of in English as something like: "The totality of all energy-ing, of all creating and of all powerful acting, both ongoing and also still in potential, where all the energy-ing, creating, and powerful acting is also intelligence-ing and awareness-ing in some special sense, and all of this is strange and wonderful, mysterious, powerful."

We can see at once how English stumbles, becomes awkward, and has to resort to invented "-ing" words when it tries to depict process.[8] (By the way, it would not do to substitute the word "energizing," above, for the invented word "energy-ing," because to energize is a different idea.) But despite the awkwardness of the English locutions one may be driven to use, it seems to me that Wakan Tanka is better described in English along the lines of a process model, as I have attempted, than along the lines of a substance model. Native American writer Paul Gunn Allen describes Native American thought as centrally focused on the "creative flux of things."

In addition, any temptation to construe Wakan Tanka as the Christian God must further leave us when we presently take a look at the pervasive Native American way of viewing space and, especially, time. If one is tempted to wonder why it is important to make the case that Wakan Tanka isn't the Christian God, let us recall that even as careful and self-correcting a student of Native American thought and spirituality as Joseph Epes Brown had to correct an early mistake of this sort, a mistake he might not have made had he been alerted from the start to a need to make use of radically other than Western categories of grammar and thought, as well as other than Christian categories of spirituality. Actually, even from the start Brown knew something about comparative religion, as his earlier footnotes reveal, for he mentions Hinduism there, but yet he did not at the start sufficiently reckon with the possibility that in Native American thought he might find something requiring an analysis that escapes the limits of English grammar and Aristotelian categories of substance and property. Walker mentions that modern Sioux when talking to whites often use "Wakan Tanka" to mean the Christian God or Jehovah, though Wakan Tanka did not mean this in traditional Sioux tradition.

A core feature of all Native American spirituality or metaphysics is the profoundly felt and believed experience and conception of the interconnectedness of all entities and creatures, the influence of all process upon all other process. This affects the Native American view of causality in ways that may be interpreted by Caucasians as some sort of superstition. But if you think of the world in terms of processes influencing or triggering other processes, it can, for example, make sense that the Navajo Chantway healing rites, used for both medical and what we would call psychiatric illnesses, employ both special sorts of big sand paintings constructed around the patient and a long chant appropriate to the type of disorder. These rites were and still are genuinely effective in healing people. The sand painting depicts the cosmos and the significant figures and features of it around the patient who is drawn back into a balance with cosmic and community influences in this way, while the chanting, as prescribed by the oral tradition, also draws the ill person back into the influence of the community, an influence now voiced and breathed out, danced and sung out, in the very presence of the assembled family and other community members.[9] These are not merely symbolic processes affecting the patient by means of faith (even though Underhill calls it a "faith cure"). These are real processes bringing into balance real sands, colours, sounds, shapes, and motions of nature. Why should we not grant that these processes could stimulate mimetic, balancing and healing processes, physically and emotionally, in the patient?

The reader can find a little discussion of causality from the perspective of a southwest Indian process model of reality in the aforementioned essays of Benjamin Whorf, who presented this perspective intelligently and sensitively and on a level that an interested reader will not find hard to grasp.

The Native American conviction of the brotherhood of all beings, based on the belief that all are Thous having each their own kind of orenda which is as sacred as one's own orenda though of a different kind, led to the belief that when, for example, one goes buffalo hunting, one thinks of the buffalo people, a four-legged people who are after all an aspect of Wakan Tanka, as voluntarily sacrificing some of their members to our human needs, in brotherhood toward our human people, and one does not slaughter buffalo for sport or beyond need. One performs rituals in which appropriate gratitude and appreciation are felt and expressed towards one's brothers, the buffalo people. Our respect, our conservation, our efforts must be toward the preservation of the species. The implications of such a metaphysics are very clear for the West, currently reaping, in ways ever more alarming, the fruits of heedless and exploitative greed toward the entities and creatures of nature regarded as mere objects and tools for our use.

It is time we turn now to the Iroquois conception of deity and pantheon. The Iroquois were unusual among Native Americans in having an all-pervasive theme of dualism running throughout their metaphysics. (The reader will have noticed by now that I have started using the word "metaphysics" whereas I was previously using the word "spirituality." The switch in terminology is deliberate: it intends to get across the idea that we are dealing here with articulated thought systems that grew up on the basis of the mythopoeic consciousness among Native Americans. These articulated thought systems may not have been of interest and concern to all members of a Native American community, nor is western metaphysics of interest and concern to everyone who lives in a western culture. But the point is that some Native Americans thought about and formulated philosophical thought just as do some westerners.)

Orenda for the Iroquois could be good or evil, that is, could be put to good or evil use. We can see this illustrated in the traditional Iroquois Creation account. The myth has come down from pre-Columbian times, and has over 300 years of recorded history. What I present below is presented by Wallace (1970).

*Before the earth existed there was a sky world that contained
land, water, animals and fish and plants, but no sun, moon,
or stars, but there was a tree of light. Manlike beings lived
there. A sky man falls in love with a sky woman who consents
to be his wife. He falls sick and dreams that unless the tree of
light is uprooted he will die; furthermore, this tree must be
done away with for the sake of the new creation of the world.
His brothers uproot the tree, which plunges through a hole
made by the uprooting. The sky husband calls his wife to sit
with him at the edge of the hole, and she conceives by the
south wind, the air of life, that comes up through the hole.
Sky husband now tells her that her new home shall be on a
newly created earth below, and that she shall be the mother of
the earth beings, and he pushes her through the hole. A
multitude of water birds assemble to break her fall, and they let
her down upon a great turtle's back. Diver birds then dive
beneath the primeval waters to bring up mud that they place on
the great turtle's back, thus creating the earth.*

*Soon Sky Woman gives birth to a daughter, Earth
Woman. When the daughter, Earth Woman, grows up she
becomes pregnant. Earth Woman gives birth to twin sons; the
elder twin is the Good Twin and the younger is the Evil Twin.
Earth Woman, now dying, calls to her side her mother, Sky
Woman, and tells Sky Woman to bury her under the ground,
predicting that corn will grow from her breasts, whose seeds must
be planted for the generations of her children that will live here.
The Good Twin now creates the sun and moon. Out of his
orenda the Good Twin now creates man and woman, some
helpful animals and plants, unimpeded waterways, and Thunders
(rains) to help with the crops. He improves the corn already
growing from his mother's, Earth Woman's, grave. He has
imparted orenda to each of his creations. The Evil Twin, in
jealousy, creates out of his orenda ugly or dangerous animals such
as bats, apes, toads and snakes, noxious weeds, the waterfalls
and whirlpools that render waterways unusable to humans, frost,
terrifying invisible menaces such as water monsters, and death
and disease. He also blights the corn to make it harder to grow
and less good tasting. He has imparted orenda to his creatures.*

Finally the Good Twin goes on an inspection tour,
walking around the earth, and he meets the Evil Twin who is
now in the form of a giant. The Good Twin asks the Evil
Twin what he is doing, and the latter says he is looking over
his creation. But the Good Twin says "It is my creation."
They agree to settle the dispute by a mountain moving contest.
The contest erupts into violence and the Evil Twin crashes
against a mountainside so hard that his face is rendered
permanently lopsided. The Evil Twin submits, as the loser,
and says that the Good Twin is the Creator.[10] *The Evil Twin*
now also agrees to drive away disease.—In some versions of the
myth, the Evil Twin creates and gives healing herbs and
healing arts to humans to whom he earlier brought sickness. He
thus becomes a healer figure who is honored in the Iroquois
medicine societies, especially in the False Face Society whose
members wear an assortment of masks many of which have
lopsided facial expressions depicting the effects of his crashing
against a mountain in his contest with the Good Twin. At the
end of the creation myth both Twins, now reconciled, finally
retire to eternal life in the sky world.

Ultimately, then, the dualisms between good and evil, health and sickness, life and death, are reconciled as the good and evil orendas of the Good and Evil Twins in the end come to operate cooperatively, their orendas now no longer in opposition. Thus on the highest conceptual level there are now complementary, cooperating orendas; on this level it can be said that the highest Iroquois metaphysical principle holds that all dualisms are ultimately complementary. But for the Iroquois in their everyday life, the antagonistic dualism of good and evil seemed often prominent, and the ultimate metaphysical complementarity was something to be worked for.[11]

One can, perhaps, relate their dualism in metaphysics to the dichotomy within actual Iroquois people between the goals of love and brotherhood. These goals were actually practiced amongst the nations that were members of their League despite their war complex that led them into revenge raids and also into imperialistic conquest of neighboring tribes outside their League. (The latter they explained as activated by the ideal of bringing the Iroquois "peace" to other peoples who would henceforth be brought under the dominion of the "superior" Iroquois.)

Likewise there was a dichotomy between the tender affection and cooperation shown family and clan members, and the torture and ritual cannibalism said to be accorded to captives taken from tribes outside the League in ever-proliferating war parties often undertaken, at least ostensibly, to console and avenge the honor of bereaved Iroquois who had lost a family or clan member killed by an outside tribe. It has been suggested (Brandon, p. 214) that reports of this torture and cannibalism were exaggerated by whites for propaganda purposes, to excuse their own cruelty. No doubt this is true. But all reports indicate that there was some of this going on, and among surrounding tribes too. No doubt, as has been suggested, it was useful to the Iroquois themselves to circulate exaggerated propaganda about these things to deter enemy attacks.

The whole war complex and all its attendant practices had virtually petered out by the mid-eighteenth century, due to decimation of the Iroquois population from over-frequent war and the ruinous expense and difficulties involved in keeping up the burden of the whole war complex. Perhaps all this is prefigured by the Creation myth's ending in the Good Twin subduing the Evil Twin—the "good" aspect of Iroquois society (love and brotherhood) finally prevailed over the "bad" aspect (the war complex, and torture and cannibalism practiced upon captives). Possibly it is also prefigured by the important myth about the founding of the Iroquois League in which a key figure, a murderer and cannibal, while one day looking into a pot of water in which he is about to boil a corpse, sees reflected there the face of an incarnated and beautiful divine male spirit who is looking into the pot from a hole in the roof at the same time. The evil cannibal thinks this beautiful face is his own, sees himself now for the first time as having potential for goodness, forswears killing and cannibalism, and helps the divine spirit found the Iroquois League to promote love, peace, and brotherhood among the five Iroquois tribes (later augmented by a sixth). However, it took the League some time to actually desist, mainly for reasons of exhaustion from wars against tribes outside the League, by about 1750 AD. (The date of the founding of the League is uncertain. A date frequently given is AD 1450.)

For the Iroquois, the brotherhood of all things and creatures seemed less easily felt and believed in than for many other Native American peoples, in view of the emphasis on dualisms in Iroquois metaphysics. In Iroquois metaphysics there is a sort of network of good entities and creatures that is constantly threatened and foiled by a network of obstructive evil entities and creatures. On the human plane, sickness and death and the thwarting of human hopes and plans by obstacles remain despite the eventual gift of healing techniques and remedies by the once evil Twin who has now become the patron of healing. There is a hint that all will ultimately end well on a higher plane—a hint of a shared life in the hereafter for good and bad Iroquois alike. There is a hint that good and evil orendas are, on some high metaphysical level, complementary and cooperative—although these complementary orendas are still not seen as an attribute of one Supreme Being; rather, the orendas of the Good Twin and the formerly evil Twin seemingly remain separate but are seen as ultimately working together toward harmony, rather than in eternal struggle with each other.

The Iroquois felt, it appears, a communion and intimate brotherhood with the entities and creatures of nature—up to a point. There is also another, opposing network of obstructive entities and creatures with whom one's communion is perhaps more conceptual than felt, for one must contend with them and try to overcome them in this earthly life at least.

In the Iroquois Creation myth, the Good Twin often gets translated in English as "the Creator," though some anthropologists call him a Culture Hero[12]—a bringer of valuable gifts to mankind—rather than a Creator. In the full Creation account there are already in existence creative figures and entities preceding the Good and Evil Twins, and also, after the Good and Evil Twins impart their respective orendas to further entities and creatures they have created, these new entities and creatures then possess and deploy their orendas independently in their own interests and thus add to the Creation.

The Seneca Iroquois prophet Handsome Lake early in the 1800s began to see in the Good and Evil Twins something analogous to the Christian God and Devil respectively, but this is not feasible if one views in terms of the whole Creation myth. The full Iroquois Creation myth in all versions shows much of the Creation already in existence before the Good Twin is born, and shows both male and female creative/generative principles or forces at work in the cosmos. It would take a stretch of the imagination to see in the original full Iroquois Creation myth only one figure who has the role of something like a patriarchal God analogous to that of Christian monotheism, namely the good Twin. Nevertheless, early in the 1800s, the Seneca Iroquois prophet Handsome Lake deeply disheartened by post-Revolutionary War reservation life and under white pressures and Christian influences, did something of this sort, thereby truncating and patriarchalizing the traditional Iroquois pantheon with its plurality and mix of male and female divine powers, as well as, some argue, altering the structure of traditional Iroquois society. He led his decimated and totally demoralized and starving followers toward the white man's method of male-run agriculture (agriculture among the Iroquois had previously been women's domain) and toward the white man's style of patriarchal nuclear family structure, and away from the traditional egalitarian Iroquois extended family structure.

Handsome Lake did not convert to Christianity, but founded his own religion which retained the traditional Indian reverence for nature, although nature was now seen as created by and obedient to only one, male Creator. Since he announced the new doctrines as having been given to him in visions—and visions and dreams traditionally carried great weight in Iroquois life—the changes he instituted carried authority in the eyes of his followers, although the latter's utterly destitute condition and the total hopelessness of their lot under the dominion of the whites, as well as considerable pressure by Christian missionaries, may have created the predisposition to try the new direction.

It is interesting to note that there are aspects in common between the Iroquois and the Sioux Creation myths. Both have an evil trickster god (the Iroquois Evil Twin can be seen as this), and a woman who falls from the sky (who, in the Sioux myth becomes later on the White Buffalo Calf Woman). But in the Sioux myth these personages are both subordinate to Skan (Sky, also energy, who announces his supremacy at once) from the start. Hence we do not have in the Sioux tradition the profound dualism between good and evil and the plurality of deities that the Iroquois tradition presents.

Traditionally, among both the Sioux peoples and the Iroquois peoples, as among Native Americans generally, people were on respectfully friendly, contractual, even equal terms with Wakan Tanka or the Good Twin or with any other bearer of orenda, and people did not abase themselves to the Power or Powers. One could perform ceremonies and rituals to bring the Power or Powers to the aid of human need and purpose (i.e., to help channel the orenda energy or energies in ways helpful to humans, but one did not feel sin or guilt or self-abasement toward the Power or Powers. If one transgressed the mores of the community there would be practical consequences, but one would not feel sinful.

The ambivalence, the love and hate, hope and fear, that we often feel toward nature, the nature which contains orendas that help us and orendas that harm us, seems better captured by the Iroquois Creation myth than by the Sioux Creation myth, drenched in passions as the Iroquois myth is, held together mostly as if by afterthought at the very end: the Good Twin to some extent deflects the harmful orenda of the Evil Twin toward a somewhat more helpful goal, namely the healing of at least some human ills. Such a turn is, I think, the late and difficult superimposition of thought, of metaphysical speculation, upon the difficult emotions evoked by the mix of goods and hurts life actually brings us; in the main, the Iroquois myth stays close to our mixed emotional experience. Our experiential ambivalence, our love and our hate toward nature as it shows us its helpful and its hurtful sides, finds less of a place to locate itself, as it were, in the Sioux Creation myth—although the latter includes Passions among Skan's (the ultimate vital energy) creations. The Iroquois myth seems to focus more on psychology, the Sioux myth on physics.

This section on deity and pantheon will end with a few brief remarks on the Native American views about the fate of human souls after death. Among the Sioux, a person was thought to have at least three souls: the first (*nagi*) was eternal; the second (*niva*) was biological and extinguished at death; the third (*sicun*) forewarned of danger and admonished for right against wrong. One might acquire additional *sicuns* (additional potentials) (Walker, 1980, p. 73). Your *nagi* was thought to be reluctant to leave loved persons and places and might lovingly linger for a while after death. Among some Indian peoples, the soul was thought to pass out of existence when living humans no longer remembered it, but for the Sioux the *nagi* was thought to live eternally as having no beginning or end. After death the *nagi* lingered for a time and then went to the spirit world beyond the pines at the edge of the earth, if you had been good during life. If you had been bad, your *nagi* after death could not find the trail to the spirit world and must wander forever in search of it. A human spirit could reincarnate. You must honor the *nagi* of a deceased person while it still lingers on earth, for if this *nagi* becomes displeased it may become dangerous as a ghost and do real harm.

Many Native American peoples believed that, at times, the souls of living persons might wander at night—especially children's souls that at night often wandered and got caught on berry bushes and had to be searched out and brought back home by shamans in order to cure the illness caused by the soul's absence (Underhill, 1965, p. 89). Adults' souls might get lost at night too, also causing illness, and the shaman might be sent for to locate and bring back the lost soul, to cure an illness.

For the Iroquois, the soul retained personal identity regardless of the form it inhabited. The Iroquois believed that the human soul could leave the human body and enter any object or place to acquire wisdom and reveal it to the person in dreams and visions. If the person refused to heed warning visions and dreams brought by the soul, the soul might leave and the person would then have no power to resist or understand the influence of good or bad spirits. You might offer a sacrifice to your own evil spirit (i.e., your own evil orenda) to satisfy it with things other than your wrongdoing, thereby avoiding giving offence to your own good spirit (i.e., your good orenda). The soul generally left a deceased human after a year, according to ancient Iroquois belief, or in ten days according to Handsome Lake's more recent belief. Iroquois souls after death went up the sky road (Milky Way) to the sky world; souls were not traditionally thought to go to heaven or hell depending on one's virtue or vice in life, but Handsome Lake's religion brought this belief into Iroquois tradition after 1800, probably as a result of Christian missionary influences. Sickness and ill fortune could be caused by evil ghosts; this could be dispelled by a ritual. There were also thought to be some earthbound hungry ghosts that could be satisfied in a ritual feast.[13]

Burial practices among Native Americans tended not to impede the merging of the deceased body with the earth; often there was exposure of the deceased body on a raised platform open to the elements, and often there was direct earth interment with no coffin. This is one of several reasons why ancestral lands were sacred; these lands were literally composed in part of the ancestors whose bodies had there rejoined the earth where they helped to nourish a continuing cycle of new plants and animals. One's community was a continuum including past, present, and future, linked among other things by the sacred physical recycling of the biological composition of its members (Deloria, 1973, pp. 175–6).

TIME, SPACE, DIRECTION

When we turn to the prevailing Native American conception of time[14] we find that this view differs considerably from the Western and especially the Christian view. For Native Americans, time was cyclical, based on the recurring sacred cycles of the seasons, and these cycles were celebrated in seasonally-appropriate thanksgiving to the sacred Powers in special religious ceremonies. Every season was sacred to the appropriate seasonal Powers as well as to all the Powers, and every day was sacred too.

There was no writing, and hence no written history. Among the Santee Sioux, a wise old man of the village might keep track of the significant events of his own lifetime and of several generations before him by means of painted and notched sticks; such an elder would serve as historian to his village and he was able to recite, with unerring memory and the aid of a word-perfect oral tradition, the important happenings of his people (wars, treaties, times of hardship, memorable times) going back for as many as five generations. Among the Iroquois, wampum belts of small, bored cylinders of seashell, of several colors, pierced and strung and woven into figures in a belt-like strip, recorded important events and treaties, and were interpreted by specially trained experts among them. But there was, as best we know, no written history in North America. There are some North American caves and rocks that bear small, stylized, old Indian-painted figures that may contain more information than we know as yet; these figures seem clearly to relate narratives, but the meaning has been lost, and also, tourists have effaced or chipped away at these sites, removing valuable fragments which it has been hard for concerned anthropologists or archaeologists to protect.

To Caucasian settlers in North America, many of whom were at least nominally of a Christian orientation, time was linear; that is, it seemed to progress in a nonrepetitive way from less worthy and less sacred times before Christ to more worthy times after Christ, or, to believers in the French Enlightenment, time progressed toward grand goals and completions, from primitivity to enlightenment. These expectations were recorded in writing. The white man might be a Jeffersonian believer in the French Enlightenment, or an earnest Christian cherishing the story of Christ's redemptive intervention in human affairs at a definite time in history that eternally bifurcated time into a dark before and a glowing after, with respect to Christ's birth (a time that progressed inevitably toward the Second Coming and the Last Judgment). He might be an ordinary post-colonial American citizen excited by the press-fed vision of the American Manifest Destiny to move westward and southward and to Americanize all terrains whose peoples could not resist. Time was for all these whites a linear matter moving in a forward direction for the better. Time was the grand stage on which inevitable and wondrous progress was being worked out over the millennia, either with the blessing of the Lord or else the blessing of human Reason. The ancient cycles of the seasons, of night and day, of planting and reaping, new and full and waning moons, awaited and prayed-for solstices, were of little secular importance to whites compared to the linear accretions of personal wealth and property. And the main spiritual and intellectual emphases of whites were not on recurring cycles but on the Christian salvation of mankind or the grand progress of human Enlightenment or the indefatigable progress of Americans ever west-ward and southward, bringing civilization and true religion to savages and improvement to land that the savages peculiarly didn't care to improve. Time is progress, not repetition!

The American Indians loved games, ceremonials that lasted for days. They loved to intensely experience the moments of one's life as suffused with the influences of all the orendas around one, every moment sacred (rather than the tendency to save up and condense the sacred into Sundays set apart from secular concerns, as did the whites). All this violated the white work ethic, for which time, as Benjamin Franklin said, is money. The American Indians did not separate their work from sacredness. For them there was ordinarily, apart from periods of ceremonials, no separation of the week into sacred and secular days, into six days of secular time and one day of sacred time.

Lest the above be presented in an overly simplified way, however, it must be mentioned here that according to Lakota Sioux oral tradition, a new dimension was thought to have been added to human life when the White Buffalo Calf Woman brought sacred ritual into human life at some long ago point in Lakota history.

For the Indians, all their activities were sacred, all activities were a coop-eration between human powers and the orendas of the nature all around, without which any human effort would surely fail. Every act was at once worshipful and practical; even religious rituals were also practical since they were necessary to ensure the successful cooperation of the orendas of animals or plants in the hunt or in the planting season.

Another persistently difficult thing about Native American attitudes for whites to understand had all along been the Native Americans' attitudes toward land, or space. The United States was founded ideologically on many ideas summed up in Locke's philosophy, as transmitted via Thomas Jefferson. Locke's *Second Treatise of Government* (containing a land philosophy that among other things summed up the English land philosophy that colonists had brought to the New World, a land philosophy that incorporated the Biblical injunction that man is to subdue the earth and its land) promoted the ideal that one of the three central aims of governments is to protect the pri-vate property of the individual man. To Locke, Reason itself shows that the preservation of an individual man's right to life, liberty and private property is the sole end and purpose of any legitimate government.[15] The US Declaration of Independence and the US Constitution were framed by men who were for the most part wealthy land-owning whites whose conception of a liberal society had at best evolved to a Lockean sort of conception of the blessings to private land owners afforded by a government that would protect their private property from the depredations of monarchs claiming to have the divine right to do as they wished. Locke had taken part in a Whig conspiracy of wealthy land-owning nobles against a "divine right" English monarch, resulting in a triumph for the rights of the land owners.

Thomas Jefferson, the great Colonial and early American statesman, had throughout his political career the cherished aim of making individual plots of land available for private ownership to ordinary citizens, preferably to farm or otherwise improve, and for a very long time he aspired to draw Indians— whom he considered to be possibly "civilizable"—into this style of life, after federal purchase of tribal lands.[16] He abandoned the plan for the Indians eventually, however, in favor of relocating them on reservations. To Locke, one of Jefferson's most esteemed ideological mentors, as to Jefferson also, it was an inestimably admirable civic virtue to independently "improve" one's private land—to cultivate it and make it produce, to put buildings upon it, to mix one's labor with it (as Locke put it) and thus to make it one's *own*. The whole natural foundation of private ownership of land was to Locke based on this idea of mixing one's own private labor with the land to improve it.[17] The aim of a modern enlightened and just government would be to protect a man's ownership of private land against unjust seizure or unjust or ruinous taxation by a tyrannical monarch.

This was for many educated colonial and early American white men the most progressive and exciting of new ideas, an idea that was being pronounced by the experts to be endorsed by human Reason itself. But long before Locke published these views in 1690, early seventeenth century England had problems of overpopulation, underemployment, and land shortage, and the early Puritan settlers thought that their colonies would solve these problems. The immediate depopulation of Indians due to European-induced diseases such as smallpox, was taken as Divine Providence's endorsement of Puritan settlement. The Indians were seen as evil and devil-worshippers by many Puritans.

There was also at this time a new doctrine in international law, called the law of *vacuum domicilium*, holding that those people who do not use their land must lawfully give way to those who would. This law was thought to be justified by the practices of Biblical patriarchs who moved into places where land lay idle, though there were inhabitants. Indians were not seen as "using" their land because (1) they did not enclose it with fences, (2) they cultivated only a portion of it, using the rest for hunting and fishing, and (3) they moved seasonally to different parts of their lands depending on the abundance of game and fish and the need to cultivate fields. English settlers did not see, or chose not to see, that Indians actually used their land in a rational and systematic way. Hence the settlers established their first settlements by expropriating land, assuming sovereignty and legal/judicial authority over the Indians and their lands, though later on the settlers sometimes gave a nominal purchase price for lands to Indians who (from the settlers' perspective) "pretended" to have title. The settlers' military force, however, was used to settle disputes.

Indians often did not understand the idea of purchase, and thought they were giving usufruct (use) rights to settlers in return for payment, while believing that they ultimately retained tribal title to their lands. The settlers did not understand, or chose not to understand, that Indians considered their land to be sacred and not subject to sale; for the settlers, land was a mere commodity in the burgeoning English agrarian and mercantile capitalism of the early seventeenth century.

For the American Indians, ultimate possession of tribal lands could only be conceived of in the sense of being communal to the tribe as a whole. True, among the planter peoples, the family matron was frequently considered to own the family's farm fields,[18] though she was not entitled personally to buy or sell this land, for title remained with the clan or tribe. For both hunters and planters, ultimate possession of the tribe's lands, its fields or forests or plains, was by the whole people. The lands were hunted or planted and harvested in common. The idea of private possession in the sense of private disposability of all or some of this tribal land would be as strange as private possession and private disposability of the air.[19] For Native Americans, humans must strive to be on respectful and reciprocal terms with the orendas of the trees, the rocks, waters, plants, animals, birds, crops, and the land itself, so that there was a sort of contractual agreement that if the tribe did its part—did not exploit the land, animals, and resources beyond need and always respected the orendas in appropriate rituals—the diverse orendas of the locale would do their part in return and would grant humans sustenance each season. If there is a poor harvest or poor hunting this year, it means that humans have had careless or incorrect attitudes or have performed the rites incorrectly, in which case the orendas refuse to do their part.

I have emphasized earlier that the orenda of each natural creature or entity is its unique life energy (which can also be thought of as its power). We need to keep in mind that this energy is reverently seen as intelligent and aware, though not in a human-like way, and also that each creature or entity is reverently seen as a living Thou, as a subject-of-a-life and hence as a "person" of sorts though not a human person. Such a nonhuman Thou might appear in a dream or vision as a sort of spirit-person or spirit-being conceived as actually present in the dream, and would be thought of as a person though not as having human-like mind or soul.

"Spirit" here is another name for intelligent, aware energy, thought of as being able to manifest itself at times apart from its body or bearer—as, for example, after the death of its body or in someone's dream or vision at a distance from its body. A human being might even metamorphose into a non-human person in a dream without loss of his or her own personhood although his or her spirit has taken on a different body; this is believed to be literally true. We need to remember that each of these "persons" is conceived of as a process rather than as an unchanging substance. The rock, the tree, the buffalo calf, are not seen as having human-like minds or souls but (following Buber's usage) I have been referring to them sometimes as Thous to indicate that they are person-like in having each its own sort of intelligent and aware energy that is used by each to maintain its own being in as close to an optimal form as possible—something like a homeostatic process, in Western terms. We can think of the orendas as person-like, from this perspective, and as each having its own "subjective aim" (as Whitehead puts it) to persist optimally in existence, and therefore as each having a good of its own, which would be to achieve its subjective aim. Furthermore, each orenda or each species of orenda can suffer harm to its subjective aim; that is, (in Western terms) it can have its homeostatic process interrupted or destroyed.

We can think of Native American rituals as a seeking of harmony with the appropriate orendas (e.g., the orendas of the corn, pumpkins, and squash that are to be planted, or the orendas of the buffalo that are about to be hunted) in such a way that you get the feel of what it is like to be a corn plant or a buffalo in order reverently to help it grow or reverently to hunt it effectively, knowing the while that, as the corn and the buffalo feed you now, your body after death will feed them in a sacred cycle. The corn and the buffalo of the past are among your ancestors, just as you will be among the ancestors of future corn and buffalo. The orendas of the corn or buffalo will refuse to do their part in the next harvest or in the next hunt if you are so out of harmony with their needs (their homeostatic processes, or the drive of their species to survive) that you plant or hunt carelessly, ignorantly, or over greedily, as by wasting seeds or killing too many members of a species beyond your need and beyond the species ability to self-replenish. (Hunters felt that buffalo, deer, and other species of game voluntarily sacrificed some of their members to human need on condition that humans help, for example, the "buffalo nation" or species to continue in existence.)

Among both Sioux and Iroquois, the people felt that the orendas must be correctly approached with rituals of petition and gratitude to ensure success, or else they would be angry and cause illness. However, these rituals can also be seen as a sacred way of intensifying one's empathic, respectful, and cooperative awareness of the need for animal and plant species to continue.

Under such widely prevailing views, American Indian men would have found the Lockean view of a man's right to have legal personal ownership and personal disposability of private property, under a rights-protecting government, impious as well as incomprehensible. (I am using the word "men" here to refer to male human beings, because Locke is in fact referring to males in his theory of private ownership, and the settlers did not, at least at first, recognize the role of planter Indian women in land usufruct rights). To the Indians, one did not ultimately possess one's own land, nor did one plan to improve (i.e., to exploit) land beyond some terracing and irrigating in dry areas, stirring up the soil with sharp sticks to receive seeds, clearing trees from time to time to make room for crops, fertilizing land at times with ashes of burned trees and underbrush, and putting up a few dwellings and ritual centers. Even this much "improving" must be done with the appropriate ritualistic spiritual etiquette, to ensure the cooperation of the orendas, and with care not to take from nature more than one needed.

Working the fields was done communally by American Indian women in companionable groups (agriculture being seen as appropriate to women's life-giving powers), and hunting and warring was hard work too and was usually communally done by the men in groups (the taking of life being seen as appropriate to men's powers).

The land philosophy of Native Americans tended to conserve the earth and wildlife, for the earth was seen as sacred and its plants, animals, streams and rocks were seen as our brothers and sisters, or sometimes other relatives. As Salisbury puts it, "The fruit of the Indian experience was an ethos in which relationships in the social, natural and supernatural worlds were defined in terms of reciprocity rather than domination and submission." (p. 10)

The overall ideals of the American Indians were conservational, in contrast to the Judeo-Christian view expressed in the Bible (Genesis 1:36) where God says that man is to have dominion over fish, birds, cattle, and the earth, and is to fill the earth and subdue it. But what was piety to the Christians was in this case impiety to the Indians. Each side seemed crazy, impious and depraved to the other. Black Elk spoke resentfully of white pressures on the Sioux to sell their land: "... only crazy or very foolish men would sell their Mother Earth," he stated (Neihardt, p. 113).

Some Indians did in time assimilate the white way of private property, at the expense of breaking with one of the deepest aspects of their own spiritual and cultural tradition. But many other Indians did not accept this way. The Santee Sioux, Charles Eastman (Ohiyesa), expressed this very eloquently in his 1916 autobiographical work *From the Deep Woods to Civilization*, as does also the Cheyenne author Hyemeyohsts Storm in his 1972 book *Seven Arrows*, recounting the break up of traditional Cheyenne culture.

A particularly important aspect of land, or space, most special to North American Indian cultures was and is the profound reverence for special terrains as sacred because most potent in orenda: places where the orendas manifested themselves most awesomely to humans. Certain lakes, mountains, waterfalls, and other locales, including the sacred burial grounds of the ancestors, were revered as of the greatest central importance to the spiritual and ceremonial life, indeed to the very soul as well as to the existence of one's tribe. This was not because some Indian equivalent of Jesus or Muhammed, as it were, had been born there or lived there, but because the people had themselves, since long ago, recurringly experienced in each generation the awesome powers or orendas of nature in these places.

Finally for this section, let us take a look at the special meaning of the directions in space for many American Indian peoples. There were four cardinal horizontal directions, North, South, West, and East, not determined by compass but by sun positions at solstices. These composed the four sacred directions, hence the number four was sacred. In addition, up (toward the Sun) and down (toward the Earth) were sacred too, and thus so was the number six. And you were yourself the intersect point between these six sacred dimensions of space, containing and reflecting within yourself all of— for example—Wakan Tanka's powers and so this seventh, intersect point was most special, and thus the number seven was very sacred. The sacredness of these special directions or dimensions was widespread among many Indian peoples; its flowering in the Plains Cheyenne people (a hunter people, allied

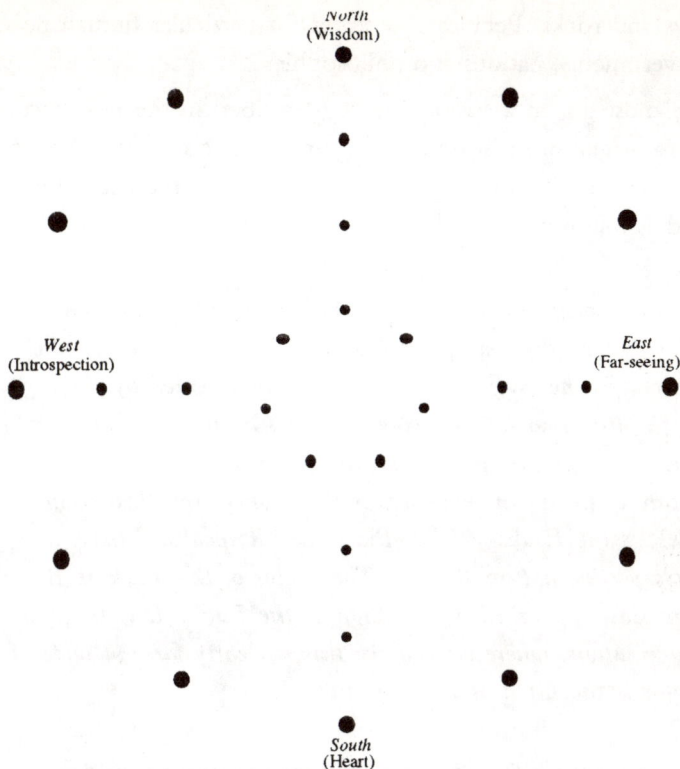

Figure 1: The Medicine Wheel (based on a diagram in Storm's Seven Arrows)

with and in many ways similar to the Sioux) is of particular interest. Let us take a look at the Cheyenne Medicine Wheel Circle (Figure 1) to glimpse the sacred meaning of the directions in space, with the caveat that to fully understand any aspect of the culture of any American Indian people we should need to experience that aspect in its full, lived context.

A Medicine Wheel Circle could be set out on the ground with a pre-scribed number of stones, but it is better understood metaphorically as a philosophy of life and of personality development that is simultaneously a spiritual development. As we shall shortly see, the Medicine Wheel Circle has some interesting things in common with Jung's personality typology and his conception of an ideally developed human consciousness and personality. From childhood, the first teaching among the Cheyenne was of the four directions or powers of the Medicine Wheel; the teacher might construct it of stones or pebbles placed on the ground before the child. Each pebble stood for an entity or creature in nature, such as animals, plants, mountains,

waterways and rocks. Pebbles also stood for particular human persons, religions, governments, nations and philosophies.

One must go on a Vision Quest (described in the next section of this
chapter) to begin one's search to determine one's initial place within the
Medicine Wheel. The four directions or powers of the Medicine Wheel are
conceived as follows:

> *To the North on the Medicine Wheel is found Wisdom. The*
> *color of the Wisdom of the North is White, and its Medicine*
> *Animal is the Buffalo. The South is represented by the Sign of*
> *the Mouse, and its Medicine color is Green. The South is the*
> *place of Innocence and Trust, and for perceiving closely our*
> *nature of heart. In the West is the Sign of the Bear. The*
> *West is the Looks-Within-Place, which speaks of the*
> *Introspective nature of man. The Color of this Place is Black.*
> *The East is marked by the Sign of the Eagle. It is the place of*
> *illumination, where we can see things clearly far and wide. Its*
> *Color is the Gold of the Morning Star.*

> *At birth, each of us is given a particular Beginning Place*
> *within these Four Great Directions on the Medicine Wheel.*
> *This Starting Place gives us our first way of perceiving things,*
> *which will then be our easiest and most natural way*
> *throughout our lives.*

> *But any person who perceives from only one of these Four*
> *Great Directions will remain just a partial man.*

> *There are many people who have two or three of these gifts*
> *[ways of perceiving] but these people still are not whole.*

> *After each of us has learned of our Beginning Gift, our First*
> *Place on the Medicine Wheel, we then must Grow by seeking*
> *Understanding in each of the Four Great ways. Only in this*
> *way can we become Full, capable of Balance and Decision in*
> *what we do. (Storm, 1972, pp. 6–7)*

It would take a person the years of his or her life to grow to include within his or her consciousness all the directions of the Medicine Wheel, and this would be the spiritual goal of one's life, enriching and opening one's consciousness to the major kinds of orendas of the earth, though not in the sense of losing one's identity. The colors associated with the four directions and the specific descriptions of the powers associated with each direction varied somewhat from one American Indian people to another, but the meaningfulness and sacredness of the directions was widespread; for example, the northerly Sioux as well as the south-westerly Keres Pueblo people attached sacred meaning to the directions.

The Medicine Wheel shows a very startling commonality with Carl Jung's personality typology (Jung, *C.W.*, vol. 6) in which he conceives of an individual as being specialized in one of the four functions or orientations of consciousness denoted by thinking, feeling, sensing, and intuiting. (He wasn't completely sure whether this specialization was innate, but thought it might be, though shaped by socialization.) One may acquire in time one or two auxiliary functions. For example, one might start out as an intuiter, then gradually acquire thinking and feeling, and then possibly a little sensation, but only a little, for Jung thought the fourth function must remain always weaker than the others—a notion apparently absent from the Medicine Wheel way. For Jung the ideal wholeness of the growing personality would consist in a gradual learning to, as it were, pick up and put down any orientation or function at will as appropriate to the situation, learning in time not to identify solely with any one of them, as one lives ever more from the Self or the wholeness of what one is. And the Self, for Jung, connects with the powers of nature, for these powers shape the foundations of human instinct, and the human psyche reflects the relations between instinct and nature in archetypal images. The Self is, likewise, the source of our idea of God.

Jung's typology has additionally the two attitudes of introversion and extroversion (making six dimensions), and the Cheyenne seventh point, the intersect between the first six, could be thought of as the Jungian Self … which represents God, too, as the Cheyenne point represents both you and the presence of Wakan Tanka in you. But the Cheyenne Four Directions do not correspond exactly to Jung's four functions of consciousness.

Jung's typology was not influenced by American Indian material on the four directions; he developed his typology early on in his work out of his own experiences with and thinking about people. Perhaps such a fourfold typology is itself archetypal.

DREAM AND VISION

The use of dreams and visions for spiritual guidance via dream contact with the orendas was a core element of the spirituality of a very great many American Indian peoples. As before, I shall single out the Lakota Sioux (a hunter people) and the Iroquois (a planter people) for central discussion to show the particular ways in which dreams and visions were used by these two peoples. Although dreams and visions were generally accorded an important role in both Iroquois life and Lakota Sioux life, we can see amongst the Iroquois tribes—and especially the Seneca tribe of the Genesee Valley (now a part of New York State), who were the leading, most numerous and most powerful tribe of the Iroquois League—a culturally central focus on dreaming as contact with the orenda of one's own inner self, and on dream interpretation. Their dream theory was psychoanalytical in a rudimentary sense. Visions played a lesser role in Iroquois life but had importance in their Vision Quests and in the rise of their prophets. Among the Lakota Sioux, visions seem to have been of greater importance than dreams, though both were seen as significant in the Vision Quest and at other times throughout life, but the Sioux did not focus as much of their time and attention on dream interpretation as a central feature of ongoing life as did the Seneca Iroquois.

Medicine men and women, and male as well as female shamans, existed widely amongst American Indian peoples, and they, as well as lay persons, made special use of dreams and visions.

A medicine person was someone who at one time, perhaps on a Vision Quest, had received specially empowering dreams and/or visions conferring upon him or her an ability to heal certain sorts of physical and psychosomatic disorders, depending on the nature of the dream or vision. In addition, the medicine person received a long training and made use of an extensive pharmacopoeia of medicinal roots and herbs, as well as possibly having later dreams and visions over and above the original empowering dream or vision. However, the medicine person did not have a dream or vision with respect to the ailment of each patient.

A shaman was someone who had been ill and close to death, had wonderfully recovered, and had received from imaged spirit beings in dreams and visions the gift of further special diagnostic dreams and visions lifelong, which the shaman needed in order to discern the particular cause of the illness of patients. In these visions the shaman was visited by a spirit being. Shamans were clairvoyant and could discern the hidden meaning of patients' dreams as well as find the wandering souls of patients who had fallen ill because of a loss of soul—in other words, shamans worked on psychiatric cases. Shamans, too, received special training.

There was some overlap in the types of cases dealt with by medicine persons and shamans, though shamans were particularly adept at finding and bringing back lost and wandering souls, having come close to losing their own in a one-time near fatal illness. A shaman could also make use of medicine herbs and roots. Both shamans and medicine persons might in addition make use of the practice of sucking out a small foreign object that had supposedly gotten into the patient's body causing illness; these procedures involved some sleight-of-hand on the part of the practitioner.

At puberty a young American Indian male or female would go alone into the woods or up onto a hilltop to fast, meditate, and experience dreams or visions during which a particular image of a guardian spirit (that is, of a particular type of orenda) came to confer special powers upon the youth or maiden. The powers varied in type and potency; the youth's or maiden's subsequent life or career would be shaped by such a dream or vision in which power to heal, or to hunt, or to predict the future, or to be successful in war, might be granted. This procedure, often called in English the Vision Quest, was of the greatest spiritual as well as practical importance to many Indian peoples and took place in many tribes across the continent. On the practical level, you found your unique career in life on the basis of your Vision Quest. (This role was often but not always within the powers thought to be accorded to persons of your sex; some males and females, however, received a spiritual mission usually thought appropriate to the role of the opposite sex, and it was socially permissible to live out this cross-sex role.)[20]

On the spiritual level, your role in life was found by means of the transmission to you of some of the special orenda of a natural entity or creature, so that your career in life was also your bond with the sacred natural world around you. You truly received a calling, and the calling was seen as a bond between you and sacred nature. Your practical role in life henceforth was suffused with sacred meaning; as has been mentioned before, there was no sharp distinction between the sacred and the secular.

Lame Deer tells us of his Vision Quest at the age of sixteen. He sat, scared, alone, and naked, on a hilltop in a hole dug into the hill; he was to stay alone for four days and nights with no food or water, wrapped only in a quilt his grandmother had made for his *hanblechia*, his Vision Quest. His family's sacred peace pipe, handed down over generations and filled now with red willow bark, had been left with him by the medicine man who had brought him here. The smoke from the pipe would go up to the spirit world, and power would come back down through the pipe to the smoker. The medicine man had also left a gourd containing forty small squares of flesh that his grandmother had sacrificed from the surface of her arm, to help young Lame Deer pray and to make him strong.

Lame Deer wanted to receive training to become a medicine man, a traditional Sioux healer, but such training would do no good unless he had a power-conferring vision now during this Vision Quest. Before starting out he had, along with four medicine men, physically and spiritually purified himself in the sweat lodge made of bent willow branches covered with blankets, in which water was poured on red-hot stones making steam that filled his lungs and made his skin tingle.

Alone in the night, Lame Deer hears the sounds of the creatures, the winds and trees, all around him. He sings and prays and cries, as is fitting for one seeking a vision. And at length:

> Slowly I perceived that a voice was trying to tell me something. It was a bird cry, but I tell you, I began to understand some of it ... I heard a human voice too, strange and high-pitched, a voice which could not come from an ordinary living being. All at once I was way up there with the birds. The hill with the vision pit was way above everything. I could look down even on the stars, and the moon was close to my left side ... A voice said, "You are sacrificing yourself here to be a medicine man. In time you will be one. You will teach other medicine men. We are the fowl people, the winged ones, the eagles and the owls. We are a nation and you shall be our brother ... You will learn about herbs and roots, and you will heal people. You will ask for nothing in return. A man's life is short. Make yours a worthy one". (Lame Deer pp. 5–6)

Then Lame Deer loses all sense of time, and eventually sees his dead great-grandfather who wants him to take his name. Then he feels power surge through him, filling him, and he knows for sure he will become a medicine man. He loses his sense of time once again, until his own medicine man/guide comes for him and shakes his shoulder, taking him down the hill now to give him food and water and to interpret Lame Deer's visions for him. Lame Deer is now no longer a boy; he has become a man.

In Lame Deer's description of his Vision Quest, we can trace the combination of various experiences. Purification in the sweat lodge and smoking the sacred pipe were preliminaries to the Vision Quest. We can also see how this boy's vocation to be was felt by him to be a sacred calling, not to be used to serve any personal ambition for wealth but to make him worthy of possessing life and to make him of service to his community. There would be no separation between the sacred and the secular in Lame Deer's life work. That this was the Vision Quest of an earlier twentieth century Lakota Sioux is a moving testimony to the persistence of American Indian traditional culture, for the rites and experiences Lame Deer describes are a profound and enduring part of the traditional culture of his people. Lame Deer, as a demoralized young man in a primarily white culture, lost his bearing later on and fell away from his calling and sowed "wild oats" for some seasons, but in later life returned to his vocation and became revered as a holy man among his people.

Visions among the Lakota Sioux could come later in life too, as well as even to a young child. It was essential to relate one's vision to the medicine persons for interpretation, and it was often deemed of utmost importance to enact the vision, using the help of others, to confer benefit upon the community who came to watch the enactment. One might fall ill otherwise, and the community might also lose an important communication from Wakan Tanka, the Great Mysterious.

I have, as indicated before, the impression that visions occupied for the Lakota Sioux the central place that dreams occupied for the Iroquois, though both peoples valued both, as did many Indian peoples. Nomadic hunter-gatherers, frequently on the move, had less time for dream recollection and dream work than did settled village dwellers such as the planter Iroquois who tried constantly to remember and interpret dreams, with the help of medicine persons and shamans. It is in part because ordinary people could and did have dreams or visions that were important to the community, and because anyone might thereby become a prophet (male or female), that Indian spiritual doctrine was more flexible than doctrinaire and showed variations from group to group of even within the same tribe. Perhaps this also accounts in part for the special understanding some American Indian peoples received from Quakers, for the Quakers, not unlike the Sioux and the Iroquois, believed that the spiritual power they revered could speak directly in any human soul including the souls of Indians.

Something was mentioned earlier about the expected traditional roles of men and women among Native American peoples. Among many of these peoples, other than the Iroquois, women were excluded from men's ceremonies. This was because women's powers were thought to center around bringing new life into the world, and men's powers to center around terminating life in hunting or war. The powers of one sex would, it was believed, interfere with those of the other sex in sacred ceremonies and also at other times; for example, before a hunting expedition, when among some peoples couples must not make love lest the life-giving menstrual power of the woman interfere with the hunting or warring power of the man. The women had their separate ceremonials. Especially in the planter cultures the women's ceremonials had and were seen as having a deeply important and central connection for the economy, for women were the agriculturalists.

The Iroquois, more than any other American Indian people, seemed relatively unconcerned about conflicting male and female powers. Amongst them, men and women participated as complementary powers in the calendar of the major Iroquois annual ceremonials, including the centrally important Midwinter Rite, with women taking the lead in some, and each sex participating exclusively in some components of these ceremonials.

In a great many Indian cultures women as well as men could be medicine persons and shamans and prophets, though among hunter peoples the medicine women often had to be older and no longer fertile and might be restricted to a pediatric practice. This restriction, however, was not the case among the Oglala Sioux. As we shall see, Iroquois women played a major role in the interpretation of the dream life of their people, which in turn was a deeply important aspect of Iroquois spirituality, ethics and health.

Let us consider in closer detail how the Iroquois thought and felt about dreams, and how they dealt with them, keeping in mind that the member tribes of the Iroquois League had each their own variants of dream theory and practice. Knowledge of Iroquois dream theory and practice during the years 1634 to the early 1700s was recorded in the reports of Jesuit missionaries.[21] Their accounts are permeated with the assumption that Iroquois dream practice constituted devil worship and was the work of the devil.

The Iroquois thought that dreams express wishes or fear. A more accessible level of the self, responsive to the daily events of one's life, could and did express its wishes or fears, elicited by everyday events, in one's dreams;

these wishes and fears could be easily read off from the dreams by the dreamer and others. A deeper and more hidden level of the self had deep, inborn wishes of its own that could indirectly express themselves in dreams in a way harder to discern and that might require the assistance of a clairvoyant shaman to discover by means of seeing into the innermost depths of one's soul.

If the wishes of either the more manifest level or the deeper level of the self were not understood and provided for, one could fall seriously ill either mentally or physically or both; hence an ill person's dreams would be taken serious note of by the patient and his or her family members. If the ill dreamer's wishes or fears were manifest in the dream, for example, as a wish expressed in a dream of talking with a certain person, or of acquiring a certain desired object, or of eating a certain food—or as a fear expressed in a dream of suffering a torture or of experiencing a particular kind of death—an effort would be made to provide the patient with the actual fulfilment of the wish, or else to assist the patient with a symbolic enactment of the fear in order to ward off a real disaster of that sort.

If the patient dreamed of certain sorts of animals or birds or other particular sorts of symbols, a medicine person from the appropriate medicine society would be sent for. For example, if the patient dreamed of a bear, a Bear Medicine Society practitioner would be sent for; if the patient dreamed of a false face, a False Face Medicine Society practitioner would be sent for. Different medicine societies specialized in different sorts of physical and psychosomatic illnesses. If the patient's dream was hard to interpret, a clairvoyant shaman would be sent for, to see—for a fee—into the secret hidden depths of the patient's soul, there to read the dreamer's deepest-level wishes. Free association was used in the process of discerning these—but it was free association on the part of the shaman, not the patient. This hidden wish when discerned might and often did involve the cooperation of the whole community in gratifying it—if, for example, the patient's deep wish was for the *andacwandet* rite that required "fornications and adulteries" (in Jesuit terms) between many couples who were not married to each other, or several dozen other feasts, dances, or rites involving participation by the community.

Some prophetic dreams, such as those in which recognized spirit beings (i.e., orendas imaged as spirit beings) or gods or goddesses appeared, might contain matters of importance to the whole community and must be shared with the whole community, lest community disaster come about. An example would be a dream in which a god or spirit being warned of a future enemy attack. Precautions and rites were then enacted by the community on the basis of such a dream, and the dreamer would be honored as a prophet or prophetess.

The most important Iroquois ceremonial was the nine-day Midwinter Rite, in late January or early February, in which, in addition to thanksgiving to the Pantheon, feasting, dancing, and singing, it was more centrally everyone's spiritual obligation to be cleansed and healed, spiritually and physically. During the day before the Midwinter Rite began, people publicly confessed the wrongs they had done during the past year. Persons with physical illnesses were attended during the Rite days by men and women members of the various medicine societies, as appropriate to the specialties of these medicine societies, for the administration of physical healing therapies.

As a major part of the Rite, it was the obligation of each member of each family to report to the family matron (i.e., the grandmother) his or her important dreams from the previous year, especially dreams involving hostility or resentment toward other members of the family or of the community. (Iroquois people lived in stable small stockaded villages of longhouses.) The family matrons had, in addition, to keep a close eye upon the dreaming of family members not only during the past year but for many years back, in order to be aware of how family members were feeling, both emotionally and physically.

During the Midwinter Rite and also at other times during the year people went from house to house in their village of up to fifty longhouses, demanding that other people guess their dreams on the basis of riddles. This was probably in honor of the Good Twin, who was thought to send messages via dreams about his will and about what is needed to preserve one's life, health, and good fortune. An example: someone, on the basis of a dream, says: "What I desire and what I am seeking is that which bears a lake within itself," meaning by this a pumpkin or a calabash.[22]

Although it was the responsibility of the family matron to keep track of family members' dreaming, during the year everyone tried their hand at dream interpretation of one another's dreams and of their own dreams too, so important did this seem to people as a way to ensure mental and physical health, and attention was paid on an ongoing basis to wishes and fears expressed in dreams. A shaman might be called in on difficult cases at any time of the year.

There are some important ethical implications in relation to the Iroquois practice at the Midwinter Rite of confessing wrongs and of telling your hostile dreams and enacting them symbolically in order to be cleansed of the past year's accumulation of anger toward family members and community members. There was in this at least an attempt to assume personal responsibility for your own "shadow side," in Jungian terms; that is, the aspects of your personality that don't meet approved ethical ideals toward family and community. The Iroquois cultural ideals called for love and brotherhood in these contexts. In assuming responsibility for (owning up to and feeling the need to rectify) your own hostile feelings towards others, there is, consequently, a diminished tendency to project your own bad and hostile tendencies upon others, that is, to see the other person as the bad one. The bad impulses within the individual were, on the other hand, permitted expression by the Iroquois, but in symbolic rather than literal enactment, and the individual was then forgiven the bad impulses by family and community. The Iroquois individual did not go on to feel lastingly guilty and sinful, but nor did he or she identify only with his or her good impulses.

PERSONAL POSTSCRIPT ON DREAMS

In considering in some detail the emphasis on dream sharing among the Iroquois, which seems to have exceeded what went on among other Indian peoples, although dreams were almost universally important to most of them, I have asked myself what would be the effect of all this on people's awareness of one another? It has been my own custom for many years to share some dreams with friends, and at one time I was a member of a sequence of small dream groups that met to share and discuss dreams over a period of some years. Also, during that time I made an effort to express in waking behavior something of my dreams' content where this did not seem to be harmful to self or others. For example, if I dreamed of talking with someone, I would actually do it (so would the Iroquois); if I dreamed of eating a certain food, I would actually eat it (so would the Iroquois); if I dreamed of singing, I would sing (so would the Iroquois), I painted pictures and wrote poems based on dream content. I cooked recipes that I quite literally had dreamed up. I got a new kitten after my former cat died, as a dream indicated my former cat wished me to do this, I walked a different route to work as I did in a dream, I made a porcelain figure of a dream motif, and many other things of this sort.

I knew that many American Indian dreamers had done this lifelong, and I was very curious to see what it would be like to do this on a sustained basis; others in the little dream-sharing groups were doing this too. As well as talking about our dreams and their meaning, we also showed each other a great many of the things we made on the basis of our dreams. Some people painted pictures with very moving spiritual content, others painted pictures of beautiful fashion designs. One woman embroidered a handsome dream motif on her jacket. Others constructed three-dimensional objects—some of indescribable oddness!—seen in dreams. One man composed and played for us a guitar song he had dreamed. Another man had us enact the roles of characters who appeared in one of his important dreams.

I undertook all the above with the intentional plan of emulating American Indian practice. Now, I cannot claim that these experiences gave me the sort of experience an Iroquois would have, for in Iroquois culture everyone did this sort of thing and the whole milieu was saturated with it, whereas in my culture few people do it regularly, so that I did not have anything like total immersion in a dream-saturated culture. Nevertheless, my experiences did give me at least some idea of what it is like to experience oneself and others in a dream-sharing and dream-enacting mini-milieu. Therefore I base the following speculations about the possible effect on the Iroquois of their dream-drenched lives, in which dream-sharing and dream objectifications were the norm, on my admittedly limited experience as related above.

It seems to me that the Iroquois would have become acquainted with self and with one another on a level very different from that experienced by most Westerners. When you and I share our dreams with one another, I get to know you as a Thou and myself as a Thou, as the subject-of-a-life, and vice versa. I see how the world seems to you. I learn what you want and don't want and what you fear. You are not to me only a vague projection screen onto which I mostly just project my fantasies about what you are like, often involving the hope of using you as a mere tool to my own purposes. Instead, I see you as being as real as myself, without my having much temptation to idealize you unduly or to see you as worse than you are. I see you as various and fluid and changing rather than as remaining just what you were years ago, and perhaps I am less tempted to try to prevent you from growing in order to try to reify you as a totally predictable object—I see you as process, not as static unchanging thing. And you have similar experiences of me, and each of us of ourselves.

All this is bound to affect our quality of life, making us feel more tolerant, more inwardly equal, more spontaneous, more playful, more serious, more spiritual, more individually creative in the arts and crafts. We are all artists, in a dream-centered life, rather than relegating art only to specialists. And we all have spiritual insights too, rather than relegating spiritual insight only to specialists. Now, Iroquois society was all of this.

Perhaps you and I would be more oriented toward inner harmony than toward technological achievement, if our lives were dream-centered; this was true of Native Americans. And perhaps our growing tolerance towards our own personality process as well as toward each other's personality process would lead to a relatively harmonious and stable and enduring community life—also true of Native Americans. Let us note that the Iroquois League still exists today, having been in continuous existence since possibly AD 1450 or so, which certainly demonstrates community stability and endurance despite all that has happened. The Iroquois still attend closely to their dreams.

And, let it be noted, the Iroquois culture had also a high proficiency in physical and emotional healing arts that was equal to or beyond the level of what Europeans had attained, they had a sound economy and lively trade, they had a strong national defense, they had a government on the basis of the consent of the governed before western countries did, they had excellent social security and welfare arrangements for all persons, and they had a highly evolved and highly effective league of nations which was more cohesive and effective and enduring than anything perhaps as yet achieved by the West.

And now I picture the eight-year-old me standing before me reminding me of how once, long ago, she climbed up one sad day into the Grandfather tree in the woods behind Orenda Drive, and how in her inwardly torn and unhappy state she became aware of a chorus of powers all around her, of the energy-powers of the living animals, plants, stones, and soil, that healed her and warmed her with the knowledge that she was not alone and unaided. She was welcomed that day into the strong and beautiful network and family of all things. I feel as if, in writing this chapter, I have been trying to understand what this was all about, in order to explain it to her and to the me of today, too, and in order to tell her that what happened to her that day in the woods made a hauntingly beautiful and strong basis for an adult spirituality that helps to give my present life some meaning, warmth, and joy.

Nothing I had read or learned or heard about before my studies of Native American spiritual concepts really helped to "get a fix on" my early experience, or to ripen it into a form that helps to satisfy my adult spiritual yearnings and to point a direction for further spiritual growth. The expression "to get a fix on" something, as currently used in American slang, originally came, I understand, from a sailor's way of locating himself by sighting certain stars, fixing his position by this means. I have located myself spiritually by means of my Native American studies.

And was the fix on these my stars rewarding? Oh yes! I have come home to a world where I am sister to animals, plants, rocks, and water, and daughter of the earth Mother and sun Father, where I am never without this family to love, revere, and relate to. Sometimes I feel as if everything visibly sparkles and shimmers with energy and life, so that nothing I look at is ordinary, and I feel a child's sense of wonder and excitement just in walking down the street. But a hard, hard price comes with this, for I anguish now more than ever about the pollution and environmental destruction of my earth-home and earth-family—which I now understand to be also my spiritual home and family. I want to save my earth-home and earth-family.

Have I become an Indian spiritually? I don't think so. Of course it isn't possible for me literally to be an Indian, but in addition my consciousness has further roots and allegiances, and my Native American studies are for me neither dogma nor destination. But I shall be forever grateful to these studies for incalculably valuable help along my way.

What have my Indian-inspired dream enactments done for my life, in the long run? More than I am able to express. The dream enactments have made everyday life rich in creativity, meaning, and self-generated activity. In my living room right now I can see seven of my dream-inspired watercolor paintings on the walls, each one holding for me a connection with the myths of meaningfulness that my dreams have woven around the events of my life. For example, one painting shows a silvery sky-woman whose hands hold a necklace of many-colored jewels; she speaks to me of many of my dreams in which jewels fell from the sky and I, and everybody else, ran to gather them, and there were enough jewels for all of us. I find it wonderful that I painted this picture some years before I read of the Iroquois myth in which the Sky Woman brings gifts to the earth!

The kitten I adopted as a result of the dream in which my previous cat who died wanted me to take a new cat into my life is now a big, beautiful calico adult feline whom I call Princess Orenda after the Indian dream princess of some other dreams of mine. This calico kitty has one side of her face black and the other side cream, and so her face teaches me, spiritually, the reconciliation of the dualisms of life, the good and bad of it all. Also I have become an increasingly enthusiastic cook as a result of trying my dream recipes, and I have been led into all manner of new explorations of life and its materials in the process of my dream enactments.

I have very few ordinary days, and no boring days, and I don't have to have a lot of wealth or land or possessions to feel inwardly rich and joyous. The poet Dylan Thomas writes of the force that through the green fuse drives the flower (by "green fuse" he means the stem of the plant); dreaming is my green fuse through which the forces of the cosmos as they affect my unconscious mind flow into my waking consciousness and help me to flower again and again. My own personal orenda is nourished by dreaming, and as a result knows itself as one of the active creators in the world rather than as mere helpless, passive pawn. And this is a kind of strength. Troubles in life will always abound, and no spiritual orientation or spiritual practice can avert the tragic personal and collective *forces majeures* of human existence. But what contact I have managed to make with the American Indian spiritual way has helped my strength to increase.

ACKNOWLEDGMENTS

My thanks to Jan Elliott, of Cherokee descent, for her many illuminating discussions with me of Native American belief and consciousness, and for alerting me to some important Native American writers.

My thanks to Richard Haynes for pointing out to me a great many important references, and for many illuminating discussions with me of philosophical issues connected with Native American belief. I wish also to acknowledge some very helpful correspondence with Stephen Lewandowski as well as his invaluable help in providing some important references. Donald Broadribb provided invaluable many-sided insights and editorial assistance. My appreciation also goes to the many students in my Social Issues and Political Thought courses, whose stimulating discussion helped many issues in this essay to come more clearly in focus.

REFERENCES

Paula Gunn Allen, *The Sacred Hoop*, Beacon Press, Boston, 1986.

Richard Ashcraft, *Locke's Two Treatises of Government*, Allen & Unwin, London, 1987.

Ian Barbour, *Myths, Models, and Paradigms*, Harper & Row, New York, 1976. (First published in 1974.)

Annie L. Booth and Harvey L. Jacob, "Ties That Bind: Native American Beliefs As a Foundation For Environmental Consciousness," in *Environmental Ethics*, Spring 1990, vol. 12, no. 1, pp. 17–43.

William Brandon, *The Last Americans*, McGraw Hill, New York, 1974.

Joseph Epes Brown, *The Sacred Pipe*, as told by Black Elk, Penguin, New York, 1981. (First published in 1953.)

Joseph Epes Brown, *The Spiritual Legacy of the American Indian*, Crossroad, New York, 1982.

William Cronon, *Changes In the Land*, Hill & Wang, New York, 1983.

Vine Deloria, *God is Red*, Dell, New York, 1973.

Vine Deloria, *The Metaphysics of Modern Existence*, Harper & Row, New York, 1979.

R. Demallie and D. Parks, *Sioux Indian Religion*, University of Oklahoma Press, Norman (Oklahoma), 1987.

Charles Eastman (Ohiyesa), *Indian Boyhood*, McClure, New York, 1902.

William N. Fenton (ed.), *Parker on the Iroquois*, Syracuse University Press, Syracuse, 1968.

William N. Fenton, "This Island, the World On the Turtle's Back," in *Journal of American Folklore*, 75, 1962, pp. 283–300.

Henri Frankfort and H.A. Frankfort, et al, *The Intellectual Adventure of Ancient Man,* University of Chicago, Chicago, 1977. (First published in 1946.)

A. Irving Hallowell, "Ojibwa Ontology, Behavior, and World View," in Stanley Diamond (ed.), *Culture in History: Essays in Honor of Paul Radin*, Columbia University Press, New York, 1960.

Eugene Hargrove, "Anglo-American Land Use Attitudes," in *Environmental Ethics*, Summer 1980, vol. 2, pp. 121–48.

J.N.B. Hewitt, "A Constitutional League of Peace In the Stone Age of America: The League of the Iroquois and Its Constitution," in Elisabeth Tooker (ed.), *An Iroquois Source Book*, vol. 1, Garland Publishing, New York, 1985. (First published in 1920.)

J.N.B. Hewitt, "Orenda and a Definition of Religion," in *Selected Papers From the American Anthropologist, 1888–1920*, F. DeLaguana (ed.), Row Peterson, Evanston, 1966. (First published in 1902.)

Marilyn Holly, "Land Philosophies," in *Agriculture and Human Values*, vol. VIII, no. 1, Winter 1990, pp. 44–8.

Beverley Hungry Wolf, *The Ways of My Grandmothers*, Quill, New York, 1980.

R. Douglas Hurt, *Indian Agriculture in America*, University Press of Kansas, Lawrence, Kansas, 1987.

C.G. Jung, *Psychological Types*, cited in the text as C.G. Jung, *C.W.*, vol. 6. Original, 1921.

John (Fire) Lame Deer, *Lame Deer Seeker of Visions*, R. Erdoes (ed.), Washington Square, New York, 1972.

John Locke, *Two Treatises of Government*, P. Laslett (ed.), Cambridge University Press, Cambridge, 1960. (First published in 1690.)

C.B. Macpherson, *The Political Theory of Possessive Individualism*, Oxford University Press, Oxford, 1988. (First published in 1962.)

James Montmarquet, *The Idea of Agrarianism*, University of Idaho Press, Moscow, Idaho, 1989.

Lewis H. Morgan, *League of the Ho-De-No-Saunee or Iroquois*, University of Idaho Press, New Haven, Human Relations Area Files, 1954. (First published in 1851.)

John Neihardt, *Black Elk Speaks*, as told by Black Elk, Washington Square, New York, 1959. (First published in 1932.)

Merrill D. Peterson, *Thomas Jefferson and the New Nation*, Oxford University Press, New York, 1970.

Maria N. Powers, *Oglala Women*, University of Chicago Press, Chicago, 1986.

Paul Radin, *Primitive Man As Philosopher*, Dover, New York, 1957. (First published in 1927.)

Neal Salisbury, *Manitou and Providence: Indians, Europeans, and the Making of New England, 1500–1643*, Oxford University Press, New York, 1982.

Gary Smith, "Utah's Rock Art," in *National Geographic*, vol. 157, no. 1, Jan. 1980, pp. 97–117.

Frank G. Speck, *Midwinter Rites Of the Cayuga Long House*, University of Pennsylvania Press, Philadelphia, 1949.

Kathleen Squadrito, "Locke's View of Dominion," in *Environmental Ethics*, vol. 1, no. 3, Pall 1979, pp. 255–62.

Sara Henry Stites, *Economics Of the Iroquois*, AMS Press edition, 1978. (First published as the author's thesis, Bryn Mawr, 1904.)

Hyemeyohsts Storm, *Seven Arrows*, Ballantyne, New York, 1972.

Leo Strauss, *Natural Right And History*, University of Chicago Press, Chicago, 1953.

Elisabeth Tooker (ed.), *An Iroquois Source Book*, vols. 1–3, 1986, Garland Publishing, New York, 1986.

Elisabeth Tooker, *The Iroquois Ceremonial of Midwinter*, Syracuse University Press, Syracuse, 1970.

Elisabeth Tooker (ed.), *Native American Spirituality of the Eastern Woodlands*, Paulist Press, New York, 1979.

James Tully, *A Discourse On Property*, Cambridge University Press, Cambridge, 1980.

Hamilton A. Tylor, *Pueblo God and Myths*, University of Oklahoma Press, Norman, Oklahoma, 1964.

Ruth Underhill, *Red Man's Religion*, University of Chicago Press, Chicago, 1965.

Ruth Underhill, *Red Man's America*, University of Chicago Press, Chicago, 1953.

Christopher Vecsey, *Imagine Ourselves Richly*, Crossroad, New York, 1988.

James R. Walker, *Lakota Belief and Ritual*, Elaine Jahner and Raymond Demallie (eds.), University of Nebraska Press, Lincoln, Nebraska, 1980.

James R. Walker, *Lakota Myth*, Elaine Jahner (ed.), University of Nebraska Press, Lincoln, Nebraska, 1983.

Anthony Wallace, *The Death and Rebirth of the Seneca*, Knopf, New York, 1970.

Anthony Wallace, "Origins Of the Longhouse Religion," in Bruce Trigger (ed.), *Handbook of North American Indians, Northeast*, vol. 15, Smithsonian Institution, Washington, D.C., 1978.

Benjamin Whorf, *Language, Thought, And Reality*, MIT Press, Cambridge, Mass., 1956.

Neal Wood, *John Locke And Agrarian Capitalism*, University of California Press, Berkeley, 1984.

NOTES

1. Originally the Iroquois League was composed of five peoples with five different Iroquoian dialects: Mohawk, Oneida, Onondaga, Cayuga, and Seneca. Eventually a sixth people, the Tuscarora, joined the League.

2. It is important to keep in mind that not everything that has orenda would be seen as sacred or holy from a Western viewpoint. Among the Sioux, a white man was called "wakan" (a possessor of orenda) at first, not because he was seen as holy in a Western sense, but because he was seen as having unfamiliar power.

3. Allen, 1986; Deloria, 1979; Highwater, 1981.

4. Adapted from Hewitt, 1902, pp. 676–78. Some of this material is also given in Tooker, 1979.

5. Hallowell's analysis of "manitou," the Algonquian word for orenda, Hallowell, 1960, is seminal in establishing the latter claim.

6. Frankfort, 1946, ch. 1; see also Barbour, 1974.

7. This reading incorporates the discerning analysis of "spirit" by Native American writer Paul Gunn Allen, as well as the important considerations

raised by anthropologist A. Irving Hallowell, and Maria N. Powers (p. 37).

8. The philosopher Whitehead points out in *The Concept of Nature* (1920) that Western languages in general heavily reflect the influence of Aristotelian categories of substance and accidents (i.e., things and their properties) on Western thought, and are unsuited to denote processes. This renders Western languages, as well as Western thinking inappropriate for discussing modern physics' ideas about energy, which is a process. Benjamin Whorf found in his study of south-west Indian people that where English commonly uses substantives (nouns) these native Indian languages use gerunds denoting process, for these Indian people think of what in Western thought are considered to be objects as actually processes. One would speak of "a treeing here" rather than "a tree here." He remarks that it is easier for these American Indians than for other Americans to grasp the energy ideas of modern physics.

9. Underhill, 1965, pp. 226–34; Vecsey, 1988, ch. 5.

10. In the Hewitt/Gibson version of the myth, although a struggle is depicted between the twins, it is not over the question of whose the creation is. Instead, the dispute is provoked by the fact that the Evil Twin menaces everything the Good Twin creates, by means of a counter-creation.

11. In the Sioux Creation story, good and evil wakan energies, or orendas, are present early on and are conceived as metaphysically reconciled *from the start* as being aspects of the one unified system Wakan Tanka, and as "moments" in a sort of cosmic balance that uses from the start both constructive and destructive energies in the balancing process. This is very different from the profound dualism of good and evil that pervades Iroquois thought.

12. Fenton, 1962, p. 285; Underhill, 1965, pp. 37–8 and 175.

13. Parker, in Fenton, 1968, pp. 61–3 and 126.

14. Allen, 1986; Deloria, 1973; Highwater, 1981.

15. Ashcraft, 1987; Hargrove, 1980; Holly, 1990; Macpherson, 1962; Montmarquet, 1989; Squadrito, 1979; Strauss, 1953; Tully, 1980; Wood, 1984.

16. Peterson, 1970, pp. 116–18 and elsewhere.

17. Locke, *Second Treatise*, ch. V, sections 27 and 30.

18. Cronon, 1983, p. 62; Hewitt, 1920, p. 533; Underhill, 1953, p. 90; Wallace, 1970, p. 24.

19. Hurt, 1987, ch. V.

20. Allen, 1986, pp. 245–61; Hungry Wolf, 1980, pp. 62–71.

21. See Tooker, 1970, pp. 83–105.

22. Wallace, 1970, p. 30; also quoted in Stites, 1904.

CHAPTER SIX

THE SACRED LAND

AUSTRALIAN ABORIGINAL

RELIGION

NORMA LYONS

I have marked my body with meaning.
The bright ochre, the white clay, and I
am become again a spirit being
who moves to the deep rhythm
of the earth breathing.[1]

Norma Lyons (unpublished)

THE PEOPLE

Australia is an island continent, the driest and most ancient land. Her flora and fauna have adapted to low rainfall. Likewise her native people, whatever their origin (for the theory of migration from South East Asia 40,000 or over 100,000 years ago is not proven), have made adaptation and are a race. Within Australia there are contrasting regions. The dramatic wet and dry seasons of the tropical north, the temperate southern woodlands and grassy tablelands, forests, mountain ranges and coastal plains, and the vast sands of the central deserts which now dominate, are separated by distances unconquerable by foot travelers. Tribal Australian Aborigines pursued a hunting and gathering lifestyle which necessitated the minimum of material possessions: men carried a few spears and other hunting weapons; women carried wooden or bark containers for food gathering, digging sticks, grinding stones, as well as any child too young to walk. They interacted with their environment in a way that was to their benefit, but which also ensured their continuing support by that land. For example, the open park-like landscape of much of the fertile regions of the continent has been enhanced by millennia of controlled burnings which encouraged regrowth of shrubs and grasses required for the flourishing of game.

Their nomadic lifestyle centered on the places, ceremonies and foods recorded in the myths of their ancestral Totemic Beings. All tribes, whether from the arid desert regions or the fertile sections of the coast, emphasized the spiritual sphere in a complex religious system which can be classified as animistic. Everywhere, the religion and way of life it ensured were instituted by mythic Totemic Beings, ancestral animal/men spirits. Although regional rituals and their mythic component differed, all rituals centered on either the renewal of the natural world or the rebirth of the individual man through his initiation into the secret-sacred symbolism of the religious life (Berndt, *Religion*, p. 4).

Because of this basic uniformity and the continent-wide concept of The Dreaming—a spiritual realm which maintains unity with the material world in the present—it is possible to study Australian Aboriginal religion by taking examples from different tribes. The religious values which emerge are relevant today not only to the Aboriginal people who seek to restore their spiritual well-being through relationship with their past and with their land, but also to those cultures which are bringing about their own destruction because of their neglect of a fundamental relationship with the natural world.

Religious beliefs and rituals shaped the lives of the original Australians and bound them to a region of land handed on by their ancestors along with the myths of its beginnings. The land was known intimately because such knowledge was necessary for survival. Tribal land was within a physical boundary, such as a ridge or watercourse or the extent of habitation by a particular species of plant or animal. It was mapped in a myth which traced the primal path of nomadic wanderings by the Totemic Ancestors. Many of these myths were lost along with the land and tribes to whom they belonged because tribal living was no longer possible for the majority of Aborigines once Australia was settled by Europeans. Government policies to assimilate Aborigines into "white" Australia failed.

Aborigines, which includes part-Aborigines, now endeavor to recapture the basis of their culture in its values of nonmaterialism, communal decision-making, and the conservative use of natural resources. Many Aboriginal people seek to restore what they can salvage of the religious beliefs of their ancestors and to maintain sacred sites entrusted to them. Their values contrast with those of the capitalistic society of Australia which upholds the individual accumulation of wealth, government by an elected few, and the exploitative "selling-off" of land, both in actual freehold sale to foreign absentees, and in mineral and timber acquisition which involves the destruction of rainforests and Aboriginal sacred sites. Because of such incompatibilities which disadvantage the Aboriginal minority, some have formed a separate Aboriginal nation within their own country. They do not, however, seek to reject the benefits of civilization or modern advances in human rights, such as the equality of women, which did not exist in Aboriginal religion, as it did not in other organized religions. They simply aim to restore the dignity of their race through a return to nonexploitative relationships between people and with the land. The spiritual strength to be gained in a sacred relationship with the environment applies universally.

Although tribal life in those traditional areas which have been developed by white settlement is now a rare thing, in many central and northern areas Aborigines continue to be in touch with tribal land and religion. Most of the religious beliefs and practices I will refer to were recorded from tribal situations early in this century, and now only a handful of people are living in a completely traditional nomadic way, making the continued practice of their religion in its purity impossible. Even so, I will speak of Aboriginal Religion in the present tense, in keeping with the timelessness it emphasizes and the truths it continues to present.

Relationship with the land

Aboriginal religion both binds the Australian Aborigines to their land and expresses a pre-existing experience of unity with that land. This sacred relationship to the land permeates every aspect of traditional life and remains the basis of values for many modern Aborigines. In the nomadic life of adaptation to an often sparse environment, tribal Aborigines seek an order and purpose which is expressed in their rites and beliefs. The religious life of the tribe is the means of controlling the natural and social environment—so much so that control through technological advance is not considered. The main aim in their religious activity is to ensure the continued fertility of nature through aiding the release of life essence, or spirit, into the land. The keeping of the religion also ensures the survival of unity within society, both in stipulating conservative use of food sources and in allocating interdependent social and religious roles. For the individual the emotions of awe and power, guilt and worth, insignificance and everlastingness—such emotions as form the basis of individual religious experience—are experienced within the context of a complex religion which verifies such feelings.

The bond between the land and the people, as individuals and as society, is illuminated in The Dreaming, the central concept behind all aspects of tribal life. The mythology of The Dreaming, often called the Dreamtime when it is being used in the sense of the creative period at the beginning of time, revolves around the equality of humans, plants and animals, and of the actual land in the form of its physical features—rocky outcrops, watercourses, sand plains and so on. A form of totemism gives expression in social structure to this equality and interdependence. In identifying as a brother or sister to a species of plant or animal, or to a food, such as honey, or to a natural phenomenon, such as clouds, or even to a part of the human body, the individual is simultaneously raised and reduced in stature. One is by being a member of any society. But in this case one is literally a child of the universe so that the individual religious dimension is potentially immense, overcoming human limitation at the same time as negating the importance of the individual. Totemism in Aboriginal religion is not just a social bond. It ties the individual to the religious dimension of The Dreaming through naming her/him as an eternal life essence of the land.

The Dreaming is a present and an eternal spiritual dimension, as well as the time of creation in the past. In The Dreaming the land was first shaped and the forms of life and ways of life came into being. Relationships and institutions necessary to maintain life and culture were established by the actions of Totemic Beings who were both the spiritual prototype and the actual ancestor of each totem. They were animal/plant/food/natural phenomena but also took human form. The relationship of these Beings to the land is the primary content of the myths of The Dreaming. They transformed the landscape as they established "tracks" through the hunting and wandering in the lifestyle which they instituted. They established the rites and ceremonies to be performed for maintenance of the land itself, rites which also serve to perpetuate the culture.

Often the Totemic Beings then metamorphosed into parts of the landscape. Features such as rock formations, caves, old trees, or waterholes have mythic explanation and retain their sacred quality. Some of the creative Beings merged into the sky or the sea. Sacred sites are those most important in the mythic history, and the concentrated power they hold makes them taboo, that is avoidance areas or areas to be entered with respect. However, the whole earth is sacred in that the Totemic Beings (or Ancestral Beings or Spirit Beings) continue to inhabit the land animistically. The Aboriginal relates in her/his religion to the whole of creation via that personal creator, the totem, of whom she/he is representative. The Dreaming is past time when "the animals and birds were all blackfellows." It is also a dimension of the present, enabling an Aboriginal to say, for example, "I am Honey-Ant" or "I am Crow," when asked "What is your Dreaming?"

The totem of an individual names him or her as an actual part of the land which she/he inhabits. Aborigines living tribally do not usually venture beyond that area or track across the land which they know, and which their ancestors knew, from their nomadic living and from their keeping of the myths and rituals of The Dreaming which mark that land with meaning. The physical features *are* the Totemic Beings, and in many instances there are sacred sites marked literally with rock paintings, sometimes carvings, believed to have been actually first drawn by these Totemic Beings. The drawings depict the mythic time of creation, and it is the religious duty of the appropriate individual of each generation to ensure the drawings are respected and kept freshly painted. The Dreaming thus enshrines a map of the tribal land which it accounts for. Myth and ritual and art and social expectations are all expressions of The Dreaming of the tribe. The religious beliefs and ritual life of the Aborigines who inhabit an area of land can be equated with "title deeds," as can the etched and polished wood or stone *churinga* which the men make and keep as a secret-sacred power source which embodies the Totemic Being. Initiated men are recognized by the tribe as having custody of that tribe's land along with its inseparable Dreaming, of which they may gain more and more knowledge in their religious lifetime.

To the Aborigine, land "ownership" is opposed to the Western concept of division of the land for occupation by a family who holds it only through force of wealth. An Aborigine is, rather, "owned" by the land, having been created by the Totemic Being who formed that territory in order to ensure its continuation through religious rites and practices. An Aborigine can say "My country knows me." The areas of neighboring tribes often overlap, giving occasion for meetings and for limited trade of valued goods, such as ochres for pigments, and mutual help in times of disaster. Several related family groups might separately roam the same area, meeting more frequently. Grievances might give rise to occasional warring clashes at boundaries, as within them, especially with those tribes of more volatile nature, such as those of the Kimberleys in the north of Western Australia. But the ownership of land is not an issue for warfare, whereas the observance of religious Law, which includes social obligations, can be enforced with the death penalty. The absence of major war results from a religious relationship to the land which negates its alienation and, additionally, was more possible because Australia was isolated from invaders until late in the eighteenth century. This absence of war was a determining factor in the stability of Aboriginal culture and technology.

The "primitive" nature of Aboriginal technology was held by colonizers to be evidence of the inferiority of the race and only in recent years has it been recognized that the culture remained static for 40,000 years and more because of the completeness of its adaptation to its environment. This adaptation incorporated the development of a complex religious system. This was not recognized in early studies of the Aboriginal people because they were usually biased ethnocentrically and, in addition, most early anthropologists distorted their findings in efforts to prove one or other fashionable theory of culture or religion. Social evolution was the theory in vogue in the nineteenth century when anthropologists first turned their attention to Australian Aborigines. Aboriginal culture was presented as a living museum piece which showed European prehistory. There was also the missionary zeal of the invading Christians who saw as an abomination any beliefs not paralleling the Judeo-Christian worship of one transcendent god. Many anthropologists, as well as missionaries, sought to elicit from the natives evidence of beliefs in a transcendent being who could be approximated to the Christian God. Questioning and hearing was thus particularly distorted in the area of religion. The assumption of all outsiders was that the changes brought with "civilization" could only benefit the Aborigines, being—as they had been proved by "science"—"savages."[2]

Truly objective study was, in any case, impossible in the nineteenth century whilst there was a vested interest in viewing the Aboriginal race as inferior. So long as the original inhabitants of the land were judged less than human, the land could be allocated to white use without a qualm of conscience by the British colonizers. First European contacts had learnt little of Aboriginal beliefs and misinterpreted their naked lifestyle and lack of possessions as being without culture. Reports were of a "miserable" people, or of primitive pagans without religion. Prejudice against dark skin reinforced the superior attitudes of white colonizers who construed that Aboriginal land use was nonexistent and therefore the land could be claimed as "unoccupied" territory, as had been done in the Americas. The one treaty which purported to have bargained 100,000 acres of land from the Aborigines in exchange for a few trade goods (the treaty of Batman at the site of Melbourne in 1835) was meaningless both in white law, which saw the Crown as owner, and in Aboriginal law which saw land as inalienable. It was convenient for the colonizers to know nothing of the beliefs of the Aborigines but to impose on them Christianity and a place in the lowest stratum of society.

Aborigines had never experienced being without a home until this disaster came with colonization. They had no concept that land could be treated as private property. For them the Christian belief that in paradise "the meek shall inherit the earth" had always been a reality. But they were separated from their tribal lands by power of the gun fired at their attempts to drive away the white intruders. Consequently, easy destruction of the Aboriginal race began once their relationship with the land of their Dreaming, the land which was the evidence of their religious beliefs, was broken by white settlement. With the fencing of private property for townships, grazing, and agriculture, Aboriginal religious expression was no longer possible. Traditional relationship with tribal land—its waterholes, rocks, trees, plants, and animals—and with the Totemic Beings who established the land and are its life, was broken. Totemic identity was meaningless in strange territory. Relationships with each other were based on this primary relationship, and all relationships required expression in ritual form at appropriate sacred places, but these rites and ceremonies could not take place. The traditional economy was not possible without that particular land allocated to them in The Dreaming and maintained for them by their ancestors. Tea, sugar and alcohol did not give sustenance. Where destruction of whole tribes, and in Tasmania of a whole race, was not accomplished directly by murder and mistreatment, or indirectly through introduced diseases, it followed upon removal of their religion and culture in the taking away of their land.

Land rights protests are not new. At the turn of the century an old Aboriginal woman caused the residents of Perth discomfort through her determination to follow the tracks of her ancestors and her Dreaming. She would regularly go from the native camp at Claisebrook, Perth, on the river's edge to a swamp at the other side of the city where traditional foods could be gathered. In doing so she broke pickets off fences and trampled gardens, regardless of such nuisance to the householders. She would also bemuse the townspeople by standing at the gate of the new Government House to shout abuse in her outrage that it had been built over the grave of her mother. Such traditional sites around Perth were dictated in myth by the primordial acts of the Wagyl, a monstrous black and winged spirit of the storm, a form of the Rainbow Serpent. Today, descendants of the local tribe attempt legal measures to protect those sacred sites which are threatened by further development and in similar fashion shout at locked gates for attention to their plight.

THE DREAMING

The realm of The Dreaming is so named by the Aborigines themselves. They include in this the dreamworld we enter in sleep. At night the land is experienced as a featureless place, as it was in The Dreaming before the dawn of creation. Also it is night when spirits of the land and of the dead most lurk, mingling with the individual spirit of the dreamer who leaves her/his body in sleep to enter the spirit world of The Dreaming. The inclusion of the individual dreamworld, a unifying functioning of the psyche, into The Dreaming, the collective myths, emphasizes the total agreement of the tribal religion with the psychic make-up of the individual Aborigine.

The prime meaning to the people whose myths these are, is the connection they express with their environment. It has been suggested that Aboriginal myths project collective psychic material onto matter, whereas European mythology has been a projection into space (Gardner, pp. 11–12). That analysis is from a European point of view, a dualistic standpoint which separates the mind from the body and the spiritual from the physical world. Aboriginal experience is monistic—spirit and matter are one. Additionally, the extent to which projection is involved is problematic. Marie Louise von Franz summarizes Jung's analysis of collective projection as a merging of the unconscious and the outer world, and tribal consciousness as merging with the external world so that the boundary of the unconscious is blurred (von Franz, p. 7). The Dreaming expresses the synthesis of all that is inner/unconscious—the symbolic world—with all that is experienced in the natural world. The ego is the link between the inner world of the unconscious and the outer environment, and Western individuals experience their ego as being inner, but for Aborigines the ego is part inner, part outer—just as their unconscious is both inner and outer. There is a unifying balance which does not require further adaptation through ego-separation and consciousness. A cultural over-valuation of consciousness and ego-separation is involved when this is called "archaic" and linked with "primitives" and children. The collective psyche of Aborigines cannot therefore be said to be "projected onto matter." Rather, it is expressed in the concept of the unity of spirit and matter. The Dreaming myths bring into Aboriginal consciousness their relationship of unity with their total environment.

We think of religion as relating to the spiritual sphere. Aboriginal religion also claims a relationship with the spiritual sphere, but, because of the unity of matter and spirit in the Aboriginal world view and the overlapping in the psyche of inner and outer worlds, it is equally a relationship to the physical world. That spirits may at times be said to operate independently from the animals, humans, landforms, heavenly bodies, or natural phenomena which they normally inhabit animistically, does not indicate a separation of spirit and matter. The earth and its spirits are the one world for the Aborigines.

The myths of The Dreaming are myths, simultaneously, of the land and the people, telling of the formation and control of both through the actions of the eternal spirits, the ancestral Totemic Beings. These Beings are pre-existent to creation, except where a Spirit Being is said to have created the Totemic Beings. In all cases, both nature and culture are formed with the first mythic wanderings, and the Western opposition between nature and culture does not become developed. Originally the Spirit Beings or Totemic Beings slumbered within the featureless land. Time began with the creative period, "the time before morning," in which these Beings established the landscape and spread life, including human life because in The Dreaming humans are not distinguished from their totem. The Spirits returned to slumber in the transformed earth, or sometimes in the sky or sea, usually at specific places, such as hills, rocks, or stars. By physically having become part of the land as they formed it, Spirits and totems never leave the land. It has their spirit, making it sacred.

The following myth is typical of The Dreaming across Australia in that it is a saga of travel from place to place with little plot other than the institution of rituals and the metamorphosis of the mythic beings into the landscape. I give a summary only of the beginning section of the myth of Jarapiri the snake/man which begins at Winbaraku, a hill in the McDowell Ranges of central Australia, taken from the full account given by Charles Mountford in *Winbaraku and the Myth of Jarapiri* which he recorded in 1960. Mountford gives photographic evidence of the specific hills, rocks, trees, gullies, and other physical features of which the myth tells. There is an abundance of other books which present Aboriginal mythology in a form edited for the interest of non-Aborigines. These do not always convey the essential theme of connectedness with the specific features of a track through the land, a "dreaming track." In Westernized versions the routine activities of wandering, making camp, establishing rituals, hunting and preparing certain foods in certain ways are omitted so that only a dramatic storyline is presented. Frequently the myths are reduced to fairy-tales and fables of little weight, stories such as "Why the crow is black." The connectedness of land and people through The Dreaming in the past and in the present may be missed by non-Aborigines who themselves lack such connection in their own myths. For Aborigines the land is the eternal book which teaches its myth to succeeding generations. And the land is a shrine built with the very bodies of the ancestral Totemic Beings who entrust men to maintain their holy place. Initiated men, only, learn and pass on the secret rituals.

In referring to the sacred stories as "myths" my intention is to emphasize their funtion as the basis of a people's culture. Myths of The Dreaming give account of creation, but creation is not limited to the past. Left in the land is a continuing source of life, a life essence, or spirit, which is now dependent upon humanity for its release. Life continues to be made available by the Totemic Beings at their sacred places, but only because men keep the Law, the religion, through ritual activities which release life essence to maintain the natural world. In this myth the life essence is called *kurunba*.

The story of Jarapiri

The story of Jarapiri begins with the creation of the twin-peaked hill Winbaraku and goes on to describe a track going north for several hundred kilometers, made through the activities of the snake/man and his companion Totemic Beings. This myth concerns the totemic origins of two tribes, the Ngalia and the Walbiri, whose boundaries coincide at this place. Both tribes share a portion of the "line of songs" of Winbaraku. Both may tell the complete story, but each has only the right to chant the songs and carry out the rituals which are located within their territory. It is through the ritual chanting of song that the sacred stories are transmitted. As in all Aboriginal creation myths, the earth was originally a featureless plain. This story differs slightly in that the landscape arising from primordial activity did not do so until after the death of the Totemic Beings and their absorption into the earth. The hill of Winbaraku and all its life, humans included, was created by Jarapiri, leader of the snakes, with assistance from other snake, animal, and insect Totemic Beings.

Jukalpi, the hare-wallaby/man, was one of the first to arise from eternal slumbering. He made a camp on an open flat southeast of the hill and walked to the north where he made a dancing ground on which to perform his ceremonies. A corkwood tree marks his camp; corkwoods, eucalypts, and desert oaks mark his path northward; and a desert oak indicates the spot at which he rested after his ceremonies. Several "songs"—chanted simple statements—tell of these tasks. For example:

Jukalpi still hopping with his feet wide apart, goes to the camp.

and

Jukalpi sits quietly in his camp.

Malatji, the dingo/man, simultaneously rose out of the plain and made a camp and ceremonial ground at locations marked by particular trees. But he has only one song:

Malatji is a piebald dog with a white head.

After these arose Mamu-boijunda, a barking-spider/man who called loudly: "Booh, Booh, Booh," and with each call a new totemic ancestor arose through the ground. The wood-gall insects, Wanbanbiri; various species of snake, including the venomous Jarapiri; and scorpions and centipedes came into being. All species were created in this way. Songs summarize the creative activities of Mamu-boijunda. He is said to have sunk into the ground at a spot where arose a mound of spherical boulders and shale which is in spider-leg-like formation. The Wanbanbiri, totemic ancestors of the wood-gall insects/people, introduced a fire-dance using long-woven eucalypt branch torches. These fire-torches can be seen metamorphosed into rock-formations, whilst ashes from the torches are become pavements of white quartz pebbles. A bloodwood tree nearby marks their ceremonial place.

At the base of one peak of Winbaraku is the camp of the blind snake Jarapiri Bomba, one of the many snake species created by the barking spider's barks. Jarapiri Bomba shares his ceremonial ground with that of the Muluguna snake who shared his camp. This is on the northwest side of the hill. The Latalpa snake and the Wala-wala death-adder/women are said to be the daughters or wives of Jarapiri Bomba. In a cave they are now white stones which project from the ceiling. There are also boulders which were the mothers of these snake/women. One large spherical boulder is Jarapiri Bomba himself. This is dangerous to go near unless a ritual throwing of sand as a warning to the blind snake of someone approaching is made, otherwise blindness will strike the intruders.

The highest peak of Winbaraku is the sacred site of Jarapiri, leader of all snakes, and his wife Jambali. Jambali is also a species of tree from which the

Aborigines of the tribe there obtain spear shafts. A rocky outcrop to the east of the peak is the sons of Jarapiri. Although Jarapiri did not introduce ceremonies of his own, he watched those of the other snake and insect species. Where he stood he is metamorphosed into a tall ghost gum tree. His body is also metamorphosed in stone at the summit of Winbaraku. This stone is the increase site for this species of snake, that is, the place at which rituals are performed to ensure the abundance of these snakes. Not only the peak but the whole hill of Winbaraku is sacred. It is taboo to camping and is treated with respect because of the various totemic ancestors who imbue its rocks and bushes with the kurunba of their totem. The sites of metamorphosis are the increase sites through which renewal of the species is ensured by ritual activity of the men of that totem. The myth is passed down orally in a series of songs which accompany the rituals. One is of Jarapiri's wife Jambali, the spear tree, and is simply her name chanted continuously. And one is of his friend Malatji, the dingo. Some of the other snakes and insects also have their campsites and paths marking the hill, and songs of their activities in The Dreaming.

A little dramatic action now enters the myth. Two women who sought Jarapiri for a husband surprised him and attempted to take him away to their camp. However, Jarapiri coiled up, refusing to leave Winbaraku. The path of the women is a slight valley, a pillar of rock is the women themselves, and small caves at the base of the pillar are the vulvae of the women.

Jarapiri did not wish to leave Winbaraku but was eventually forced to by his sons. The totemic ancestors who left Winbaraku with Jarapiri, going north, were Jukalpi, the hare-wallaby, Malatji, the dingo, the Wanbanbiri, the wood-gall insects, and the Latalpa and Wala-Wala snake/women. Jarapiri, was still coiled to resist capture by the two ardent women as he was finally dragged away from his hill by his sons. He managed to take his wife with him as he passed the camp, a creek bed marking the place where they were dragged. Songs tell this part of the story simply:

The totemic people traveled northward in a straight line.

and

The young snakes dragged Jarapiri and his wife along the ground.

The summary given of the myth thus far is merely of the beginning of the mythic track which has songs and rituals related to the landscape all along the way. The Dreaming track continues with further camps and ceremonies. There is a spring called Jambali which was the home of the snake/tree/woman Jambali and her child. The route then follows gullies and crosses clay pans and vast sand drifts. One place is Mara, a totemic place for dingoes, where Malatji, the ancestral dingo, slept beneath a bush. Here the group of totemic ancestors split into two parties and meet up again at a waterhole where several days of ceremonies are held. At one point Jarapiri escapes underground to Ngama to the east, but he emerges to rejoin the others. Where the track reaches the limit of the land known by the two tribes who share this myth, it is said that the ancestral travelers continued northward into unknown land and nothing further is known of them.

A sketch of the complete myth has been given following the fuller summary of its beginning in an endeavor to show how myth is tied to tribal territory both on the large scale and in its minute details of the land. The religious arts—song, dance, painting—evolve from the myth, as do the sacred ceremonies which bring the tribe together at regular intervals, and the social relationships between the totems.

The Wunambal story

The creation myth of the Wunambal and related tribes in the Kimberley in the tropical northwest of Western Australia, while demonstrating some regional differences, carries the same implication of man's role in maintaining the world through keeping the rituals and way of life of The Dreaming. Once again it is the life essence of the land which must be manipulated through religious activity. Ungud, a python who is identified with the rainbow and the earth and water, and Walanganda, the eaglehawk and lord of the heavens, together dream the Totemic Beings in the primal night. The Wandjinas, spirits of the monsoon clouds, and all the plants and animals were thus first dreamt by these dual creators who then painted their images and imbued the paintings with spirit so that they could roam the land. About a dozen named Wandjinas feature in many cave painting sites. They are in human form, with large eyes but no mouth, and robed and haloed. (This dress has raised theories of shipwrecked Arabic or Asian sailors.)

It was the Wandjinas who formed the landscape in their wanderings, before laying down onto the wet rocks to die, leaving behind their painted image. To the Wunambal people to whom this myth belongs, the Wandjinas are the controllers of lightning and rain. These cloud spirits must be both placated, to prevent destructive cyclonic gales, and their creative aspect wooed for the fertilizing monsoon rains. Man's part in maintaining the cycle of life is to retouch the paintings each year to maintain the life of the Wandjina spirits and to ensure their reappearance as rain clouds. Ungud and Walanganda are examples of Spirit Beings. Walanganda became the Milky Way after his creative dreaming and painting. Ungud, a form of the Rainbow Serpent, sank into all deep waterholes.[3]

In the Wunambal myth, Spirit Beings created the Totemic Beings. The distinction is made by Swain and others that Totemic Beings are benign and sympathetic, less dangerous than the more powerful Spirit Beings (Swain, p. 56). Also, unlike Totemic Beings, Spirit Beings are most often a composite of several powerful natural phenomena, such as the Rainbow Serpent which is symbolic jointly of the dangerously powerful storm spirit, relied upon for its life-giving rain, and another danger in the Aboriginal world, the often deadly, yet edible, snake. Ungud, the Rainbow Serpent, is of the earth and Walanganda, "he there above," is of the sky, combining the soaringly majestic eaglehawk and the Milky Way. These are great spirits, more encompassing and powerful than the Totemic Beings, as is shown in the creation myth. This does not mean that the Spirit Beings are transcendent of the physical world. The Rainbow Serpent, in varying forms across Australia, is in particular often mistakenly said to be a transcendent spirit. Maddock calls it a bridge between totemic and transcendental powers (Maddock, p. 85). This might be the case were there a transcendent world according to Aboriginal thought, but there is not. The spiritual world of The Dreaming is united with the physical world.

Creation is on a grander scale in the tropical Kimberley myth of the Wunambal than in the desert myth of Jarapiri; but in the desert it is the minute creatures and the snakes which are evidence of the continuing life essence in the land, while in the Kimberley it is the dramatic northern monsoon which annually renews nature. Rain may not fall for years at a time in the inland deserts. In the Jarapiri myth it is Jarapiri, the venomous snake, who takes precedence over the other snakes and insects. He is referred to as a Totemic Being, rather than a Spirit Being, because of acting directly in creating the landscape with others. Also he is identified with a specific creature and is not a symbolic combination as are Ungud and Walanganda.

In both places, desert and tropical, Aborigines identify with the life essence of the natural world in myths of The Dreaming. The natural and the spiritual world, from both of which humanity is inseparable, are united.

TOTEMS AND INCREASE

"Totem" is the word used by anthropologists to translate from Aboriginal languages the complex Aboriginal system by which identification with the natural world is made. Whatever meaning the word held for the North American Indian tribe from whose language it was taken, in English it was used in a simple sense of "mark" or "badge" and does not adequately convey its function for Aborigines. They themselves tried to convey more in saying it was their "friend."

An individual is linked to a totemic ancestor through being born into one of two totemic moieties, or four or more sections or subsections, which make up the tribe. The totem is similar to a family name and is usually allocated patrilineally. As well as determining potential marriage partners to be of the opposing moiety, as against totemic relations who are sexually forbidden, the totem allocates social and religious obligations. There is also a personal, or conception, totem decided before birth, usually by the mother. Occasionally the two totems coincide, so that in effect that person has only one totem. Frequently the sexes have opposing totem names. The moiety totem has the weight of social and ritual obligation.

A totem may be any part of nature, from the sun or rain to an insect, a rock, or a part of the human body, such as teeth or the sexual organs. They are grouped in related oppositions. Black cockatoo may be opposed to white cockatoo, for example, and crow or black lizard may be linked with black cockatoo on the principle of like coloring. Or animals or insects associated with water may be grouped as subsections opposed to those who inhabit dry places. Whatever a totem, it is a part of the natural world, and of some positive or negative value in tribal life. The totem spirit, Totemic Being, is recognized as the spirit which animates both the people of that totem and the creatures and things of that totem, much as a hologram exists in any portion of its material. The human is identified as of the same being as her/his totem, and, as we have seen in the section on The Dreaming, the identification extends via the Totemic Being to the land itself.

Totems are given when a woman first knows she is pregnant, often with quickening. Customs vary, but in some way the locality of that happening determines the totem. Maybe a totemic place nearby, or a particular totem may synchronistically make its presence known. The totem may be the food the woman has eaten, food from that place. Dreams may be involved, telling the father or mother or a tribal elder of the totemic spirit of the child. There is said to be transferal of a Spirit Child from a totemic depot nearby where it has been dormant with other spirits of that totem, those of humans as well as the totemic animals or things. These Spirit Children are equivalents of the life essence, *kurunba*, in the myth of Jarapiri. The physical facts of conception resulting from sexual intercourse are known, but are not seen to relate to spiritual origin. From the Kimberley in Western Australia is recorded an account of the means by which babies, that is, spirit children, enter the world, having been sent down in the rain:

> *Our fathers found us in the form of fish or turtles but the Wandjina is our real father. He put us in the water from the sky. We now call our name from our earthly father, but we came from heaven through the water by dreams.*
>
> (Crawford, p. 34)

The individual spirit is seen to be united to the physical world prior to birth, during life, and after death. In dreams the spirit wanders in The Dreaming, the spiritual dimension of the material world. At death the spirit leaves the person's body but remains in the real world, often at its totemic place. The world, thus full of spirits, is experienced as a dangerous place. The Australia of subsistence wanderers is in any case a place of danger. Although poisonous snakes and spiders are the only deadly creatures, the climatic hazards are life-threatening.

The myths of the Wilmen (or Wheelman) tribe of southern Western Australia revolve around primordial acts of the birds, and other creatures in transformation into the land. For example, Cubine, the Mopoke (boobook owl) chased Norn, the Black Snake, into the sea at Cape Riche where now the snake lies as the reef and the bird is a rock which stands guard against it. As with other tribes, there are, additionally, stories which serve to reiterate the Law, the moral values which bond person to person. The Wilmen have many such fables, such as that which concerns the opposing attitudes, to the sharing of food, of the wedge-tailed eagle and the crow. They say that during a long, dry summer when many waterholes had dried up, a pair of Waalich (Wedge-tailed Eagle) found permanent water but decided to keep it for themselves. When asked by a pair of Wording (Crow) for water, they showed them only a muddied and fast-drying place. The Waalich themselves continued in secret to enjoy fresh water, but were soon found out by the cunning Crows. The Crows then secretly shared the good water whilst giving pretense of drinking at the muddied pool. When the Waalich realized this, there was fighting between eagles and crows which still continues. For the Wilmen, the eagles violated the law of absolute honesty and equality in sharing food and water. Although the crows are well-known by them as greedy, lazy, and cunning, this behavior in contrast is not immoral because food may be obtained by any possible means, but food must always be shared, which law was broken by the Waalich, not the Wording.

The Wilmen arrange their totems in a rare example of a hierarchy. Totems are ranked thus:

1. Birds and creatures that fly
2. Animals and creatures that climb
3. Animals and creatures that jump or run
4. Flying insects
5. Creeping insects
6. Lizards
7. Snakes
8. Trees
9. Grasses

In the Wilmen Dreaming the sun is said to be the land of the dead, a paradise of warmth and plenty which contrasts with the environment of the tribe, the district inland and eastward of Albany, which is cold and wet for over half the year, with cold nights throughout. It appears from the hierarchy of totems, from which moieties took a balanced division, that those life forms less earthbound are given most value, in keeping with the tribe's myth of the sun as an ideal land. Nevertheless the totems remain of the natural world, as is the sun (Crawford, p. 34).

Some measure of control of the environment is sought by religious means, but the overall goal of religious activity is to maintain the natural world. The fertilizing life essence of the earth is maintained through ritual, and its dangers averted. But, as Gould stresses, the rituals are more an expression of man's harmony with nature than manipulation (Gould, p. 128).

Such is the overlap of magic, sorcery, and religion in Aboriginal ritual, that the boundaries are often not delineable. *Magic* is defined as direct control of the environment, emphasizing procedures, with relative disregard of any spirits involved. *Sorcery* is the manipulation of the world through influence upon the spirits who control it. *Religion*, supreme in this hierarchy, involves a relationship of obligation to the spirits. But religion can only be defined in this way within a dualistic definition of the world in which matter and spirit exist separately. Aboriginal religion is monistic, the animistic spirits being unified with the material world they enliven. It is a religion because it concerns the human relationship to the spiritual, but magic and sorcery are involved because of the unity of spirit and matter. The rituals of increase which maintain the fertility of the totemic species or the regularity of totemic phenomena can be delegated to magic and sorcery only if religion is defined in dualistic terms.

Totems are the link uniting the spiritual and natural aspects of the world, as these aspects are united in The Dreaming. Men imitate the totemic rituals instituted by the Totemic Beings. Totems have been called a symbolic link to the spiritual world in The Dreaming, but the link is also to the material world, as C. and R. Berndt emphasize (Berndt, *First Australians*, p. 294). The rituals which maintain the totemic life essence are symbolic of humanity's role as a spiritual being to relate to the environment in a sacred way.

Myths of The Dreaming are continually re-enacted in dance and song and ritual and sacred art in the ceremonial life of the tribe. Ceremonies are related either to initiation of the men (not only at puberty but ongoing for those men who desire further access into the wealth of secret religious knowledge held by their elders), or to the maintenance or increase of the natural world, including humanity, often referred to as fertility rites. Initiation may, in fact, be seen as a form of increase ceremony in that it maintains the supply of men, custodians of the fertility of the land. Increase is dealt with in this section, and initiation and the secret-sacred will follow in the section on sacred knowledge.

Increase rites

Increase rites range from elaborate costumed and choreographed ceremonies taking much time and cooperation to prepare and perform, to simple private practices such as the rubbing of yams over the body in order to increase vitality. (Here the massage and positive thinking may enhance the effect.) The Totemic Being is evoked in the chanting of the myth, that is the poem or song which tells the story of the relevant part of The Dreaming, as illustrated in the myth of Jarapiri. The men performing the ritual are vehicles for the life-giving power of the mythic beings who continue to influence the material world. They are "following up The Dreaming," making the myth come alive in the present. In their role as the Totemic Beings of the totems, men are responsible for the increase of the totem species through performance of the rituals.

The myth of Jarapiri includes increase sites for all the totemic creatures and animals it features. For example, Ngama, a rocky outcrop which is known as the home of Malatji the dingo. Near Ngama is a large boulder which is the metamorphosed body of the leader of the dingo pack and so has *kurunba*, life essence, of dingoes, the native dogs.

> About the middle of winter, the tribesmen perform a ceremony at this rock to increase the supply of wild dogs. An old Aboriginal man, taking a large stone and chanting the appropriate songs, breaks off fragments of the flaking stone. This action releases some of the kurunba contained in the rock, which, flying into air "like a mist" (as the Aborigines describe it), fertilizes the female dogs, thereby ensuring a plentiful supply of young dingoes during the August pupping season. (Mountford, p. 64)

Stone churingas are also used in increase rituals. Worms records an Aranda man telling of this ritual.

> My father gathered in the cup of his hand a little powder by scraping the small stone tjuringa [=churinga] named Djuning andera (kangaroo fat tjuringa) and he sprinkled the powder about. We fatten the kangaroos not with grain, like cattle, but by sprinkling this powder. In this way the kangaroos become fat when the weather grows cooler. (Worms, p. 13)

Blood may be let from the arm vein and ritually drained over sacred stones which are Totemic Beings, so giving them new life. The effects of such remineralization of the earth may be seen by the outsider as merely symbolic. However, it is because they are also symbolic of the Aboriginal religious attitude to the earth and its creatures as being sacred—to be treated with respect in order to be maintained—that such rituals "work."

Central to sacred ceremonies are the churinga, the sacred boards or stones which are said to contain the Totemic Beings and which are marked symbolically with records of their mythic track in The Dreaming. Ritual chanting of the myth accompanies the creation of churinga for initiates—they are said to have been "sung into," that is, made sacred by containing the myth of the Totemic Being. Similar singing rituals accompany other artistic preparation for ceremonial rituals, such as body painting and decoration. The churinga boards are ochred and greased, and stones are similarly polished, to ensure the continuing life essence. The red ochre is seen as blood, and the grease as body fat, thus emphasizing the human "life essence" shared by the Totemic Being, inanimate things included. This regular care inadvertently serves to preserve the churinga boards in protecting them from damage by weather or termite attack.

Often Totemic Beings are also represented in rock paintings, as with the Wandjinas. The renewal of these paintings prior to the onset of the wet season in the summer months is the responsibility of the custodian of the particular site, a man of that totemic place. The ritual repainting is with the same red, white, and yellow ochres, and charcoal, and the lines of the figures are carefully retouched. The painter himself becomes the creative Wandjina Spirit Being. He chants:

I paint myself anew, so that the rain can come.

On completion he blows a mouthful of water onto the painting, symbolizing the bringing of the rains by the monsoon spirits, the Wandjina. When the humidity in the caves increases with the arrival of the rains, the paint takes up moisture and comes glowingly "alive," with the fresh colors glistening. The painter has ritually given new life to the Wandjinas, as they, in the rain, bring life to the land.

The totemic relationship can be seen to be reciprocal. It symbolizes the unity between humans and the natural world, and humans and the spiritual world. Ritual actions unite religious beliefs with the environment in imitation of the sacred activities of The Dreaming in a spiritually charged world. Sacred ritual continues creation in a united world.

SACRED KNOWLEDGE

Sacred knowledge is only to be attained by men. Aboriginal tribal society is blatantly sexist. The importance of being male is, in the northern and central regions, emphasized by the "ceremonial unveiling" of a boy's masculinity in circumcision. In large areas of southern Australia, circumcision has been unknown, and is said to have spread from the north, leading to theories of its origin from foreign seafarers. Where it is not practiced, there are other ritual mutilations to mark initiation, such as tooth removal, nosepiercing, or decorative scarring of the body. These can also be either preparatory or further stages of initiation in circumcision. In some regions there is added mutilation of the penis a few years later by subincision, a practice unknown elsewhere in the world. Blood-letting from this subincision scar or from a vein in the arm is common in rituals and ceremonies. The symbolism of initiation is predominantly that in submitting to pain, even risking death under the primitive conditions of the operations, the boy gives recognition to the primacy of the social solidarity of the tribe over individual suffering. The essential purpose of undergoing these painful initiations as social bonding is also the interpretation of the role favored by Gould over the many symbolic interpretations which have been made (Gould, p. 118). The knowledge of the Totemic Beings which begins to unfold for the initiate has a similar theme of bonding: he is not only a part of the society of men with social obligations, but he is representative of part of the natural world and has responsibility toward the whole land of the tribe for its continued fertility.

Initiation is purposely made frightening by the men. Women and children know only the basic story of the relevant mythic events of the Totemic Beings who are said to have established the rites, for example, in killing and restoring to life the ancestral men or animals. As boys they are encouraged to believe in such stories literally, and nothing of the rituals is told to women and boys. Boys are taken into the company of men at an age around puberty, which can be as young as seven, depending on local custom. Women take part in the ceremony only in a minor and preliminary way, driving the boys away, wailing or chanting, or being driven away by the men. Like the boys themselves, the women are fearful, knowing that there is a real risk of death in the possibility of excessive bleeding or infection. The boys do not show this terror in their behavior or they would fail their society. Initiation rituals may take weeks or even months to complete. When circumcision is involved, there are several weeks of seclusion until the wound heals. Following are longer periods of isolation in the bush during which time they perfect their hunting skills and knowledge of vital water holes and the other sacred places which are mapped in the myths. Through hunting they repay the debt owed to religious teachers who are occupied with sacred tasks and may also be too old to hunt. The newly initiated may be sent on missions of introduction to neighboring related groups where there are potential wives. The physical marks of initiation or additional adornments of manhood, such as string belt, or headband, or hair bun, announce that he is now a keeper of the Law, that is, of social obligation and sacred myth and ritual. The marks of manhood are signs of power and as such are a sexual attraction.

Men undertake, on behalf of the women also, the sacred rituals which maintain the land. Lesser rituals mark the passage to womanhood, and women may take part on the outskirts of men's ceremonies in singing and dancing, with bodies daubed and painted to a lesser degree. Women may scar their bodies, too, or show grief by the removal of a finger joint. Their own rituals, for example, in love magic, are kept secret from men. The absolute control over sacred rituals by men is not because men are seen as intrinsically more sacred than women, but that men assume more importance and power. As in the histories of the vast majority of organized religions, religious power perpetuates the power of men over women and children. Men gain social privilege and influence through advancing in their religious career. In Aboriginal society it is the only "career" possible. A man's talent, whether in music, art, medicine, or organization, is expressed within religious ritual or ceremony. All men must have a general knowledge of all these arts in order to fulfil their religious obligations, but to what extent and in what area he pursues sacred knowledge is up to individual choice. Between men there is equality. Individual assertiveness is not approved, even in an elder. Decisions for the tribe are made by discussing at length the many issues and opinions involved, until eventually a mutual agreement is reached. But the Law which embodies correct behavior is the religious knowledge held by the elders, so that the elders are effectively in control. The Law specifically excludes women from any knowledge of the sacred rituals. Death is the penalty for serious violation, by men or women, of the sacred secrets. For lesser offences severe punishments are meted out, for example, the Aranda of central Australia punish with mass rape a woman who sees a sacred object. The religion, its secret rituals and their levels of meaning, is a secret society of men.

At initiation a man first receives his personal churinga, a sacred power source which concentrates his Totemic Being. Small churinga may be secreted on the body, tucked into the hair or bound under the arm. As well as being used in rituals this is a personal power source which gives strength over the game on hunting expeditions or can impart life energy when held over the sick or injured. The churinga may be a bullroarer, a flat-toothed board of a few centimeters or longer which is attached to a string. It imparts an eerie whirring sound when swung, varying in tone according to its length and teething. The sound is effective in raising emotions of uncanny fear and awe. The effect is multiplied in those who never know the source of the sound. The effect is even more multiplied in those who believe it to be the voice of a Spirit Being or Totemic Being. Women and children hurry away back to their camp at this sign, so that men are free to conduct their secrets. The source of the noise in the bullroarer is one of the secrets first revealed to the boy in initiation. Later he will learn the way to craft such objects, to "sing into" them their sacred power as they are created.

The creation story relating to the voice of the bullroarer varies regionally. For the Wulamba of the coast of Eastern Arnhem Land, in northern Australia, the Spirit is Kunapipi, "Old Woman" or "Mother," who brought life into being through creation of the Totemic Beings. The bullroarer is named her secret name of Mumuna, somewhat mimicking its sound, because it is her voice. She used to kill and eat the ancestral men until she was attacked and killed by the Eaglehawk, who heard her cry out *brr* as she died. This sound, as her blood, went into every tree so that Eaglehawk was able to cut down a tree and fashion the first bullroarer, recapturing the sound her blood made as she was dying. Eaglehawk also let blood from his arm as a ritual action to avert punishment for her death. With other Totemic Beings, Bandicoot and Native Cat, he mixed this blood with ochre and the red soil of anthill for ritual daubing of their bodies. The unity of life essences in blood, red gum of the eucalypt, and red ochre of the earth itself is captured in the sound of the bullroarer. It symbolically represents a sacred unifying life force, as does Kunapipi herself.[5] In other tribes there is similar mythic explanation of the bullroarer as the voice of a Totemic Being.

The religious ceremonies all revolve around myths of the Spirit Beings and Totemic Beings as re-enactments of their primal activity. Abbie has pointed out that, in respect of the ceremonies recounting the life of a spiritual being, Aborigines show devotion in the same way as many other religions (Abbie, pp. 133–4). The performance of the ceremonies requires much cooperative preparation. The coming event may require travel by the whole tribe to the relevant sacred place where a camp is set up at some distance from the dancing ground so that women are removed from its vicinity. Often there are interconnecting grounds related to sections of the ritual activity. The grounds are cleared of any regrowth and surrounding marking stones tidied. Nearby are hidden the sacred boards and stones which will be brought out at the most sacred point and their myth and its levels of meaning, recorded in the sacred markings, retraced by their totemic owner. Men of one totem may have the responsibility to organize the ceremony but men of the other moiety take part and witness the sacred objects and share in the secrets. Preparation for ceremonies may include the construction of sand paintings, or sacred headdresses or poles made from feathers and string, or the body painting of one another with symbolic designs, equally as sacred.

Painting is a sacred activity to which a boy is introduced after initiation. Bark painting is a ritual expression in itself. The painter is taught the myth of the symbolic designs before he is allowed to use that symbol so that he "sings into" his work the myth it represents. The work of a novice who may only use, say, two colors and three designs may well be more aesthetically pleasing than the more complex paintings of his elders, degrees of artistic creativity naturally varying. But that of the elder is the more sacred by virtue of the higher degree of meaning he can impart to it.

H. Morphy has described the particular way the Yolngu of northern Australia make their paintings sacred. For them bir'yun, "brilliance" equates with spiritual power in their bark and body painting. A bark painting begins with a geometric design of several colors. Onto this background is carefully marked a fine crosshatching in white, a process which can take a week of steady work. The result is a shimmering effect which seems to bring the painting alive. This is said to give the painting spiritual power, and it does have an emotional impact on the viewer. The "brilliance," or spiritual power, is also created in body painting for ceremonies by sticking on white birds' down to highlight sacred designs which are painted in blood. Blood acts as an adhesive for the feathers but is also itself sacred through its life-giving power. The men thus painted obtain a sense of easiness and joy, a feeling of lightness—the same physical effects said to be felt by the person from whom blood is let. A similar increase in the sacred power of paintings is that described earlier of the effect of moisture enlivening the ochre of the Wandjina cave paintings.

In all their arts, which are brought together in ceremony, Aborigines are recreating the sacred. Dance and music are primarily sacred, as is painting. The acquisition of sacred arts and knowledge is a lifelong process. Men learn through taking part in the ceremonies, both the preparation and performance. Also there is opportunity to learn from the elders in a more casual way in everyday activities and times of relaxation. These arts may be used simply as entertainment—for "playabout"—but the sacred songs and mimes cannot be used in this way. There is, in "playabout," scope for individual creativity in new songs which can become permanent in the culture, but cannot be used in sacred ceremonies. By song is meant a hypnotic steady chanting. The songs are of simple repetitive statements, as those of Jarapiri, but often are movingly poetic in their imagery. The singing is spiritually evocative and is intensified in this effect in its sudden silences. I have experienced its command even under the adverse conditions of the intense atmosphere of a chronic psychiatric ward's crowded day room. Although the words were unknown to us, staff and patients became reverent, immediately removed from the mundane by the calming yet uplifting effect of a lone Aborigine's singing.

The songs are accompanied in ceremony by tamping and clapping and rhythmic movement. Clapping sticks, and in the north the didgeridoo, give musical accompaniment. Mime is much used in dance, expertly portraying the actions of the ancestral men/animals of the totem. Sign language is a highly developed secret language between men incorporated into ritual. The mesmerizing effect of the long ceremonies has been reported by male anthropologists who have taken part. When the heightened emotions of the men are combined with the physical effects of blood-letting rituals or rigorous dancing, an altered state of consciousness in which they experience themselves as the superhuman Totemic Being is likely. This individual experience of unity seems to be what is expressed when men say they are "making themselves," that is, they are making themselves into the Totemic Being—becoming sacred (Berndt, *Gunwinggu*, p. 114). The individual psyche of the Aborigine is already largely merged with his fellows and his land, so that perhaps for him the experience of the ceremony is not a jolting alteration of consciousness from its everyday functions.

Erich Neumann, writing on the nature of mysticism, speaks of tribal or early life ego-identification with non-ego as "the archetype of paradisiacal wholeness." (Neumann, p. 378) Tribal Aborigines maintain this psychic state of unity through the religious culture which relates them to their environment. Neumann and Joseph Henderson differentiate between this experience of original unity—"source" mysticism—and a "last stage" mysticism, where the ego is transformed by the world taking form wholly outside it (Neumann, p. 414 and Henderson, pp. 84–5). This categorization is relevant only in cultures where increasing ego-separation is the cultural norm. In the ordinary consciousness of the tribal Aborigine, the ego is dispersed in people, totems, and landscape—a state allied to both source and goal in The Dreaming. It may be, that if mystical experience is defined as the experience of unity with the sacred, then tribal Aborigines are mystics, even though they would not experience a change in consciousness which is normally associated with mysticism. Her or his everyday experience is of unity. In sacred ritual, men express their unity with each other and with a unified world. This high level of unity is both a reflection of, and in turn is mirrored in, the individual Aboriginal psyche.

When Aboriginal religion was first discovered by anthropologists and described as "primitive" they meant this in the derogatory sense of at an early, childlike, stage. The childlike comparison can also be used in a positive sense in that it is children who have a unified experience of their world. Aborigines, too, have an inner state of unity, that is, the psychological freedom from being controlled by only a partial complex and instead a relating with the whole being. Jung theorized the unity of inner and outer worlds to exist at a deep unconscious level. This unity of inner and outer has been demonstrated in the Aboriginal religion in which the people experience unity as pre-existent and therefore do not symbolize it as a god. The Dreaming imagery of land and spirits combined in primordial featureless form predating creation is symbolic of such primary unity. The childhood experience of unity is gradually lost in developing through the many separations necessarily involved in growing up in Western society—from parents and lovers into ego-consciousness; from an integrated world to a culturally learned separation from matter; from body into mind—to list the major dualities. In contrast, tribal Aborigines are able, through their totemic links, to grow up without withdrawing into their unconscious their primary identification with the world. To "become as children," Christ's message, is to become again a unified whole. Aboriginal religion is "primitive" only in that it is a "pure" religion which expresses our most sacred relationship, that with all things.

Individual unity is not pursued separate from the group. The kadaicha man, or medicine man, is the most lone in his individual amassing of secret-sacred knowledge to increase his spiritual power, but he is not considered to be more sacred than other men, even though more spiritually powerful. In Aboriginal tribal society, individuals do not acquire charismatic power, or mana. The sacred remains outside of humanity in the physical world. Elders are given great respect because of their relationship with and knowledge of the sacred, but they are not powerful as individuals. Kadaicha men have been described as mere sorcerers who practice sleight of hand with quartz stones, bones, or pieces of string in order to effect cures. Their negative effects on enemies is also often seen as being obtained through suggestion. But their personal accounts tell of a lifetime of introduction into esoteric knowledge, often from father to son, and an inherited predisposition to psychic experiences through altered states of consciousness seems mandatory.

Records of their experiences, as collected by Mircea Eliade, tell of seeing ghosts and communing with the dead underground, or walking with a Totemic Spirit through trees or beyond the clouds. They tell of being killed and cut open and filled with stones and restored to life, or of doing this to others (Eliade, *Zen*, pp. 423–9). Their inner life is suggestive of schizophrenic experience, in which the outer spiritualized world becomes internalized. The individual psyche suffers unconscious invasion in both cases. The kadaicha man appears to have the fluid ego boundary of the schizophrenic. As with schizophrenics, his difference separates him and his abnormal power is feared. It is also valued in that he has secret knowledge of the spirits which can be used by him to the benefit of the tribe. He is not shunned, but neither does he possess personal charisma—the mana usually found with medicine men of other tribal cultures. He is relatively alone in the world of The Dreaming when it is usual to relate to the sacred environment in unity with others.

The Berndts stress the relationship of unity between people and land. But Ronald Berndt has defined sacredness in Aboriginal religion as having to do with relationship between body and soul, man and Totemic Beings, and man and The Dreaming (Berndt, *Religion*, p. 26).

The relationship between body and soul, or, jointly, man and The Dreaming includes that between man and Totemic Beings. These relationships that Berndt defines are subsumed in the relationship of people and land. This is the sacred relationship in Aboriginal religion.

The sacred knowledge of the tribe which gives expression to this sacred relationship is not obtainable by individual endeavor or merit, but only in the relationships between its custodians, the men and their elders. The land is kept a sacred place by those who maintain its unifying life essence. The land itself contains The Dreaming, its spiritual revelation. Sacred knowledge is of the sacred land.

THE PRESENT

The Aboriginal religion is capable of making adjustment, of incorporating a changing environment or psychological change, when that need arises. There are relatively new cults in Arnhem Land—new in having originated in the last centuries—such as that of the Old Woman or Mother, Kunapipi, which have this century been recorded in their spread south and west from the northern coast. These are incorporated within the traditional totemic theme of relationship to the land.

However, there was no opportunity for the religion to demonstrate adaptation at the time of forced settlement, when white interference stamped out attempts to continue the religious gatherings. More recent confrontation with white culture and dislocation from tribal lands has been shown by Eric Kolig, in his study of the Aborigines of the Fitzroy area, to have effected adaptation in Aboriginal religion. Fortunately, changes in white attitudes have also been reflected in government policies which assist Aborigines to maintain and adapt traditional ways, while sharing the benefits of civilization. Kolig shows Aboriginal religion to have adapted to the situation at Fitzroy Crossing where various tribal groups who migrated from their traditional areas in the 1960s and 70s camp around the European settlement. There are about seven hundred people overall in several camps which include white-educated part-Aborigines from surrounding pastoral stations (ranches) and full-bloods from the desert to the south. Traditional tribal separations and totemic affiliations are being overridden in order to create a unified Aboriginal society at a new place. It is the land around Fitzroy Crossing which is now seen as relevant to the Aborigines, although they keep identity jointly with their place of birth. Children born at Fitzroy Crossing are said to belong to that place.

An Aborigine will always first enquire a stranger's place: "Where are you from?" This is not small talk or curiosity about your current travel. The most relevant identification an Aborigine can make is with her/his place of birth, her/his land. Equally, they identify with their own people, part of that land. An Aboriginal child will bring before a visitor her/his most treasured posessions: they shyly but proudly present for inspection not toys or dolls but other children, their sisters and brothers, cousins and friends. Anyone who could be in the remotest sense related is addressed as Cousin, Aunty or Uncle, if not Brother or Sister, so that the next questions, having found out your area of origin, is to enquire as to whom you are related.

In the move to towns the tribal myths and places are not forgotten. Aborigines have demonstrated their determination to protect their "deserted" sacred sites from destruction by mining companies, as at Noonkanbah in 1979–80. Even though these places are not attended full time by tribal people living around them, their people still make pilgrimage. The old patterns of religion, the timings of ceremonies, are compromised to fit in with the employment of men on cattle stations (ranches) during the dry season. Increasing individuation through Westernization is allowed for, so that the kinship rules for marriage are less rigid. Although Totemic members still organize the traditional ceremonies, regular gatherings are held in tents, and storehouses have been built to house the sacred totemic boards. If they had come into the European community earlier this century, these people would have lost such ongoing connection with their religion. Even in the early 1960s, under the influence of Christian missions, the Gogo community in the same northwest area disposed of all their traditional sacred objects.

In the first half of this century it was a sorrier situation for Aborigines in settled areas. In the southwest of Western Australia, the entire population of Aboriginal people were denied human rights and removed under law from their camps on the outskirts of towns where they had been forced as landless beggars by white settlement. As a preliminary to assimilation, Aborigines were then kept in slave-camp conditions at Christian missions well removed from view. The main location was the Methodist Mogumber Mission at Moore River, north of Perth. Here they were institutionalized into Christianity and into skills which could make them useful as servants to white masters. Their life decisions were made by a "protector," always with his goal of assimilation uppermost. Any signs of being native, including native religious rituals, were severely punished.

Even under such extraordinary conditions of different language and kinship groups gathered in a place unknown to most—in fact a place traditionally feared by the local Aborigines as belonging to evil spirits—a community of Aborigines, the Nyungahs (simply "Men") survived in spite of the white intent of their imprisonment. The Nyungah are thus without their traditional land, even though they know of the localities of their ancestors. But most of their religious traditions have been lost. Many did adapt to white ways and were able to incorporate their Aboriginal identity within this. Many others cling to the traditional values of communal living and remain on the outskirts of Australian society—"the fringe dwellers"—as they have named themselves. The Nyungah peoples have not lost their religious connection with their land, shown when they recently fought and won a long court battle against the state government to prevent commercial development of a sacred site, a home of the Wagyl, beside the Swan River in Perth, only to have the decision overturned at a later date by the same government.

Where it is possible, some Aboriginal groups seek a return to more traditional lifestyle. They do not reject the benefits of civilization, and this is not a complete return to the past, but they need to escape the destructive aspects of towns, such as alcohol. Tribal lands may not always be retrievable, nor tribal religion. Land rights have been granted to some groups who were fortunate never to have lost connection with their tribal land, for example the

Aranda at Hermannsburg in central Australia. Some tribally organized but landless groups have been able, through government assistance, to lease cattle stations—perhaps those on which they at one time worked without pay—in order to once more have their own place, even though it may not be traditional land laden with religious meaning. The Out-Station Movement allows for several small kinship groups to live a tradition-oriented lifestyle away from, but with the support of, a central cooperative which provides supplies and health services. Financial independence for the group can be realized through an enterprise such as cattle raising, and some tribes have even sold mineral rights, but with knowledge that the area involved did not entail violation of a sacred place. The place of religion in their life may now be filled by Christianity, or maintained by an adaptation of traditional ceremonies related to the land, or left empty.

The destruction of the Aboriginal people, of their land, and their religion, is a source of shame for all Australians. The sacred relationship between land and people which has been demonstrated to have existed in Aboriginal religion gave Aborigines a psychological unity which is not easily attained in the modern society which ousted it. As Aborigines can benefit from the technology of the twentieth century which was introduced into Australia, all Australians can benefit from the Aboriginal religious value of a sacred relationship with the real world.

In recent years some environmentalists have begun to recognize the same identification with the world which Aboriginal peoples experience. The deep ecology of modern theorists such as Arne Naess[6] offers a "new" consciousness for Western culture, yet deep ecology is fundamentally the intuitive wisdom of indigenous people worldwide. They are part of their world, not master of it. The intrinsic right to existence of all things is recognized, rather than acting on the assumption that Nature is merely a source of fulfilment for our physical and psychological needs.

Deep ecology arises from the experience of organic wholeness with our world, as does Aboriginal religion. In its relationship of oneness with the world, Aboriginal religion is not different from Buddhism or Taoism. Some Christian radicals and mystics (such as Saint Francis) have demonstrated the truth of such relationship to dogma-bound churches. For those whose spiritual needs are not met in Western society, such unity can be a new way of seeing. An experience of oneness allows a social vision which is nonhierarchical, noncompetitive, less regulated, and very much anticonsumerism. Deep ecology, in which nature is recognized as part of the self, accords with Jungian depth psychology.

Psychologist Carl Jung recognized that at a deep level (deep in Western people because of its suppression in the development of rationality and the individual ego) the human psyche merges with the outer world. This is not a "primitive" level, although in ethnocentric studies it has been misinterpreted as less desirable than the consciousness of separateness normal for westerners. Separateness from the natural world has proven self-destructive in allowing the environment to be treated as an expendable resource. Now the future of the earth may depend on all cultures rediscovering the truths of indigenous people who have maintained tribal connection with their land and the consciousness this engenders.

The world's history of imperialist expansion in order to take foreign land for individuals has temporarily separated humanity from its natural experience of unity with its environment. The new environment of individualism is experienced as "other" rather than "self." An initial childhood experience of unity with the world is lost to the dualities created in the many separations the individual is forced to make by family and society in the individual's development. In contrast, tribal Aborigines are able, through totemic bonding and relationship, to grow up without the primary human experience of identification with the world having to make withdrawal into the unconscious. Tribal consciousness is of a merging of the individual with the outer social world and the environment. The collective psyche of Aborigines is expressed in their concept of the earth and its spirits as a unity.

All humanity has an instinctual pursuit of unity which balances the dualities created by consciousness. A duality of the material and spiritual world is a mental construct which, for Western society, has allowed the overvaluing of acquisitiveness and political power which facilitates individualism. Our culturally enforced ideas and behaviors are based on the assumption that spirit is separate from matter. This leads to the spiritual then being dismissed as non-existent. In Aboriginal thought there is a unifying balance which has much to offer those of us who have overvalued ego-separation, rationality, and the Western ideal of consciousness. The psychological wholeness of unconscious connectedness for the individual is matched by social cohesion and a meaningful relationship with one's world—the one world of matter and spirit united.

Because we are one species, all races have areas of potential functioning which are undeveloped at the expense of dominance of an alternate way of thought and interaction. In the hands of ethnocentric anthropologists, environmental determinism led to the erroneous but persistent belief that some races are more primitive than others. If we look again, this time from a holistic stance, at what primal or indigenous people can share with us to our benefit, it is their relationship with the environment which offers us salvation. All Australians can benefit from the technology this century enjoys, and we can all also benefit from recapturing and maintaining a sacred relationship between a united society and a land of continuing providence, which is the primary function of Aboriginal religion. The Dreaming teaches that psyche both fits with and merges with the world.

Bill Devall and George Sessions recognize that we must learn from the wisdom of indigenous people who maintain an equilibrium with nature. We must learn we are not outside nature, but "of" it. We must learn to value the diversity of nature, and that a landscape is a living being to which we will respond if it is being destroyed. The lesson of ecology is that humanity is not the center of life on earth.

This thinking is subversive to the dominant culture in the same way as is Aboriginal religion. The old wisdom is bound to resolve into a "new" consciousness of identification with the humility of nature. "To the extent that we perceive boundaries, we fall short of deep ecological consciousness," says Warwick Fox, who is an ecologist who makes the connection between deep ecology and transpersonal psychology (Devall and Sessions, p. 65). It is not just in our way of seeing, but must apply to how things are done in our society. Devall and Sessions give the example of regional organization into bioregions rather than political states. This was the method of land use in practice by Australian Aborigines prior to white settlement. Deep ecology aims to develop in the dominant society the dispersed ego-boundary which is behind the normal consciousness of traditional Aboriginal groups.

A Mowanjin Aboriginal speaks of the fight for his tribe's traditional land: "It is our longing. All our belonging is there."

Unity has commonly been the conscious goal of religions, but in many religions that goal has been ironically unreachable, except momentarily, because of the divisions the religion itself perpetuates. (In Aboriginal religions the division of the sexes is in contrast to its many unities. Carl Jung demonstrated that consciousness itself entails the division of the psyche into oppositions. The universal experience of men and women as divided may be an initial cost of consciousness for humanity, false though such division has proven.) For Western individuals an instinctual personal pursuit of unity is hindered by culturally enforced ideas and behaviors which are based on the assumption that there is a duality of the spiritual and the material worlds. In contrast, for Aborigines the unity of spirit and matter is the basis of religion. Their religious practices express symbolically their union with the world. Through the concept of The Dreaming, Aboriginal religion emphasizes the unity of past and future time in the present. To be at one with the environment implies to be in tune with the present. In Aboriginal religion the timeless spiritual world of The Dreaming and the continuous material universe, of which humanity is part, are unified.

Such a concept equates with that of the ancient Chinese in the Tao, which is variously inadequately interpreted and translated, for example, as Nature, Non-Being, The Way, The Word (as in the Gospel of John). Jung most approved of Richard Wilhelm's "Meaning." The Tao is the connecting principle, the Ultimate Reality, in a monistic world view. In Australia initiated Aboriginal males bore the ritual responsibility to maintain this unity, and in doing so they maintained the world as a sacred place. This revelation of the world remains of the utmost meaning to humanity.

REFERENCES

A.A. Abbie, *The Original Australians*, A.H. & A.W. Reed, Wellington, Auckland, Sydney, 1969.

R.M. Berndt, *Kunapipi. A Study of an Australian Religious Cult*, Cheshire, Melbourne, 1952. (Referred to in the text as Berndt, *Kunapipi*.)

R.M. Berndt, *Australian Aboriginal Religion*, Brill, Leiden, 1974. (Referred to in the text as Berndt, *Religion*.)

R.M. & C.H. Berndt, *Man, Land and Myth in North Australia: the Gunwinggu People*, Ure Smith, Sydney, 1970. (Referred to in the text as Berndt, *Gunwinggu*.)

R.M. & C.H. Berndt, *The World of the First Australians*, Ure Smith, Sydney, 1976. (Referred to in the text as Berndt, *First Australians*.)

I.M. Crawford, *The Art of the Wandjina. Aboriginal Cave Paintings in Kimberley, Western Australia*, Oxford University Press, Melbourne, 1968.

Bill Devall and George Sessions, *Deep Ecology, Living as if Nature Mattered*, Peregrine Smith Books, Salt Lake City, 1985.

M. Eliade, *Australian Religion: an Introduction*, Ithica (N.Y.), 1973. (Referred to in the text as Eliade, *Australian Religion*.)

M. Eliade, *From Primitives to Zen*, Collins, London, 1967. (Referred to in the text as Eliade, *Zen*.)

R.L. Gardner, *The Rainbow Serpent, Bridge to Consciousness*, Inner City Books, Toronto, 1990.

R.A. Gould, *Yiwara. Foragers of the Australian Desert*, Collins, London, 1969.

E. Hassel, "Myths and folktales of the Wheelman tribe of South-Western Australia" in *Folklore*, Sept. 1934, Dec. 1934, June 1935.

J.L. Henderson, *Cultural Attitudes in Psychological Perspective*, Inner City Books, Toronto, 1984.

E. Kolig, *The Silent Revolution*, Institute for the Study of Human Issues, Philadelphia, 1981.

K. Maddock, "The world creative powers" in *Religion in Aboriginal Australia an Anthology*, University of Queensland Press, St Lucia (Queensland), 1984.

H. Morphy, "From dull to brilliant: the aesthetics of spiritual power among the Yolngu" in *Man*, Vol. 24, 1989.

C.P. Mountford, *Winbaraku and the Myth of Jarapiri*, Rigby Limited, Adelaide, 1968.

E. Neumann, "Mystical Man" in *The Mystic Vision. Papers from the Eranos Yearbooks* (ed. Joseph Campbell), Routledge & Kegan Paul, London, 1969.

T. Swain, *Interpreting Aboriginal Religion. An Historical Account*, Australian Association for the Study of Relgion, Bedford Park (South Australia), 1985.

M.L. Von Franz, *Projection and Re-Collection in Jungian Psychology. Reflections of the Soul*, Open Court, LaSalle (Illinois), 1980.

E.A. Worms, *Australian Aboriginal Religions*, Nellen Yubu Missiological Unit, Kensington (New South Wales), 1986.

NOTES

1. Norma Lyons (unpublished).
2. An overview of historical interpretations of Aboriginal religion is presented by Swain.
3. For fuller accounts of the paintings and myths of the Wandjina see Crawford's *The Art of the Wandjina* and Eliade's *Australian Religion: an Introduction*.
4. Ethel Hassel recorded the beliefs of the Wilmen before the turn of the century and her notes were edited by D.S. Davidson for publication.
5. The Kunapipi myths and ritual were recorded by Berndt, 1952.

6. Arne Naess, *Self-Realization: An Ecological Approach to Being in the World*, Roby Memorial Lecture (Murdoch University, 1986). *Ecology, Community and Lifestyle* (Cambridge University Press, 1989).

CONCLUSION

*Symbols are to express ideas. When ideas have been
understood symbols should be forgotten. Words are to interpret
thoughts. When thoughts have been absorbed words stop.*

Tao-sheng[1]

The conclusion to a book such as this is bound to be highly subjective. To clarify one point straight off, it has not been my intention to argue for the adoption of one religion rather than another, or any religion at all, for that matter. My intention has, rather, been to present as best I am able a reasonably coherent, psychologically and historically based description of the principles which have made some religious cultures what they are today. In doing this I have had to be somewhat unfair. In regard to Christianity, for example, I can be criticized for not having mentioned or discussed many of the non-Catholic groups, not only Presbyterians, Baptists, and Methodists but most non-mainstream groups as well, for example: the Waldenses (a group which originated in the twelfth century and continues to exist at present in Italy); The Church of Jesus Christ of Latter Day Saints (commonly known as the Mormons, primarily centered in the United States); the Pastoral Meetings among the Quakers (those who have "pastors"—a paid ministry—in contrast to the silent meditation Meetings), found in abundance in the United States and also, through missionary activity, widely spread in Africa; and so on. The reverse criticism might be made of the chapter on Buddhism, in which Zen has been given undue importance if we are to consider space devoted to a group's concepts a measure of its importance, and to Tibetan Buddhism which can hardly be called typical, not to mention everyday practice of Buddhism among the peasants in contrast with the rarefied atmosphere of the monasteries. But I have not set out to present an introductory textbook of Comparative Religion, or any kind of textbook. It was not even my conscious intention to make the religious cultures form a sort of geographical

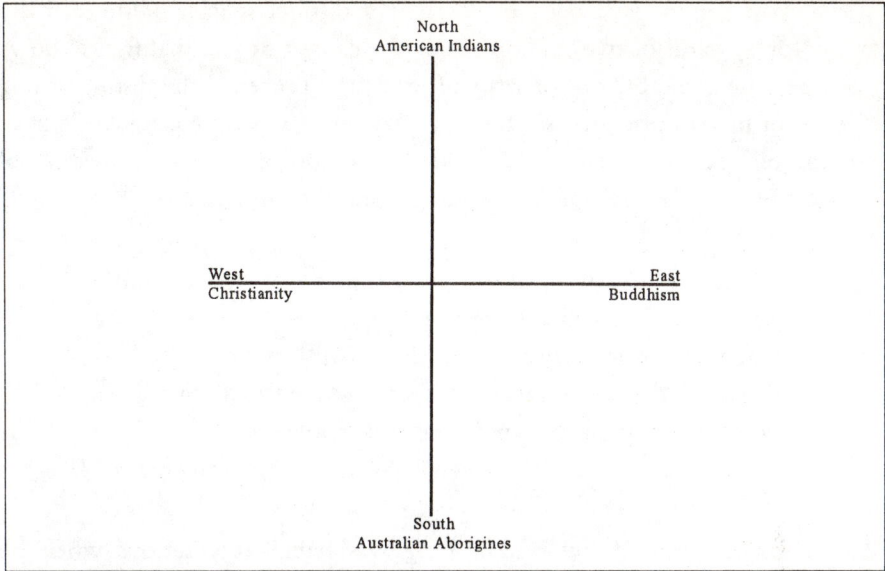

North
American Indians

West   East
Christianity   Buddhism

South
Australian Aborigines

Figure 2: Geographical orientation of the religions discussed in this book

mandala, even though that has been the effect of my choice of subjects as can be seen in Figure 2. Perhaps Mysticism might provide the missing center for the design, since all four sides partake of it in one degree or another.

If I were attempting a textbook presentation of comparative religion, it would be unpardonable to leave out some of the most influential religious movements in world history, Hinduism, for example, Islam, Judaism, the now nearly defunct but once mighty Zoroastrianism, the Gnostic movements which once came near to dominating the West, and other ancient religious movements such as those of the Babylonians, Egyptians, perhaps even the Hittites (in the area we now call Turkey) or the culture of Ugarit (whose one-time geographical location is now within the borders of Syria), and of course the Greeks and the Romans. Not to be too chauvinistic, the "Far East" ought not to be left out. Consider: Lao-Tzu and Taoism, Confucius and the way of life he founded ... Actually brief references have been made to most of these at one point or another in the book, enough to explain a point being made, but not enough to warrant being called satisfactorily discussed.

If I try to describe the kernel thought throughout this book, it is something like this:

We human beings have been evolving as a distinct species of the primate family for upwards of two million years. We cannot stop at that figure, however, because some billions of years of evolution preceded the distinguishing features of human primates, so that in a very literal sense we can say we have billions of years of evolution behind us (as does every other species, of course). In his far more poetic way Jung made the same point:

> [The] whole psychic organism ... still preserves elements that connect it with the invertebrates and ultimately with the protozoa. Theoretically it should be possible to "peel" the collective unconscious, layer by layer, until we come to the psychology of the worm, and even of the amoeba.
>
> (Jung, C.W., vol. 8, paragraph 322)

Though it sounds whimsical, Jung was being very serious when he wrote that, as any reader will see who bothers to look up the complete text from which the quotation has been taken.

We have become used to thinking of evolution as the adaptation of an organism to its environment, but it is something of a wrench when we are asked to delineate just what "environment" refers to. A little thought helps us realize that environment refers to far more than to physical surroundings. To make a ludicrous over-simplification, it could be said that Konrad Lorenz won the Nobel Prize for pointing out that social interactions between animals have an instinctual base tracing back to evolutionary development. Bees form highly complex social communities. So do ants. So do human beings. Environment includes not only the physical surrounds but also all living beings, including those of your own species. So now we have a revision:

Human beings have some millions of years of evolution behind them which determines not only their physical and mental structure, but also their social customs and relationships.

Actually, of course, this is no great profound thought, nor did it originate with me. Charles Darwin himself argued the point at great length. And so did Sigmund Freud. But we need to move yet one more step, and here we must tread carefully. That step is to take active account of the highly limited character of our knowledge of reality. And those basically unknown aspects of reality, of which we have no adequate or even partial knowledge, also must be included in the term "environment."

Here, I fear, I feel a bit of uneasiness stirring in me. The world is full of "occultists" (the pop term nowadays of course is "New Age"), by which I mean people who claim to know—as much intellectually as emotionally— those realities of which conventional culture is unaware. What makes me uneasy about these people is that whenever some such claim is made, there stir within me Lao-Tzu's opening words in the *Tao Te Ching*, "The Tao that can be told is not the eternal Tao. The name that can be named is not the eternal name."[2] In other words, anything that a human being can express is by virtue of that very fact not an eternal truth. More philosophically and more succinctly: *What can be conceptualized or even named is not truly real.* Bringing together the teachings of both Plato and the Buddha: *That which we are familiar with, even in the most esoteric way, is merely a part of the phenomenal world and has no Reality.* To be sure, my viewpoint does not strike the reader as terribly radical, since it is very much in vogue at present to invoke modern nuclear physicists, especially those fond of contemplating the possible implications of Quantum Theory, to show that what we assume to be reality really isn't. It is frequently pointed out that both time and space are constructs of human thought and do not exist in and of themselves. Albert Einstein is the prophet cited for this insight. We are aware that our distinction between mass and energy is illusory, Einstein's $E=MC^2$ is the sacred scripture quoted for that. But what troubles me is the conviction on so many people's part that now we, or at least they, *know*—*know* in the Gnostic sense of having arrived at ultimate truth.

If the *homo* branch of the primates continues to exist for another two million years, I have not the vaguest idea of what the processes of evolution will have made of it, but I feel rather certain that most, if not all, of what we now think we know will no longer be part of the mental processes of those beings. I suspect this will be true as much of what the "New Agers" claim to have discovered as of what our orthodox sciences claim. I also tend to suspect that those hypothetical future beings will themselves suffer the illusion that they "know Reality" and that they will be just as wrong as we are. And their wrongness will, just like ours, approach ninety-nine percent, or perhaps a wee bit more, of what they think they know.

Now all this is rather unpalatable if it is taken seriously. We have a very strong emotional need to have something to hold onto. Thus the importance of religions to us, along with their close cousins, scientific theories.

The two "native" religious cultures, of the American Indians and of the Australian Aborigines, as they have been described in the last two chapters, seem to come closest to accepting that the human beings in the world are a natural part of the nature of the cosmos. The world's major religions have tended to stress a break between human beings and all the rest of reality. This is quite the opposite of, let us say, traditional Australian Aboriginal views. From their viewpoint there is no difference in essence between a large rock, a particular species of fish, bird, or animal, and a human being (or clan of human beings). They are all three the same. This is not "prelogical thinking," as has often been claimed, it is logic which is totally rational, it is merely separated from the mainstream of what became "Western" logic a very, very long time before Aristotle attempted to determine what logic is. The result of that separation is that we have to set aside the entire set of cultural presuppositions which dominate us in order to see along the lines of a different train of logic.

For one thing, Aboriginal culture does not reify time in the way that we are used to. To be sure, Einstein did, to some extent, force us to accept that time is not a thing. It is not clear whether we have also been able to conclude that time does not exist in any absolute sense. We do, after all have clocks and they are measuring something. If there is no "real" time, then what is it they are measuring? The big thing, of course, is our knowledge that time flows in only one direction. We can with surety say that an event took place, we cannot with equal surety say an event will take place.

But, now, let us skip over to another pathway of thinking. We know that everything changes, that seems to be one of the very few points that virtually everyone agrees with. If we do not take it too literally, we could even say that time is our way of expressing the experience that change constantly occurs. Maybe our clocks are just attempting to break down the process of change into ever more discrete units so that we can cope with change by quantifying it somehow. If we did not need to quantify change, we really would have no particular need to formulate theories of time and to construct an apparatus to measure it. An Aborigine is just as capable of making a sundial as a European or an Asian. But, so far as we know, no tribal Aborigine ever did in fact make a sundial. Or, if some one or more persons did, the idea did not catch on because sundials are totally absent from Aboriginal culture. Why?

Let us look at this conundrum from the viewpoint of the Aborigine's track of logic. Events as such are unimportant, from an Aboriginal point of view, except in so far as they exist now. An Aborigine's Dreaming is not a mythical tale of an event that took place in the far distant past. That is Westerner's logic, and consequently the Westerner's way of presenting Aboriginal beliefs in books. But what is actually experienced by the

Aborigine is that there is a particular Rock in a particular place, a particular plant/bird/insect/animal, a particular person or clan of persons, who all share the same essence. There is at least one more form of that Essence, what for convenience has been called the "Spirit Beings" although the word "Spirit" comes from white people's cultural traditions, not from Aborigines.

In the West we have had to invent a term rather recently as cultures go: "Nature." If we are willing to include under the term "Nature" all that is real—including all the aspects of reality of which we are totally unaware at present—then maybe we can approximate to the Aborigine's conception. Here, now, at this time and place, as the Westerner would say, one part of reality is manifest. It is manifest as that Rock, it is manifest as that Bird, it is manifest as that Person. And though not visible, it is manifest as that "Spirit Being," or "Totem." Or, in the special sense described above, "Nature."

If we realize, if our culture realizes, that we are an aspect of Nature in that very wide sense of "all that is real," it may not be too big a jump to make to give up our belief in the priority of human beings and give equal value to Rock, to Bird, to Person, to Spirit Being.

Something rather remarkable happened when I wrote that last paragraph above. Isn't what I wrote equally valid as a description of the essential basis of Buddhism? Did the enormous logical gulf between Buddhism and Australian Aboriginal culture somehow suddenly become bridged? Put another way, both classical Buddhism and traditional Aboriginal culture have no interest in Aristotelian logic. Both hold, implicitly at least, that the type of rational thought which is so dear to us whites is just one of many possible logics, and can claim no absolute reality as its basis—nor can any of the others.

Jung, who was very familiar with the major philosophers, attempted to give a sort of definition of our much beloved words "reason" and "rational." I will quote a portion of his discussion:

> The rational is the reasonable, that which accords with reason.
> I conceive reason as an attitude whose principle it is to
> conform thought, feeling, and action to objective values ...
> Human reason ... is nothing other than the expression of
> man's adaptability to average occurrences, which have gradually
> become deposited in firmly established complexes of ideas that
> constitute our objective values. Thus the laws of reason are the
> laws that designate and govern the average, "correct," adapted
> attitude. Everything is "rational" that accords with these laws,

everything that contravenes them is "irrational."
(Jung, C.W., vol. 6, paragraphs 785–6)

Without attempting to lay upon Jung responsibility for the use I am making of this quotation, I am suggesting that the attitude which a culture has adopted in respect to the normal environment is what that culture calls rational and reasonable. "Normal environment" means the total environment as it exists in itself, the natural outcome of natural events. Over the past centuries many of us have forgotten what the natural environment is, except for those uncontrollable times when earthquake, volcanic eruption, or other "natural disaster" destroys our self-imposed delusion that we control the earth and all of Nature. "Objective values" is the set of values we place on whatever is outside of ourselves. I am suggesting that what we call reason or rationality are not fixed laws of the universe or "laws of nature" but our culturally and, perhaps, genetically transmitted ways of relating to our environment. And I dare to add here that there are many possible rationalities or forms of logic. What we consider to be logic is actually one culture's way of dealing with the constants of which their experience of life is constituted. Because for so long we in the West have been isolated, or have isolated ourselves, from close contact with any form of thought other than that which was transmitted to us via Greece and Rome, we have come to the conviction that *our* thought forms are the only ones possible, or at least the only ones worth taking into consideration.

Religion has often been accused of distorting our view of and relationship with Nature. The conflict between Religion and Science has received enormous emphasis, not merely in the past few centuries but even back in Greek times. Yet this conflict really amounts to little more than a tempest in a teapot. It is the same procedures of reasoning and logic which we invoke, regardless of which side we favor. What happens, of course, is that religion tends to be somewhat more conservative and thus to lag behind science in its acceptance of new viewpoints. But Western religion and Western science are rooted in the same basic patterns of viewing reality.

Would Western psychology have developed the concept of a psyche, if it did not have the religious concept of a soul already at hand? The original identity of these two concepts is easily visible to anyone who attempts to read and understand Plato, who uses the Greek word *psyche* for what we at the present time differentiate into soul and mind.

To return to the topic of "logics," logic is the name we give to the procedure of reasoning, and reasoning is the link we make between our mental processes and the environment, physical, social, or spiritual, in which we find ourselves. Wakan Tanka as spoken of by an American Indian, or The Dreaming as spoken of by an Australian Aborigine, are very difficult concepts for us to understand primarily because they are part of different logic-systems than that on which our Western religions and philosophies (and consequently sciences) are based.

The Australian Aborigine begins with the assumption that the world, the cosmos, is a single whole. There can be no "acts of God" distinct from "acts of persons" simply because that involves the splitting of reality into two distinct parts. Our Western love of dualisms is powerfully entrenched in our way of thinking and has given our religions and our sciences their distinctive basis. Not only do we make mind/body, world/heaven, human/God distinctions, but we make animate/inanimate, animal/vegetable, hereditary/learned, and countless other dichotomies. The very machine with which I am writing these words is based on a dualist principle: the electronic principle of present/absent, the binary signals by which our computers are made to function. Present-day Western theories of neurology operate with the same concept as computer technology, the presence or absence of a chemical stimulus being taken as the method by which the nervous system, and thus thinking, works. Even Western physics has played around with the idea that matter is counterbalanced by anti-matter, so that there are, or must be, two "universes." Is our chronic Western desire to find some kind of a God or a Spirit in every religion no more than our obsession with dualities—our obsession that there must be something to counterbalance the material world?

To accept the unitary basis on which Aboriginal, American Indian and also Buddhist principles are founded might make not only our traditional religious and philosophical systems meaningless, but much of our scientific theorizing as well. Neither Aborigine, nor American Indian, nor Buddhist has the need or even the cultural capacity to conceptualize a God in the way the West does, because the fundamental premise on which their logic is based is that reality is one. There is the cosmos in which we find ourselves, and that is that. If some outsider wishes to add on a God, there is no objection *per se*, but it seems obvious to them that the God being added is an integral part of the cosmos, and consequently just one more factor in Nature to cope with.

The thesis behind this book, however, is not specifically that there are multiple logics, or argument for or against any particular system of logic, but that there is a specific role which religion plays in human existence. Succinctly, that role is to form a bridging link between the participant and the whole of the environment. It is, as it were, the "two-million-year-old person" within us coming through to our awareness. It is the experience of being-at-one-ness (the literal meaning of Jung's term "individuation"). And once again I feel I must emphasize that the whole of the environment means far more than environmentalists tend to mean, it means the unitary whole of reality.

In the chapter on American Indians there was considerable attention given to the concept which in the history of Western philosophy has been called "entelechy" or "telos." This concept has so dropped out of our Western secular culture that only remnants are to be found here and there. Though the words trace back to Aristotle, the concept was already basic to Plato. The closest we can come to it in modern English would be something like "goal." In the chapter on American Indians it was stressed that to understand the American Indian viewpoint it is helpful to use the principle adapted from Martin Buber, of viewing and relating to everything existent as a "Thou," a "person" having in and for itself an innate purpose and value, if we are to enter the conceptual world of the American Indian.

The remnants of this concept still existing in our modern Western culture are to be found in very unexpected places. For one, in commercial advertising. Many advertisements use as a theme that some product, usually edible, is "the way Nature intended it to be." In modern Western science this suggestion, that whatever turns up "in Nature" is intended for the well-being of modern human beings, is subject to very devastating criticism. But what is important here is that the advertisements are effective because they appeal to the feeling that "Nature" has plans, or purposes. At first glance this seems to be merely a watered down version of "God has plans and purposes," with the word "Nature" substituted for "God" so as to appeal to believers in religion and at the same time to nonbelievers. In the Western religions it is assumed that everything in "Nature" was created by God for human beings to exploit.

The appeal of "the way Nature intended it to be" as a slogan goes much deeper, however. It assumes that everything in existence has an innate function, an innate purpose. We rarely pause to justify this assumption, but if necessary it could be rationalized by appealing to Darwin's theory of the survival of the fittest, since the conclusion to be drawn from his theory would be that whatever exists is most adapted and suitable for existence. "The way Nature intended it to be" would, from that viewpoint, merely be a personification of the process of natural selection. And the accompanying proposition that *homo sapiens* is the peak of a meaningful process of evolution would go unchallenged, despite its obvious origins in the Judeo-Christian religious philosophies.

But more and more, as the geographical environment in which we live deteriorates, even we in the West are coming to see that "the way Nature intended it to be" is more akin to the idea of homeostasis than to the proposition that there is a natural hierarchy in evolution. The trees, the waterways and their composition, the animal and plant life, and, in general, everything that concerns the environmentalists, are now coming to be understood as a delicate balance and regardless of what theory we wish to adopt as to how that delicate balance came to be, we are learning to our dismay that even "minor" changes can have far-reaching and even disastrous effects.

The discussion of the two "native" cultures has focused on the stress each lays upon the maintenance of Nature, of ensuring that the homeostasis in nature is preserved unchanged. In both instances, this stress has been embodied in the conception that everything in existence is a "Thou," a "person" to be respected in the same way that respect is shown to fellow human beings. And, in so far as Aboriginal totemism is concerned, that all persons are manifestations of the essence of existence that is found equally in all geographical objects and all other living beings.

"Essence of existence" appears to many Westerners as a concept difficult to understand. "Life essence" is an easier concept, but unfortunately it does not express what "essence of existence" means to express. Again, Buddhism comes to mind, for its primary goal is to remove the "essence of existence" from us, for us to move into the realm of nonbeing. A primary difference between Buddhist thought compared with American Indian and Australian Aboriginal thought is that the American Indian and Australian Aboriginal cultures have as their effect and more or less conscious goal the maintenance of the essence of existence, while the Buddhist goal is to become totally free of it.

The danger, of course, is that the Westerner assumes that "nonbeing" means death, and that "essence of existence" is merely a long-winded way of saying life. But Buddhists, American Indians and Australian Aborigines are fully as aware of death as all the rest of humankind, and have their own myths and beliefs about the nature of death and beyond. They all have made it abundantly clear that the alive/dead dichotomy is not what they are talking about.

Where, then, can we find anything in Western experience which can give some sort of clue to what they are getting at? The mystics, perhaps. We have already found it difficult to disentangle basic Buddhist experience and practice from that of some of the major mystics. I pointed out that among them are some who find it impossible to describe their mystic experience with any terms or concepts familiar to us, and have had to fall back on dichotomous negatives to express it: it is nonlife and it is nondeath, it is nonknowledge, it is nonignorance, it is nonvisible, it is noninvisible, it is nonfeeling, it is non-nonfeeling, it is nonrational, it is non-nonrational. As we saw that it proved to be necessary to invent an English grammatical form to convey American Indians' perception, "there is a tree-ing here," a phrase which is not identical with "there is a tree here," so among the mystics it is necessary to recognize a new category of nonconcepts, the ultimate necessity of stating that the essence of existence cannot be put into the conceptual world at all. And we have to cope with the Buddhist paradoxical statement that the essence of nonexistence is identical with the essence of existence.

I rather think that among the mystics we are dealing with yet another logic, a third logic to be added to the Westerners' logic based on dichotomies and to the "native" logic based on totality. To understand all three logics I think we must give up the hope that any one of them can be converted into one of the others. The three logics are not three ways of expressing the same thing, they are three separate tracks along which the mind may travel, all of them equally valid in and of themselves.

Until the early decades of the twentieth century there was no place for such subjects to be discussed adequately, because of the conviction that all of reality is knowable and potentially known. In its first years Depth Psychology shared this conviction. When Freud expressed his theory of the unconscious, he defined it as consisting of a more or less disorganized mix of experiences, thoughts, and feelings which could and should be brought to the light of conscious reason. Ideally the unconscious could be totally emptied, as blocks to acceptance of its contents were removed.

Jung's caution in following Freud on this point slowly gave way to a very different manner of envisaging unconscious processes. Apart from elevating feeling to an equal level with thought, he insisted on the unknowability of much that is unconscious in our mental processes. Unknowable because not expressible.

Jung's insistence on a clear demarcation between what is known and what is merely hypothesized has not met with universal approval, largely because, I suspect, of our apparent emotional need to find certainty upon which to rely. Thus it is difficult to find a detailed discussion of Jung's ideas as applied to fields other than psychiatry and psychopathology that does not take one side or another of some controversial topic of which Jung purposefully steered clear.

For example, there has been much controversy, both among laypeople and analysts alike, as to just what constitutes the "self" in Jungian thought. One rather amusing aspect of this controversy is the editorial demand by some publishers that in psychological writings his term "self" should be printed with a capital S (Self) while others demand a lower case s (as I have been writing it). The question is not merely one of deciding whether we are dealing with a special use of a technical term which should be distinguished from its everyday meanings in some orthographical way, although this is involved. There is also an ideological dispute, namely: is Jung's term intended to refer exclusively to the "structure" of the psyche of the individual human being, or is it meant to refer to a sort of universal Self, akin to the Hindu Atman, in which all human beings partake? An extraordinary amount of mental wrestling has been devoted to this question. The reason such a dispute is possible is that Jung himself refused to get involved in the discussion, stating (quite wisely) that his interest was in the psychological functioning of the patients with whom he worked, and not in metaphysical speculation. Jung explicitly denied, repeatedly, that his concept was that the Self=God—and equally that he claimed that the Self≠God. This, he said, is speculation about metaphysical matters about which he was neither qualified nor interested.

This particular point is important in that a number of religious arguments can be constructed around the concept of the self. In Jung's presentation, the "self" is the name given to the directing center in the psyche, an analogy on the psychological level to the DNA coding which controls the nature and development of the physical body. Jung pointed out that there is no distinct definable point at which physical mechanisms (e.g., the nervous system) leave off and psychological functions (e.g., thought, emotions) begin.[3] It appears to me to be desirable to err on the side of caution and say that the "self" is a term for the directing principle held in common by the physiological and the psychological aspects of the human individual. Consequently, the precise relationship of physiological, psychological, and spiritual to one another can be circumvented—which is highly desirable given that all attempts to determine whether any demarcation exists between the three, and, if so, how they are to be understood, are entirely hypothetical.

Another area of importance in relation to this question of the "self" is whether it is to be limited to human beings, or whether it extends to all living beings (animal? vegetable? viral?). The comment from Jung, quoted earlier in this chapter, that in theory it should be possible to peel away the layers of the collective unconscious and ultimately reach the psychology of an amoeba, leads to the conclusion that unconscious psychological processes take place in all living creatures, and consequently it must be as possible to speak of the "self" in/of a tree or bacterium fully as much as in/of a human being. It is significant that in the quotation Jung spoke only of unconscious psychological processes. He largely avoided the difficult question of whether conscious processes also take place in some or all living beings apart from humans, although he was willing to moot this possibility quite seriously (Jung, *C.W.*, vol. 8, paragraph 956).

So far I have been discussing the unitary ("monist") principle at the heart of Buddhism, American Indian thought and Australian Aboriginal culture, and the possibility of linking up Jung's concepts of self and individuation, with the stress being on the experience of being-at-one-ness, being-at-one-ness with all of reality, whether it be related to the psychiatric concern of disintegration of the psyche, the sociological concern of disintegration of society, or the environmentalist concern of disintegration of the world's ecosystem. In Western development of science, particularly the areas devoted to microphysics and to astronomy, there is a companion interest (it cannot at this stage be called a concern) in the integrity or nonintegrity of the universe.

Where, in all this, does Christianity come in? It is a flippant, though frequent, answer to say that Christianity does not come in at all, and is consequently rapidly fading away. The same can be said of all religious cultures, however. Buddhism, Hinduism, American Indian and Australian Aboriginal cultures are all, for one reason or another, fading rapidly away. Where, ideologically speaking, does Christian thought fit into the picture? It has already been pointed out that Christian ideology, except for its mystical strands, is based firmly on dualistic principles in contrast to the other religious systems we have been examining. Is there any "being-at-one-ness" at the heart of Christian experience? The answer seems to me to be located in the Christian concept of Christ. Doctrinally speaking, Jesus Christ has been formally defined as "fully human and fully God"; that is, an integral, indivisible amalgamation of all that is human and all that is God. Being-at-one with Christ is the total experience of being-at-one-ness, expressed in the feeling-doctrine that in the Mass the bread and the wine are literally the body and blood of

Christ, so that by taking these into your digestive system you are literally integrating yourself and Christ.

As I have found when various persons have read earlier drafts of this book, this last sentence tends to arouse a lot of opposition—primarily among Protestant Christians, because the Protestant Reformation rebelled against the literal interpretation of the Eucharist (Holy Communion) which is a key doctrine of the Catholic Churches. There was not (and to my knowledge still is not) much or any consideration given to the point that feeling is as much a rational function as thought. A feeling-doctrine has as much human validity as a thinking-doctrine. Both Protestants and Catholics alike tended to limit their discussion to debate about the intellectual meaningfulness and validity of the doctrine, or the lack thereof. Western dualistic logic is probably not capable of coming to terms with the unitary-based and (in this instance) feeling-based doctrine of the union of Christ and the material world without loss of any of the God-quality or human-quality of Christ. Nevertheless, vast numbers of Christians do find a being-at-one-ness in Holy Communion, momentary as it might be (as is satori in Zen) in terms of time. Christian theology as developed in the early centuries AD took time to be an aspect of the material world, and foreign to ultimate reality—in much the same way as Buddhism.

This then to me is the religious dimension, the experience of being-at-one-ness with all that is, neither identified nor distinguished from that all-that-is, neither superior nor inferior to any other part or aspect of all that is. Neither crown of creation/evolution, nor inconsequential part of an on-going process which has as its goal something greater. Just an integral and necessary part of all-that-is.

NOTES

1. Tao-Sheng, quoted in Fung Yu-Lan, *A Short History of Chinese Philosophy*, The Free Press, New York, 1948.
2. Lao-Tsu, *Tao Te Ching* (tr. Gia-Fu Feng and Jane English), New York, Vintage Books, 1972.
3. Jung *C.W.*, vol. 8. Lengthy discussion in "On the nature of the psyche."

INDEX

A

Abraham, 92
Academy, Plato's, 62
Active Imaginary Vision, Active Imagination, 150
Acts of the Apostles, 80, 137, 140
Adam, 73, 116, 124
Africa, 5, 56, 254
African tribes, 5
Ahriman, 85
Ahura Mazda, 85, 131
Akhenaton, King, 10
Alexander the Great, 33
Allen, Paul Gunn, 180
American Indians, 4, 5, 8, 104, 109, 120, 130, 131, 143, 155, 232, 257, 261, 262, 263, 264, 266
Amish, 5
amoeba, 256, 266
anaesthetics, 134
Ananda, 25
angels, 89, 90, 93
Anglican Church, 78
Angra Mainyu, 85
anima, 96
animism, 166, 219
animistic spirits, 235
Anti-Christ, 85
Anti-god, 87
anti-matter, 261
apostle, 43, 57, 58, 64, 73, 76, 78, 87, 90, 111, 126, 132, 140, 142, 146, 149, 151
Apostles' Creed, 43, 87
apparitions, 95, 97, 143
Arab religious movements, 10
Aramaic language, 58
Aranda, 247
archery, 47
archetypes, 139, 140, 155, 242
Arhats, 34
Aristotelian logic, 181, 259
Aristotle, 170, 171, 258, 262
Asia, 23, 56, 85, 218, 230, 258
Asoka, King, 23
Atman, 17, 18, 28, 142, 153, 155, 265
atonement, Christian doctrine of the, 61
Australian Aborigines, 4, 5, 6, 8, 104, 109, 143, 155, 218–50, 257, 258, 259, 261, 263, 266
auto-suggestion, 41
automatic writing, 150
autonomous complexes, 136, see also complexes, theory of

B

Babylonians, 146, 255
Baha'i, 12
Banzan, 27
baptism, ritual of, 78, 110
Baptists, 254
bark painting, 241

being-at-one-ness, 266, 267
belief systems, 8
belief, meaning of the word, 8, 75
beliefs, as intellectual statements, 7
beliefs, Christian stress on, 61
Bergson, Henri, 170
Bernadette, Saint, 94
Berndt, C. & R., 235, 244
Bible, 56
binary signals, 261
birth of Jesus, 93
bitheism, 87
Black Elk, 172, 173, 174, 175, 176, 178, 180, 196
blindness, psychogenic, 137, see also hysteria
blood letting, Aboriginal, 236
Bodhidarma, 44
bodhisattva, 26, 32, 42, 43, 45, 90, 120
body, 139
body painting, 241
body-mind split, 142, see also psyche
body-psyche unit, 48
Bombay, 11
Bonpos, 40
Brahman, 17, 18, 65, 153
brain, 95, 96, 97, 102, 137, 138, 148, 149, 150, 151
brain, visual centres of the, 138
bread and wine, ceremony of, 76, 77, 80, see also Eucharist
"breaking through", 114
breathing control, in yoga, 37
Buber, Martin, 7, 8, 109, 112, 119, 122, 171, 177, 194, 262
buddha nature, 28, 42, 45, 99
Buddha, life of the, 16
Buddha, The, 16, 18, 19, 20, 21, 22, 23, 24, 25, 26, 27, 30, 31, 32, 33, 36, 43, 45, 47, 48, 49, 50, 60, 61, 72, 73, 75, 82, 83, 84, 99, 102, 120, 121, 123, 257
Buddha, Western misconception of, 26
buddhahood, 26, 31
Buddhas, 116
Buddhism, 3, 4, 5, 7, 11, 16–51, 57, 60, 61, 68, 72, 73, 74, 75, 77, 79, 81, 82, 83, 86, 96, 98, 99, 100, 102, 103, 109, 116, 117, 120, 123, 127, 154, 156, 247, 254, 259, 261, 263, 264, 266, 267
Buddhism as anti-rational, 27
Buddhism as introverted intuitional, 27
Buddhism in India, 11
Buddhism, gods in, 21
Buddhism, role of beliefs in, 72
Buddhist attitude towards other teachings, 60
buffalo, 174
Bulgaria, 116
Bunyon, John, 144
Bushmen, 5

C

camel, 82
capitalism, mercantile and agrarian, 193
caste system, 22
Catholic Church, 5, 78
cause and effect, 20
center, 154, *see also* no-center
center, concept of the, 153
center, no need for a, 153
center, psychic, 142
Cheyenne people, 196
China, 43, 116, 118
Chou dynasty, 118
Christ, 267, *see also* Jesus Christ
Christ complex, 136
Christ, descent into hell of, 43
Christian Science Church, 7, 12, 69
Christianity as an extroverted thinking religion, 35
Christopher, Saint, 59, 60
Church of Christ, Scientist: *see* Christian Science Church
Church of Scientology, 4
churinga, 222, 236, 239
circumcision, Aboriginal, 237, 238
city, divine, 146
clans, 3
codes of conduct, 9
collective unconscious, 67, 68, 139, 140, 152, 153, 225, 256, 266
Comforter, the, 88
communion mysticism, 114, 118, 125, 139, 141
Compassionate Buddha, the, 22, 83
complex, Christ-, 136
complex, Jesus-, 126
complex, unconscious, 126
complexes, theory of, 86, 135, 136
conatus, 170, 171
Confucianism, 3, 255
consciousness, 67, 143
consciousness, surface, 149
consciousness, tribal, 225
Constantine, Emperor, 62
constellations, 138, 154
Conze, Edward, 51
cosmos, 153, 154
Councils, Christian Church, 62, 63, 65, 66, 91
craving for existence, 74
Creation story, 163, 177, 178, 182, 184, 185, 186, 187, 188, 227, 230, 231
Creative Beings, 221, *see also* Totemic Beings
creative evolution, 155
creedal statements, 11
cross, as symbol, 45
crucifix, 45
crucifixion, 58, *see also* execution of Christ
Culture Heroes, 186
cypress tree, 44, 45, 46

D

Damascus, 125, 126, 136, 140
dance, 108

Dante Alighieri, 144
dark night of the soul, 133, 144, 151
Darwin, Charles, 256
David, King, 10
David-Neel, Alexandra, 38, 40
dead, salvation of the, 87
death as final escape from existence, 19
death instinct, 49, 50, 70
death, as punishment by God, 73
death, life after, 69
death, not known by the unconscious, 69
Declaration of Independence, 191
Deep ecology, 247, 249
demon possession, 85
demon, vision of, 129
demons, 85, 86, 89
Depth psychology, 22, 148
depths of the soul, 143
depths, inner, 143
descent into Hell, Jesus', 87
determinism, 103
Devil, 85, 86, 99, 101, 186
dharma, 48, 49, 120
Dianetics, 4
dichotomous categories, 169
dingo, 228, 229, 230, 236
Dionysius the Areopagite, Pseudo- *see* Pseudo-Dionysius the Areopagite
directions, sacred, 196
disintegration of society, 266
disintegration of the psyche, 266
Divine Comedy, The, 144
divine spark, 152
DNA, 265
Donne, John, 119
Doors of Perception, The, 130
Dorjee Naljorma, 38
drama, Greek, 65
dream theory among the Iroquois, 200
dream theory, Iroquois, 204
dreaming tracks, 226
Dreaming, The, 6, 219, 220, 221, 222, 224, 225, 226, 227, 229, 230, 231, 232, 233, 235, 236, 237, 242, 243, 244, 250, 258, 261
dreams, 95, 96, 143
dreams and visions, 138
dreams, Aboriginal view of, 233
dreams, prophetic, 205
Dreamtime, The, 220, *see also* Dreaming, The
drug-induced states, 139
drugs, 132, 141
drugs and mystical experience, 134
dualism, 28, 44, 182, 184, 185, 187, 210, 225, 248, 261
dualistic logic, 267
dualistic principles, 266

E

Earth Woman, 168, 183
Eastman, Charles, 176, 179, 196
eating fish on Fridays, 5
Eckhart, Johannes, 111, 114

heroes, Greek concept of, 63
Herrigel, Eugene, 47
Hewitt, J.N.B., 164, 165, 166, 167, 169
Hillman, James, 96
Hinayana, 120
Hindu concepts of God, 17
Hinduism, 5, 17, 18, 19, 20, 22, 23, 24, 26, 27, 28, 35, 36, 51, 64, 72, 73, 75, 81, 103, 110, 122, 123, 127, 131, 142, 153, 181, 255, 265, 266
Hittites, 255
Holy Communion, 76, 110, 121, 267
Holy Spirit, 64, 65, 66, 68, 74, 78, 79, 88, 89, 93, 94, 99, 101
Host, 45
Huxley, Aldous, 130, 132
hypnogogic state, 150
hypnosis, 150
hypnotism, 137
hysteria, 126, 137, 139

I

"I am", 92, 114
I and Thou (Buber), 7, 171
id, 67, 68, 69, 70, 86, 104
identification with non-ego, 242
Ignaz Martin, Thomas, 138
illumination, 22
Imitation of Christ, The, 121
Immaculate Conception, 93
immortality, 70, 71, 146
immortality, Gilgamesh's search for, 144
immortality, herb of, 146
increase, rituals of, 235
India, 9, 16, 43, 116, 131
India, Buddhism in, 23
individuation, Jung's concept of, 48, 148, 245, 262, 266
initiation, Aboriginal, 238
inner depths, 143
insanity, 132, 141
inspiration, 68
inspired mysticism, 132
instincts, 140
intellectual morality, 137
introversion, 199
introverted religions, 120
Inward Light, 123, 143
Iran, 4
Iraq, 4, 90
Irondequoit, 161
Iroquois, 160, 161, 163, 164, 165, 167, 168, 182, 184, 185, 186, 187, 188, 189, 190, 193, 195, 200, 203, 204, 206, 207, 208, 209, 210; creation story, 167; dualism, 184; League, 166, 167 184, 185; pantheon, 186; territory, 160
irrational meaning of the word, 260
Isaiah, 118, 121
Islam, 4, 8, 12, 23, 29, 42, 63, 72, 75, 80, 81, 101, 109, 110, 111, 115, 116, 122, 255
Islam, spread of, 23
Israel, 4

Italy, 92

J

Jambali, 229, 230
James, William, 133, 134, 135, 138, 149
Japan, 42, 43
Japanese Buddhism, 123, *see also* Zen
Jarapiri, 226, 227, 228, 229, 231, 233, 235, 236, 242
Jefferson, Thomas, 190, 191, 192
Jeremiah, 111
Jerusalem, New, 147
Jesus Christ, 7, 26, 31, 32, 33, 43, 45, 57, 58, 59, 60, 61, 63, 64, 65, 66, 67, 68, 69, 72, 74, 75, 76, 77, 78, 79, 81, 82, 83, 84, 85, 86, 87, 88, 89, 90, 91, 92, 93, 94, 95, 97, 98, 99, 100, 101, 110, 114, 115, 116, 121, 122, 123, 124, 125, 126, 127, 135, 136, 137, 140, 141, 190, 196, 254, 266, 267; alleged insanity of, 132; theological concepts about, 63
Jewish morality, 61
Jewish rituals, 61
Joan of Arc, 122, 132, 138, 149; alleged insanity of, 132
Job, 85
John of the Cross, Saint, 133
Jordan River, 79
Joshu, 44, 45, 46
Journal of George Fox, 120, 127, *see also* Fox, George
journey as an image for mystical experience, 143
Jove, 63
Judaism, 4, 8, 9, 11, 12, 26, 29, 42, 56, 57, 58, 61, 62, 63, 64, 67, 72, 73, 75, 76, 78, 79, 80, 81, 84, 85, 89, 91, 92, 109, 110, 111, 112, 118, 122, 125, 255
Judgement, Last, 71, 88
Jukalpi, 227, 228
Jung Institute in Zürich, 160
Jung, C.G., 3, 27, 35, 48, 50, 67, 68, 69, 70, 77, 86, 104, 123, 126, 135, 136, 137, 138, 139, 143, 148, 150, 152, 153, 160, 161, 176, 197, 199, 207, 225, 243, 248, 249, 250, 256, 259, 260, 262, 264, 265, 266

K

kadaicha man, 243, 244
Kant, Immanuel, 170
karma, 7, 18, 20, 21, 30, 31, 42, 49, 68, 73, 100, 102, 103
Kimberley, The, 222, 230, 231, 233
Kingdom of God, 58
Klaus, Brother, 132, 138
knowing all things, 152
koan, 43, 44, 45, 46
Kokushi, Dai-o, 48
Koran, 63, 75, 117, 132, 152
Kubi, Baba, of Shiraz, 112
Kunapipi, 240, 244
kurunba, 227, 229, 233, 236, *see also* life-essence
Kutagara Hall, 25
Kwan-yin, 26

Totemic Beings, 218, 219, 221, 222, 224, 226, 227, 230, 231, 232, 235, 236, 237, 238, 239, 240, 242, 244
Totemic Spirits, 244
Toynbee, Arnold, 27, 35, 99, 110, 119
tradition, role in Christianity and Islam, 75, 92
Transpersonal Psychology, 249
Treaty of Batman, 223
tribal consciousness, 225
Trinity, 7, 66, 67, 68, 75, 85, 88, 94, 138, *see also* Father, Son, Holy Spirit
Trinity, vision of the, 138
trust, meaning of the word, 75
tumo, 38, 40
Turkey, 62, 80, 90, 92, 255
Twins, Good and Evil, 183, 184, 185, 186, 188, 206
two million year old person (Jung's phrase), 68, 143, 262

U

Ugarit, 255
Ultimate Reality, 35, 36
unconditional love, 87, 88
unconscious fantasies, 138
unconscious, the, 139, 148; *see also* collective unconscious, personal unconscious
Underhill, Evelyn, 142, 143, 148, 149, 150, 152, 181
Ungud, 230, 231, *see also* Rainbow Serpent
union mysticism, 114, 139, 141
Unitarian Church, 78
unitive experience, 114, 118, 140
unitive mysticism, 155
unity of past and future time, 250
unity with the land, 220
unity, experience of, 248
unity, state of, 243
universe as random, not a cosmos, 154
unknowing, 113, 148
Upanishads, 17

V

vacuum domicilium, 192
Varieties of Religious Experience, The (James), 133, 135
Vedas, 17
vegetarianism, 23
Vishnu, 17, 75
Vision Quest, 177, 179, 198, 200, 201, 202, 203
visions, 97, 126, 138, 139, 140, 143, 148, 151, 203; in Iroquois culture, 187; nature of, 95; *see also* dreams
visual centers, 138

W

Waalich (Wedge-tailed Eagle), 233
Wagyl, 224, 246, *see also* Rainbow Serpent

wakan, 164, 172, 174, 178, 179, 180; meaning of the word, 164
Wakan Tanka, 173, 174, 175, 177, 178, 179, 180, 181, 182, 187, 196, 199, 203, 261; does not mean God, 174
waking dreams, 149, 150
Walbiri, the, 227
Waldenses, 254
Walker, James D., 175
Walker, James R., 176, 177, 178, 179, 181
Wandjinas, 233, 237
water of forgetting, 30
water, as an image of nirvana, 34
Way of the Mystic, 143
West, Morris, 56, 104
Western Australia, 4
wheel of rebirth, wheel of reincarnation, 29
Wheelman, 233
White Buffalo Calf Woman, 187, 191
Whitehead, Alfred North, 171, 194
Wholly Other, The, 31
Whorf, Benjamin, 182
Wilhelm, Richard, 250
Wilmen, 233, 234
Winbaraku, 226, 227, 228, 229
Winnebago tribe, 130
wishing jewel, as an image of nirvana, 34
women: exclusion from men's rituals, 239; in Aboriginal Australian culture, 218; in American Indian agriculture, 195; role among the Iroquois, 204; role in Buddhism, 24; subjection of, 83 *see also* Sexism
Wording (Crow), 233
worlds, many, 42, *see also* reincarnation
worm, psychology of, 256
writing, systems of, 83

Y

Yahweh, 67
yoga, 36, 40, 41, 43
Yoga of Psychic Heat, 38
yoga, Buddhist, 36
"You are That", 17
Yugoslavia, 97

Z

Zaehner, R.C., 130, 131, 132, 134
Zarathustra, 11, 85
Zen, 7, 27
Zen Buddhism, 7, 8, 27, 28, 38, 40, 43, 44, 45, 46, 47, 48, 49, 51, 123, 152, 156, 192, 205, 230, 254, 267
Zen paradoxes, 27
Zeus, 63
Zoroaster, 11, 85
Zoroastrianism, 11, 13, 23, 42, 71, 75, 85, 87, 104, 116, 131, 255
zygote, 153, 154, 155